A SUNRISE BRIGHTER STILL

Frank Waters in July 1981 during a presentation at the Penrose Library, Colorado Springs, honoring his career.
Copyright © 1991 by Myron Wood.

A SUNRISE BRIGHTER STILL

THE VISIONARY NOVELS OF FRANK WATERS

ALEXANDER BLACKBURN

SWALLOW PRESS

OHIO UNIVERSITY PRESS

ATHENS

Swallow Press/Ohio University Press books are printed on acid-free paper ∞

96 95 94 93 92 91   7 6 5 4 3 2 1

Library of Congress Cataloging-in-Publication Data

Blackburn, Alexander.
  A sunrise brighter still : the visionary novels of Frank Waters /
by Alexander Blackburn.
      p.   cm.
  Includes bibliographical references and index.
  ISBN 0-8040-0947-3.
  1. Waters, Frank, 1902– —Criticism and interpretation.
I. Title.
PS3545.A82Z55   1991
818′.5209—dc20   91-18370
                                                                        CIP

For **FRANK**

CONTENTS

FOREWORD BY CHARLES L. ADAMS ix
PREFACE AND ACKNOWLEDGMENTS xvi

1. INTRODUCTION 1

2. *THE LIZARD WOMAN* AND THE EMERGENCE
OF THE DAWN MAN 19

3. *THE YOGI OF COCKROACH COURT:*
AN AMERICAN BOOK OF THE DEAD 34

4. *PIKE'S PEAK:* THE SEARCH FOR
THE SUPREME UNIVERSE 52

5. PASTORAL, MYTH, AND HUMANITY IN
PEOPLE OF THE VALLEY 69

6. THE ALLEGORY OF EMERGENCE IN *THE MAN
WHO KILLED THE DEER* 90

7. ARCHETYPAL PROMISE FROM APOCALYPTIC
PREMISE: *THE WOMAN AT OTOWI CROSSING* 112

8. CREATIVE MAN 132

NOTES 144   BIBLIOGRAPHY 156   INDEX 166

FOREWORD

WHEN I WAS asked by Alexander Blackburn to write an introduction to this seminal examination of Frank Waters's works, I was struck with a vague sense of insufficiency—not as a scholar or as a writer but somehow with an uncertainty as to my role as the messenger who would present this vital book to the world. As I saw it, the task would be somehow to convey a message not only about this study of Waters's novels but about the man himself.

Knowing Frank Waters as both man and writer has been an exceptional and rewarding experience, one of the deepest of my life. From his very approach to living, I have been able to witness examples of the dualities that are so much a part of his writing. He is at once humble and proud, obscure and well known, observer and visionary, chronicler and poet. In this day of the literary superstar, Frank Waters is the rarest of all writers—one who is not bigger than his art. He has repeatedly stated that he wishes to be known not for what he has done or how he has lived, but solely for what he has written. But how can the man be separated from the writer? He is, in the essence of his own dual nature, this fusion of modesty and stature, an integral living part of everything that he has written.

On 25 July 1990 National Public Radio's Bob Edwards informed listeners, "Writer Frank Waters turns eighty-eight today. Waters was published first in the 1930s; some of his books are considered classics, and . . . he's been nominated for the Nobel Prize for literature. Yet Waters continues to practice his craft in relative obscurity." Thus, even as Waters approaches ninety, the perpetuation of the myth described by his career-long label, "the best-known unknown author in America," continues. Ironically, he is now receiving nationwide birthday greetings sent to the "relative obscurity" of his native Southwest.

In introducing this current critical evaluation of Waters's novels, however, it would be well to note in regard to the myth of his obscurity that he does have seven honorary doctorates, as well as honorary life membership in the Western Literature Association and in the Rocky Mountain Modern Language Association. In addition, he is an honorary life member of the National Honor Society of Phi Kappa Phi and received a grant from the Rockefeller Foundation. He also has been a National Endowment Fellow and, as Bob Edwards noted, has since 1985 been nominated annually for the Nobel Prize.

It is true that Frank Waters has never had a best-seller, and has never been a media-marketed writer. But he does have seventeen books currently in print, some having been originally published over half a century ago. And there have been, undoubtedly, over a million copies of his works printed, including novels, biographies, ethnographies, and collections of essays. Waters, himself, has said of this phenomenon of having had slow, steady sales rather than a best-seller, "Every writer, whether he admits it or not, hankers after fame and fortune. That I did not attain them was the best thing that ever happened to me. I was compelled to keep following the carrot dangling before my nose by doing still another book."[1] And with most of those books still on the market and still selling, it is quite possible that Bob Edwards may be the very last person who can legitimately use the myth of Waters's obscurity.

Indeed, in this present volume, Alexander Blackburn pretty much ignores the question of why Waters seems to have been destined to have his reputation advanced primarily by his satisfied readers rather than by the literary establishment. However, in a letter to the Swedish Academy, sent in support of Waters's original Nobel Prize nomination, Dr. Blackburn did take up this issue, and I think some of his observations deserve attention here.[2] Blackburn noted as a primary reason that Frank Waters "comes from and writes about the least-understood area of the United States, the Southwest," that Waters has "rejected the dominant mechanistic-materialistic aspects of American and Euro-American civilization," and that he writes about "such relatively unpopular subjects as the American Indian, Hispanic-Americans, and the ancient civilization of Mesoamerica." Furthermore, Blackburn emphasized that Waters "champions the cause, a universal cause, of racial and ethnic reconciliation." Obviously such raw material rarely translates into best-sellers. Blackburn then went on to note Waters's use of Jungian psychology and Eastern philosophy and his direct confrontation of the possibility of the destruction of the world's ecosystem and of humanity itself through nuclear annihilation; and he added, almost as an afterthought, that Frank Waters "eschews all political ideologies and religious and nationalistic credos." While these reasons, formulated over five years ago, perhaps help to explain why Waters failed in the past to receive much attention from the national literary establishment, they may also explain not only his ever-growing popularity in foreign lands (he has been translated into Swedish, Dutch, French, German, and Japanese) but also the current phenomenally expanding interest in his work. Many people (and I count myself in their number), lay readers and scholars alike, agree that Frank Waters is our most important living writer.

Frank Waters was born in Colorado Springs, Colorado on 25 July 1902. The story of his life there, as well as that of his parents and grandparents, is fictionally chronicled in *The Wild Earth's Nobility* (1935), *Below Grass Roots* (1937), and *The Dust within the Rock* (1940) and has been retold in the monumental novel *Pike's Peak* (1971), a one-volume version of those three books. His maternal grandfather, Joseph Dozier, became quite wealthy designing and constructing a variety of buildings in Colorado Springs, many of which are still in use. He lost his money, however, pursuing an obsessive search for gold in the boom town of Cripple Creek on the site of Pike's Peak itself. For Waters the mountain came to stand for many things. Quay Grigg has noted that "[d]uring his youth in Colorado Springs, Pike's Peak became a central feature of Waters's inner landscape. . . . The image of the mountain has truly possessed Frank Waters; and he, it."[3] And many critics have noted the continuing presence of "mountain as influence" in all of Waters's works.[4] In various books, the ubiquitous mountains are sometimes male, sometimes female, sometimes androgynous. They can be benign or malignant, exploited for their mineral wealth, or drawn upon as great sources of psychic power.

In any case, his early exposure and relationship to the rugged landscape of the Rockies seems to have permanently embedded a profound understanding in young Frank Waters, and readers soon become aware of the presence and magnitude of the mountains in all of his works.

Perhaps the most influential nonlocal element in Waters's childhood was an almost yearlong visit in 1911 with his part-Indian father (perhaps one-half Cheyenne), to the Navajo reservation in New Mexico. This was not Frank's first contact with Native Americans. His father had taken him frequently to visit the Kiowas, Utes, Arapahoes, and Cheyennes, who traveled annually to

Pike's Peak to make votive offerings in the springs at its base. But it was his first opportunity to watch his father clerking at a trading post, interacting comfortably with the Navajos, moving freely in and out of the white and Indian worlds, and it undoubtedly afforded him a view of Native Americans, and a possible white relation to them, that has lasted him a lifetime.

Waters's father died in 1914, when Frank was only twelve. The boy and his widowed mother moved back into the big, boxlike family house occupied by the Doziers, where Grandfather Dozier continued for the rest of Frank's maturing years to be the primary male influence. A theme of major importance in all of Waters's work, the resolution of conflicting dualities, possibly originated in the need the growing boy felt to resolve the two sides of his own inherited nature: his grandfather's manifestation of the rational, materialistic, aggressive aspects of the white culture and his father's embodiment of the intuitive, spiritual, patient aspects of that of the Indian.

The family interest in mining dictated that Waters would major in engineering in college. From 1921 to 1924 he endured the dry, sterile engineering curriculum at the Colorado College in Colorado Springs. But in 1924, without taking a degree, Waters left formal education to support himself with a variety of jobs ranging from digging ditches in the oil fields of Casper, Wyoming, to working as an engineer for the Southern California Telephone Company. It was in southern California, on the Mexican border, that Waters wrote his first adult work, *The Lizard Woman*. In this initial full-length literary venture Waters makes the first of many literary attempts to depict a character's ability to achieve a synthesis of opposing dualities, here a young engineer who fuses a moment of full awareness of nature with a kind of spiritual enlightenment. Thomas J. Lyon rightly notes that the protagonist

> attained a spiritual exaltation comparable, in the way Waters describes it, to Buddhist *satori*. He had overcome, or been granted relief from, his baggage of white-engineer sophistication and rationalism and had been permitted to link directly to the world in unmediated experience. This moment may be seen as the prime one, the touchstone, of Waters's own life. . . .[5]

In addition to providing scholars with this "touchstone," *The Lizard Woman* is also of interest because it foreshadows many of Waters's research and writing interests of later years.

Also written at this time and also set on the Mexican border were Waters's only published short story, "Easy Meat" (which appeared in the *North American Review* in 1931)[6] and *The Yogi of Cockroach Court,* written in 1927, rewritten in 1931 and 1945, and published, unsuccessfully, in 1947. While *Yogi* was successfully reissued in 1972, there was, perhaps, legitimate reason for its initial public rejection: in no other work does Waters deal so openly with the dualities of human existence, and this work includes among its characters half-breeds, drug users, prostitutes, percentage girls, and lesbians. Here perhaps more than in any of his other works, Waters's compassion for *all* people is demonstrated. As one critic put it, "Frank Waters has an amazing ability to portray emotions in the people he writes about. In this case, they are undoubtedly the scroungiest human beings on earth, yet before the end of the book, you'll find yourself laughing, crying, hurting—even grieving for them."[7]

From 1932 to 1939 Waters worked on the Colorado mining trilogy mentioned earlier. Also during those years, he wrote *The Earp Brothers of Tombstone,* a history, biography, and exposé of that clan of itinerant cardsharps, gunmen, saloon keepers, and con men, and *Midas of the Rockies,* a biography of Winfield Scott Stratton, the former carpenter who struck it rich in the gold fields of Cripple Creek. The latter, an immediate success (it has never gone out of print), is a definitive biography. But it became more than that: ". . . it is a large-canvas survey of an era."[8] Researching this biography gave Waters the opportunity to immerse himself totally in impressions and statistics of the great mining scenes of the times, and enabled him to write, in 1939, that his trilogy was "the first major work covering a mining background, and with a thoroughness that will not be duplicated for a long time, and never by a casual, popular novelist."[9]

As Waters moved away from his semibiographical novels, he began to write some of his finest and most lasting fiction. I shall avoid discussing here such masterpieces as *People of the Valley, The Man Who Killed the Deer,* and *The Woman at Otowi Crossing,* dealt with so thoroughly in Professor Blackburn's present study. However, simultaneously with the above imaginative literary activities, Waters was developing, in his nonfiction, his ideas of the relationship between the people and the land of the American Southwest. Many of those ideas are presented in two major nonfiction works, *The Colorado* (1946) and *Masked Gods: Navaho and Pueblo Ceremonialism* (1950). As early as 1943, Waters had commented in a letter to the editor of the Rivers of America Series, "I have been writing *The Colorado* for the past twenty years, though the words themselves have yet to be put on paper."[10] During the next three years, most of which were spent writing propaganda briefs in Washington, D.C., Waters somehow managed in his "spare time" to put the words of *The Colorado* onto paper and created his monumental study of the history and the people of the great Colorado pyramid. Here he developed on a grand scale his examination of the relationship between the land and its inhabitants. A basic tenet of this work is that life in the total environment of the American West cannot be fully perceived by the usual Euro-American rationalistic outlook. Rather, a mystical outlook—perception through intuitive awareness—permits a person to experience an attunement that results in personal psychological adjustment. Waters then applies that concept to the American people, to the Native Americans, who, he suggests, had this "apperception" (which Lyon calls "perception squared"),[11] and to the waves of white settlers, who did not. The Indian, psychologically in tune with his perceived environment, is patient, intuitive, introvertive, and respectful of the land. The white is quick, eager, rationalistic, extravertive, and power-oriented. Waters depicts the conflict between the two groups as something far deeper than a military-political struggle. Rather, he suggests a psychological conflict deep within the character of each. While the conquering whites are depicted as just that—conquerors of people, of rivers, of the land itself—Waters is careful not to depict the Indian as Noble Savage. Rather, linking these ideas with his growing belief in the evolution of consciousness, he suggests that overemphasis on either point of view is ultimately destructive and that what is needed—what is possible—is a synthesis of the apparently opposing points of view into a wholeness in both individual and mankind.

These ideas are developed further in *Masked Gods* as Waters suggests that the problem is not simply white orientation or Indian orientation but that the conflicting dualities are present in each individual, in any time or place. The dichotomies are part of human nature, and are part of outer nature as well. Waters suggests that the Pueblo and Navajo Indians have long recognized these conflicting forces which make up the universe and human nature; and recognizing as well the need for internal harmony and harmony with one's environment, they havé, for centuries, used ritual to portray the cosmic dualities and to dramatize their equilibrium. Thus, the focus of these ceremonies is on universal harmony and on psychic wholeness. Waters postulates that the Indians may have intuitively perceived through their necessary closeness to the forces of nature a universe greatly similar to that being discovered by modern science. He cites the evidence of contemporary atomic physics, biology, and astronomy that describes a universe of interdependence, of mutuality—a "process reality." This is the reality that has been dramatized in dance by the Navajos and Pueblos for centuries. It is also the reality that Waters, a consummate storyteller, has, over the years, been gradually dramatizing in his fiction.

That the Indian view is being approached by modern science Waters sees as hopeful evidence of mankind's achieving the synthesis necessary for its survival and as evidence of an evolution of consciousness already in progress. In his most recent nonfiction publications,[12] Waters develops and affirms his belief in earth's transcendent pattern of evolution and in the responsibility of mankind, as earth's highest developed life form, to perceive its own ultimate cosmic function. In a recent interview for television, Waters mentions such scientists as David Bohm, Stephen Hawking, Ilya Prigogine, and Rupert Sheldrake, and suggests that there is now even more greatly increased speculation on the validity of the intuitive Indian concept of the unity and interconnectedness of all things. And in his 1987 revisions to *The Woman at Otowi Crossing,* I believe we can see additional evidence of Waters's increased assurance of this eventual scientific validation.

Thus, while these ethnographic and philosophic theories were taking shape in Waters's nonfiction, they were finding dramatic form in the novels he was creating over the years, culminating in the redemptive vision of *The Woman at Otowi Crossing* and resulting, when viewed as a total oeuvre, in the "living myth," the growth and development of which Professor Blackburn here so effectively traces. Frank Waters's tales of the people of the American Southwest have revealed a living myth that speaks directly to our time. It is almost a validation in itself that over the years Waters's readers have never stopped growing in number as more and more people come to realize the value of the vision he offers us.

Yet all my observations of Frank Waters's work still do not fully address the problem of presenting this particular book to its public. There has been one other element in its production that should be noted, one that can only be described by a term familiar to any student of Waters's thought. That is the synchronicity which has brought a scholar of Alexander Blackburn's stature to produce this current volume. Dr. Blackburn's literary background is impeccable and his analytical skills demonstrably superior. But his study and understanding of Waters's writing go beyond mere credentials and experience in the craft of criticism. Dr. Blackburn is himself a novelist, an editor, a teacher of literature and of creative writing. He is also a man of extraordinary sensitivity and intuition. Here, in a manner which would make any messenger feel inadequate, he brings all those talents into focus to reveal the complexity of Frank Waters's life work.

CHARLES L. ADAMS

PREFACE AND ACKNOWLEDGMENTS

FRANK WATERS IS a major American writer of the twentieth century. Author of more than twenty books of fiction and nonfiction, continuously nominated since 1985 for the Nobel Prize for literature, and arguably, on some grounds, as great a novelist as his famous contemporaries William Faulkner, Ernest Hemingway, and John Steinbeck, Waters is nevertheless outside his native Southwest relatively unknown. Indeed, for many readers this critical study, which is limited to what I have called his "visionary" novels, must serve as an introduction to a writer of whom they have never heard or whose beauty and depth of imaginative expression they have not previously or fully appreciated. If I have succeeded in leading both the general reader and the literary specialist to the discovery of Waters, this book will have served its purpose.

There is a steadily lengthening list of articles and essays about Waters, but Thomas J. Lyon, the distinguished editor of *Western American Literature,* has heretofore been the only literary critic to devote a book to him. Lyon's pioneering *Frank Waters* is a richly insightful survey (to 1973) of Waters as both novelist and philosopher. Obviously it leaves room for an expanded and revised point of view. Whereas Lyon gives the impression that "ideas" in Waters's narratives may represent superimposed intellection, I believe it can be shown that philosophical concepts are inherent in the fictional forms. Lyon, moreover, tends to view Waters in a context of the American West. Waters's western regionalism notwithstanding, he is, as I hope to show, first and foremost an American novelist in a recognizable American tradition. Finally, of course, some of Waters's most important work has been published since the appearance of Lyon's book—*Mexico Mystique: The Coming Sixth World of Consciousness* in 1975, *Mountain Dialogues* in 1981, and the revised edition of *The Woman at Otowi Crossing* in 1987. Not only is it now clear that *Otowi* is a literary masterpiece to be ranked beside or above Waters's acknowledged fictional masterpieces, *People of the Valley* and *The Man Who Killed the Deer,* but also from the perspective of the early 1990s we can see that Waters, like Herman Melville before him, is a mythopoetic and prophetic writer whose vision, universal in import, has anticipated the principal spiritual concerns of our time. Waters, it turns out, has simply gone further than most "modern" novelists (and a whole host of our contemporaries is not yet "modern" in this sense): he has perceived and given dramatic form to what Pierre Teilhard de Chardin called "the most prodigious event, perhaps, ever recorded by history since the threshold of reflection," an event taking place in our minds, namely, "the definitive access of consciousness to a scale of new dimensions and in consequence the birth of an entirely renewed universe."[1]

Some of Waters's popular audience—for he *is* popular with untold thousands of readers—may see him as a New Age guru. The tag is nebulous enough to be acceptable because his creative mythology of Emergence qualifies as a redeeming counterpoint to world crisis. To the extent that many people today are acquainted with revolutionary discoveries in neuroscience or with subjective experience of such phenomena of mind as expanded awareness and thus participating in what Marilyn Ferguson calls the Aquarian conspiracy,[2] Waters does loom as a writer of astonishing relevance. But the pervasive dream of our popular culture—that after a dark, violent age we are entering a millennium of love and light—dilutes the transcendental meaning of Waters's vision. Although his speculations in *Mexico Mystique* about ancient astrological lore may confirm, for some, a sense of personal, social, and global transformation and may, for others, assuage fear of catastrophic changes in the near future, his essential view, elucidated in almost all his books for more than sixty years, is not narrowly historical and sociological but psychological and cosmological, having to do with our human search for a wholeness, a harmonious Self inherent in Creation from the beginning. As physical events (overpopulation, pollution of the ecosystem, technological innovations) bring psychic parallels (discarding of old values, new beliefs, revolutions), so the oppression of the separation of mind from instinct must lead, in Waters's view, to the emergence of a new faculty that will dominate both instinct and reason during the coming cycle. This is an evolutionary view involving a long and painful process, inevitable perhaps but not necessarily impending.

Still, Waters is strongly attracted to the possibility of an increased awareness operating in society. As we approach a historical verge, sudden "emergences" such as those dramatized in his novels have the representative effect of resolving crisis this side of nuclear annihilation and the partial or total collapse of world culture. He calls into question some of the deepest assumptions of Western civilization—concepts of linear time, material progress, the separation of mind and matter, the priority of the will of individuals—in order to point the way to creative enlargement of self and society, not to lament the passing of a shattered world, as so much of modern literature from Tennyson's *Idylls of the King* to T. S. Eliot's *Waste Land* and Faulkner's family chronicles has been inclined to do.[3] In fact, in his rejection of ego-dominance and its attendant Western cult of individualism, Waters comes closer to the view of Eastern mystics—and New Age thinkers—than to that of most American and European writers. The authentic consciousness that he envisions is one liberated *from* ego and will *into* the richness and wonder and mystery of a meaningfully interrelated universe. If this is a "mystical" vision, it is much in accord with post-Einsteinian discoveries in the physical sciences and post-Freudian, Jungian theories of mind.

We are, then, just coming around to seeing what Waters has been seeing all along. We are ready, so to say, to find accommodation for a writer with a wisdom and a substance of hope to match the decorum of a high style irradiated by warmth, humor, and vitality.

The question arises about why the academic world has been slow to recognize Waters. But since it is not just Waters alone but a number of other impressive writers, all from the American West, about whom we speak as neglected, the conclusion may be that academics have yet to discover America. That is the premise of A. Carl Bredahl, Jr., in *New Ground: Western American Narrative and the Literary Canon*. He argues that western writers have been neglected because they have discarded eastern and southern assumptions of imposing self and enclosing landscape and have reconceptualized the individual's relationship to the land. Although I was unacquainted with Professor Bredahl's book when I wrote the introduction to this study, we are in agreement: students of American literature will soon be discovering the West—and Waters.

Among the first to discover Waters, and to whom I owe a debt of gratitude for their leadership, are Thomas J. Lyon of Utah State University; Joe Gordon, director of the Hulbert Center for Southwestern Studies at the Colorado College; John R. Milton, editor of *South Dakota Review* at the University of South Dakota; and, above all, Charles L. Adams of the University of Nevada, Las Vegas, founder of the Frank Waters Society (which holds an annual meeting conjointly with the Rocky Mountain Modern Language Association) and editor of *Studies in Frank Waters*. Giving generously of his time and knowledge, Dr. Adams read this book as it was in progress; while I assume responsibility for its views and misdemeanors, his friendly but firm comments have sometimes saved me from falling on my face. It has also been my wonderful privilege to enjoy the friendship of Frank and Barbara Waters. When I needed to clarify a point, Mr. Waters has always been there to help, but I've tried not to abuse a privilege. He is, among all the writers of my acquaintance, the most modest and self-effacing; therefore his forbearance during assaults of critical praise is an exemplary quality, and I hope I have not put it to too severe a test. To my wife and colleague, Dr. Inés Dölz-Blackburn, who shared with me her insights into Waters's novels, I owe, as always, especial thanks. Finally I wish to thank Ruth Wild for her typist's wizardry and devotion in preparing the manuscript, and the members of the committee on research and creative work of the University of Colorado, Colorado Springs, for granting aid for that endeavor.

The author gratefully acknowledges permission to reprint from his entry entitled "Frank Waters," in *Dictionary of Literary Biography, Yearbook 1986,* edited by J. M. Brook (Gale Research, 1987) and from his essays that appeared originally in *South Dakota Review* 28, no. 1 (1990):5–18; *Western American Literature* 24, no. 2 (1989):121–36; *Journal of the Southwest* 30, no. 4 (1988):535–44; and *Studies in Frank Waters* 6 (1984):48–63; 7 (1985): 11–15; 8 (1986):68–98; 10 (1988):89–113; and 12 (1990):77–96. For permission to quote from Frank Waters's letter to Mabel Dodge Luhan, dated 14 February 1941, the author also gratefully acknowledges the Collection of American Literature, Beinecke Rare Book and Manuscript Library, Yale University.

ABBREVIATIONS

Deer	*The Man Who Killed the Deer*
Dust	*The Dust within the Rock*
Lizard Woman	*The Lizard Woman*
Nobility	*The Wild Earth's Nobility*
Otowi	*The Woman at Otowi Crossing*
People	*People of the Valley*
Pumpkin	*Pumpkin Seed Point*
Yogi	*The Yogi of Cockroach Court*
Tanner	Terence A. Tanner, *Frank Waters: A Bibliography*

INTRODUCTION

THE PRIME TASK of mythology is through vision to carry the human spirit forward. When poetry and imaginative literature arise from and exhibit the mythic mode of consciousness, they can be properly described as visionary: vision is a birth of something new that makes possible the work of creation, freeing spirit from the passing phenomenon of time to achieve a realization of an imperishable life that lives and dies in all. There must always, of course, be a place for a literature which expresses our current spiritual and cultural condition. Even literature which sees our condition as "alienated" can be authentically revelatory. But to experience the world in this way, as if it were a wasteland in bits and pieces, suggests a disability, whereas, as Colin Falck persuasively says in *Myth, Truth and Literature,* "there must always be the possibility of a literature which reaches beyond this disability to a greater wholeness and which aims to cure our spiritual condition rather than merely to express it."[1] The vision that tries to transcend spiritual disabilities "in order to re-connect with the most central meanings of human life"[2] has the high aim of revealing a new world—a new mind. This is the aim of the visionary novels of Frank Waters.

A mountain man, as he calls himself, born in 1902 in Colorado Springs and endowed with both Euro-American and Native American heritage,

Waters has written more than twenty books of imaginative literature and philosophy that light a way out of the figurative wasteland and that reclaim and reconstitute ancient integrative myths which are relevant to modern life. His has been an arduous and isolating quest which has led him to reexamine the Old World traditions of Judeo-Christian and Hellenic cultures from the perspective of other worlds of antiquity. The quest has taken him literally to some of the wildest and most remote regions of the American West and Mexico, to knowledge of their peoples and cultures, and spiritually to mythologies originating thousands of years ago in the Orient. Not in Europe, from which deracinated American writers have so often sought nourishment, and not in the urbanized, industrialized regions of the eastern United States, but in the true continental heartland, Waters, like the seeker in all mythologies,[3] has come under the protection of the Cosmic Mother—of the archetypal feminine or the powers of the unconscious—and found in the depths of fathomless being that the human body is "but a microcosmic replica of the macrocosmic body of all creation" (*Pumpkin,* 137). Departing from a doomed and tragic culture, returning to archaic depths, and then surfacing to teach the lesson of life renewed: this pattern of quest is evident in the life and works of Frank Waters.

What is this heartland, sometimes regarded as a recent frontier or a cultural backwater inimical to imagination?[4] It is not a geopolitical Lebensraum but a space-time continuum. The heartland is the geographical heart of the continent, provided that one ignores national boundaries and thinks of North America and Mexico as a single entity; it is the historical heart of ancient American civilization; and it is the mythical heart of a self-subsistent country of the soul. These dimensions of geography, history, and myth fill the stage of Waters's novels and nonfiction. The geographical heartland emerges from Colorado and New Mexico, expands to include the vast region drained by the Colorado River, and finally encompasses an area stretching from the Rockies down the spine of the Sierra Madres to Middle or Central America. Throughout the heartland beats the living pulse of the past, as evinced in Navajo and Pueblo Indian ceremonialism, and historical orientation locates the true heart in pre-Columbian Mexico among Mayan and Aztec cultures. Its center would be the sacred city of Teotihuacán, with its mythically central temple of Quetzalcoatl. Symbol of union between heaven and earth, matter and spirit, Quetzalcoatl is in Waters's interpretation a self-sacrificing God-Redeemer who taught that the mythical Road of Life is within man himself. This road of life is not individual man's brief diurnity but humanity's evolution, which, more than a mechanical process of geological and physical change, takes place on psychic levels as well and can be "hastened or retarded by man's perception of his responsibility in the cosmic plan" (*Masked Gods,* 179). The road of life is, then, an ethic based on regard for all forms of life and is a psychological affirmation of a new world to emerge, where an "enlargement and unification of personality" transcends dualities to achieve a unified stage of consciousness (*Masked Gods,* 183). Waters's quest through the dimensions of the heartland has yielded a creative mythology, Emergence, and this myth is the heartland's answer to the wasteland.

The quest of Frank Waters has been for and within the heartland and warmly and mystically evokes the feeling of "being within, communing with past ages" (*Pumpkin,* 167). The superlative message of the quest is the interconnectedness of all living systems—from the subatomic to the human to those of the planets and stars. Yet to *be within,* one does not have to depend on teachings of past civilizations or the discoveries of modern science. One can realize an emergent intuition through nature itself, in ordinary living, as Waters shows in this passage from *Mountain Dialogues:*

> It is my habit, weather permitting, to observe a moment of meditative stillness each morning when the sun first tips the rimrock of the mountain range behind my adobe. The place for it is always the same. An unprepossessing spot on a slight rise in the waist-high sagebrush, flanked by a clump of huge gnarled junipers—cedars, as we call them. . . . Here I stand, sniffing the early morning breeze and spying out the vast landscape like an old coyote, as if to assure myself I am in the center flow of its invisible, magnetic currents. To the sun, and to the two oppositely polarized peaks, El Cuchillo and the Sacred Mountain, I offer my morning prayers. Then, letting the bright morning rays of the sun engulf me, I give myself up to a thoughtless silence. . . .
>
> It doesn't come immediately, the crisp morning is so invigorating. There isn't a cloud in the sky. The earth emerges pristinely pure, virginly naked in its beauty. The snow-tipped peaks of Jicarita and the Truchas to the south, down toward Santa Fe, rise sharply into the blue. Beyond the slit of the Rio Grande to the west, the upland desert rises to the southern thrust of the Colorado Rockies. And to the east and north, directly behind me, the Sangre de Cristos curve in their great semi-circle. From down in Arroyo Seco, a mile below, sounds the clear pealing of the church bell. Reluctant wisps of smoke rise from the adobe village. Around me, the magpies are stirring awake. . . .
>
> But end it does. Abruptly, without warning, just as sleep overtakes you. As if one had suddenly broken through an invisible barrier, to be becalmed in an immeasurable, profound quietude, broken only by the voice of silence itself. . . .
>
> And so it is this deep silence, this white silence, that I experience during my moment of meditative stillness in the sagebrush at sunrise. All the sensual morning sounds seem to merge into one sound, the steady ringing in my own

ears which merges into the steady hum of silence itself, the voice of the living land, or perhaps the sound of the moving universe itself. *¿Quién sabe?* I myself have never questioned it. [49–54]

"There is not even silence in the mountains," laments the seeker in T. S. Eliot's *Waste Land.*[5] So how does Waters's experience of silence return us to wonder and to the energies of hope? The answer is simple, embedded almost imperceptibly in the symbolism of his sunrise ritual. He stands, like everyone, at the apex of the cross that is oriented to the four directions of the world, and he further reminds himself of the eternal dualities in nature and in humanity. He is conscious of being at one with the four elements, with the sun father and cosmic mother, with plants and animals, and with the nearness of fellow human beings for whom the bell is pealing. But as thought dissolves into apperception of and acquiescence in the mystery of being, he becomes momentarily a part of all creation. There is nothing separated from anything else. All is one.

The American West has its share of great writers, even though critics may argue over hierarchy. It seems to me, without engaging such an argument contentiously, that Willa Cather (the merits of *My Ántonia* notwithstanding) and John Steinbeck (the merits of *Grapes of Wrath* notwithstanding) are decidedly writers of the second rank, whereas Waters, Wallace Stegner (*Big Rock Candy Mountain* and *Angle of Repose*), and Walter Van Tilburg Clark (*Ox-Bow Incident* and *Track of the Cat*) are decidedly of the first. But it is Waters who may one day be seen as having revealed the complex civilization of the West as William Faulkner revealed that of the South. That Waters is a major *American* writer is in any case an opinion difficult to abjure. Two of his books, *The Man Who Killed the Deer* and *Book of the Hopi,* have sold many hundreds of thousands of copies. Almost all his books have enjoyed slow but steady sales. His reputation for greatness, however, has been largely the result of "discoveries" by the reading public. Like another great prophetic writer, Herman Melville, Waters has been more or less ignored in his lifetime by the literary establishment.[6] Scholars in the field of Western American literature have recognized Waters. But scholars east of the Mississippi River have omitted him, as well as other writers of the West, from the canon of American literature. For example, in Frederick Karl's 1983 book, *American Fictions 1940–1980* (part of whose subtitle is *A Comprehensive History*) there are six references to Steinbeck, but Stegner is mentioned only once (in a footnote), and there is no mention whatsoever of Clark, Frederick Manfred, Paul Horgan, or Waters.[7] *Comprehensive* does not yet include the West. Waters has not been singled out for neglect, but the universality of his vision hasn't been noticed either. Obviously, where the national literature is concerned, not all writers of the West can be, or will for much longer be, anathematized as regionalists, as fabricators of horse operas and moral fables, or as exiles from culture and tradition. Moreover, sooner or later scholars and critics may recall what Eliot in 1919 asserted in "Tradition and the Individual Talent": that the "whole of the literature" of one's own country "has a simultaneous existence and composes a simultaneous order," and that the "existing monuments form an ideal order among themselves, which is modified by the introduction of the new (the really new) work of art among them."[8] The art of Waters is *really* new, truly original. Judged by the standards of the past, he will eventually be found to have affinities with the religious tradition of Ralph Waldo Emerson, Henry David Thoreau, Walt Whitman, Melville, and Eliot. Whatever may be the future consensus about Waters in relation to the national literature—or to world literature for that matter—he is not easily put down. If he isn't a "regionalist" in the pejorative sense, neither is he a "mystic" in that sense. Regionalism in fiction is not a limitation which seals universality away; and mysticism is the expression both of a tradition common to all the great civilizations of the past and of a tradition indigenously American.

Perhaps the only fair procedure is to compare Waters's perception of reality with the perceptions of other American writers. He belongs to a literary generation which includes Faulkner (b. 1897), Hemingway (b. 1899), Thomas Wolfe (b. 1900), and Steinbeck (b. 1902). Three of these novelists (Faulkner, Hemingway, Steinbeck) won the Nobel Prize for literature, and a fourth (Wolfe) exercised considerable influence on American writers in the 1930s and 1940s. As a stylist in prose and as a celebrity to aficionados of excessively masculine behavior, Hemingway is probably the best-known writer of his generation. Steinbeck, though less admired than Hemingway, has appealed to popular sentiments about oppressed peoples. Faulkner is esteemed by writers and critics as the greatest imaginative writer of the United States in the twentieth century. And yet none of these white male writers has a social and sexual understanding which accords to women equal status with men, and none has a worldview which convincingly transcends the experience of their time. By contrast with writers of his own generation, Waters may be seriously considered as the twentieth-century American writer who in searching the meaning of his experience through the mode of mythic consciousness has reconciled the dualities of male and female awareness, reason and intuition, and has come upon a worldview that is tantamount to an affirmation of faith.

A comparison of Waters and Faulkner may establish points of reference about the nature of vision in fictional art.

Both novelists are regionalists with universal themes—Faulkner from a part of the South once called the Old Southwest, Waters from a part of the West now called the Southwest. Each writer had a strong-willed Southern grandfather with pioneering spirit, by whom each was influenced.[9] Both novelists felt burdened from an early age with a region's history of racial conflict and of a dominating materialistic civilization. Both revolted against the onslaught of this civilization, against conventional social forces inhospitable to the imagination, and both strove to free themselves and their heroes from historical systems, designing narratives that acknowledge the reality of society only to question it as a source of moral standards and spiritual values. Both novelists create mythical kingdoms—Faulkner his Yoknapatawpha County, Waters his heartland. With symbolic art each novelist has produced a core of literary classics: Faulkner's *Absalom, Absalom!, Go Down, Moses* (which includes "The Bear"), and *The Sound and the Fury* usually contend for top honors in the affections of readers, with *As I Lay Dying* and *Light in August* orbiting nearby, not to mention a galaxy of superb short stories, whereas readers of Waters plump for, in varying order of preference, *The Woman at Otowi Crossing, The Man Who Killed the Deer, People of the Valley,* and *Pike's Peak* (which includes "The Wild Earth's Nobility"), may feel endeared to *The Yogi of Cockroach Court,* and often find greatness in all or part of such nonfiction as *The Colorado, Masked Gods, Book of the Hopi, Pumpkin Seed Point, Mexico Mystique,* and *Mountain Dialogues.*

The two novelists—and I am concerned primarily with Waters as novelist—relate technique to vision. Faulkner is a kind of verse dramatist whose authorial omniscience releases him from theatrical conventions and permits him to present large dramatic actions that focus a civilization in its complexity. This technique gives Faulkner the privilege of making an internally consistent world, of defining human action against a background of code and ceremony, of creating characters with a force of will behind their words and acts, and of devising strategies to establish a high style of tragic and comic decorum.[10] Authorial omniscience works to similar effect in Waters's fiction. Consistently seeing his material as mythical, he too creates characters who are larger than life, though moving to the patterns of a visible world; he too, because his sense of the past brings antiquity to bear upon the temporal present, defines human action against a convincing background of code and ceremony. Faulkner's technical innovations are incomparable in their way: interior monologues that spring from various levels of the mind; multiple, restricted points of view; layered and overlapping narratives; and the delay of focus while temporal events loop around in a limbo of arrested motion. Waters is not as experimental as Faulkner, but so great is the burden of his commitment—"to comprehend the incomprehensible," as Martin Bucco has remarked[11]—that innovativeness has been a necessary component of his art. The "multimedia," symphonically orchestrated tapestry of *People of the Valley* makes of that imagistic novel a metaphor for the earth's vibratory rhythms. The nonverbal silence of Native Americans in *The Man Who Killed the Deer* is communicated through italicized passages of poetic beauty and force. A carefully concealed dramatic irony wires character and event together in all of Waters's visionary novels and makes the very complexity of unraveling the strands one of the enriching values of his art. Nowhere is this complex irony employed to more intense effect than in the interior monologues of the protagonist of *Pike's Peak,* a mystic who perceives an Absolute Consciousness in the universe yet madly projects the imagery of his unconscious mind upon a mountain, as if the secret of life lay in it and not in himself. In *The Woman at Otowi Crossing* the structural and thematic counterpointing is as sensitively organized as that in *Go Down, Moses,* and the technique of multiple, restricted points of view in *Otowi* permits Waters to freight all the crude particularity of social realism into the realm of his heroine's spiritual totality and yet maintain the integrity of literary form. At their rapturous best, both Waters and Faulkner are poets in the generic sense: makers of worlds.

At the Faulkner and Yoknapatawpha Conference at the University of Mississippi in 1981, Elizabeth Spencer explained some "worries" about her fellow writer and Mississippian. She worried that Faulkner had tried to pass off his legend of the Snopeses, the emotionless, double-dealing poor whites ignorant of aristocratic manners, as social observation on the order of that in European novels. Since the confidence man in American literature is always a more mythical than historical figure, I hesitate to share this concern.[12] I do share, however, her worry about Faulkner's treatment of women characters: they are usually depicted as prime sources of evil or as nonnurturing neurotics or as mindless earth mothers. Spencer's third worry is, I think, crucial: Faulkner's nihilism.

> I think personally that Faulkner may have been stimulated by a nihilistic approach, finding in it that source of a feeling of danger—threat, doom, the impossible event—which informs many of his strongest works. Violence is one thing—I don't mean only violence; but beyond violence, beyond tragedy even, lies the blank-out, the complete destruction, the totality of blackness, darkness, nothing, nothing.[13]

The sympathetic reader of Waters is also going to have worries, but they are of a different kind. One worries, for instance, about the relationship of art and idea, whether the pressure of philosophical and psychological insights may affect the validity of artistic knowledge, which is knowledge of things as experienced. If Waters were not incurably devoted to capturing the wonder of life, perhaps his truths might not jolt us into shared experience. But, I believe, they do this and more, for the ideas, which are inseparable from the aesthetic expression, have the power to expand our experience. Spencer's worries about Faulkner do not carry over and apply to Waters. First, Waters's social observation, which includes in its sweep the history and ways of life, of thought and feeling, of four cultures, Euro-American, Native American, and Mexican American—a fourth culture, that of the Asiatic American, is depicted in *The Yogi of Cockroach Court*—cuts to the human marrow and engenders the sort of respect one might grant to a Joseph Conrad, Joyce Cary, D. H. Lawrence, or E. M. Forster. *Pike's Peak,* for example, is more than a story of pioneer settlement in the West, more than a story of the growth of a small city and of the interaction of its social forces, and more than exposition of gold-mining enterprises that bring fabulous wealth or financial disaster to certain individuals, just as Melville's *Moby-Dick* is more than a story of whaling. *Pike's Peak* is a parable of American history and society: experiences of exile, conquest, and colonization, of the dreams of a better life, of faith in mechanical progress, and of belief in a divinely ordained mission to the wilderness are gathered at the heart of the continent, and found wanting. Second, Waters's treatment of women characters is tainted neither by misogyny nor by sentimentalized idealizations of the Eternal Feminine; perhaps unique among major white male writers of his generation in the United States, he depicts women as fully human and in one instance, *People of the Valley,* portrays a female protagonist who incarnates the androgynous ideal. The social and sexual aspects of Waters's fiction reflect an instinctive soundness and balance in his vision of life.

When we consider the third of Spencer's worries, Faulkner's nihilism, this matter of an artist's vision of life brings into sharp focus a contrast between Faulkner and Waters. According to Cleanth Brooks, one of Faulkner's most ardent admirers, the value of a writer lies in the totality of his perception of our world as it involves ourselves, and a writer most fulfills his role when he gives us a vision of reality that renews a tradition. Vision is not a game "to pick out . . . the mounting wave of the future and then to ride it triumphantly onto the beach."[14] Vision, Brooks contends, is a product of a spiritual environment, and the concerns of visionary art are finally to be understood by reference to such environmental premises. Brooks is, I think, right in this view of the significance of vision in our critical evaluation of a writer in relation to tradition. However, he identifies the spiritual environment in American literature with Puritanism. Even Hemingway, apparently, may apply for canonization as long as his fictionalized tests for courage and endurance are made analogous to a sinner's experiencing of salvation. Faulkner shares with Puritanism, we are told, a cardinal belief in "the sense of the importance of the human will" in "the unmediated encounter between man and God" through which man gains "salvation by individual effort."[15] Because Faulkner usually views nature as radically evil and eschews the concept of grace, it is through discipline that his heroes achieve something of value, and his novels are accordingly dramas of moral choice. Reality in Faulkner is said to be perceived via a "required initiation . . . analogous to the crisis of conversion and the character's successful entrance into knowledge of himself."[16] But what vision of "reality" are we talking about when, instead of being a totality, it is reducible to the moral dogma of a special belief? Intuitively Faulkner was attracted to a *timeless* reality, I suggest, but had only a marginal confidence in the truth to be derived from it. There is an emptiness, a darkness— one can call it nihilism or attribute it to a conviction of Original Sin—but at all events a failure of spirit in Faulkner in that the mythological basis of knowledge has been reduced to merely a form of belief and epistemology. To the extent that his vision is preobjective and prelogical, it is mythic, but to the extent that he abandons the mythic mode of perception for a rational mode of explanation, he has not forged a literature of the imagination that we can trust.

From the foregoing we might propose some expectations about vision in literature. Vision may prove prophetic, but prophecy is not calculated. Vision might be expected to reveal the essential wholeness of humanity, without separations of gender, race, and culture. Vision might also be expected to reveal reconciliation within man himself, as between conscious and unconscious polarities of mind, or meaningful relationship between man and nature. Vision, too, might be expected to renew a tradition of faith, a nonlocalized and nondogmatized tradition of faith, in a timeless reality pervading temporal experience and assimilating contemporary humankind into the mystery of origins. Such vision arrives and assumes epistemological authority from numinous depths of creative imagination, from the mythic mode of consciousness which in Jungian aesthetics involves the animation of archetypes or primordial experiences that have repeatedly occurred in the course of generations. The methods of this vision are not simply, however, originality and unlimited freedom. Vision imposes restrictions. While it uses methods other than those of ordinary thinking, it must be something that, sooner or later, ordinary thinking will understand and accept. Otherwise vision would be bizarre, not creative. And so, I think, vision reveals something new as a result of the artist's being open to the world and endowed with the capacity to add his or her perception of reality to culture, thereby introducing a new cultural canon. This function has always been associated with shamans, seers, and poets whose dreams come spontaneously and unbidden and really have little to do with objective "facts" which call for "explanation." The visionary knows that the vision *is* a myth, one that brings real truths that have every right to be called profound, though they remain outside the possibility of full test or full congruence with conventional codes. In itself the mythic vision is already a satisfying explanation of all the main events in the world, already an integrated awareness in which fact and awareness have not become *dis*united.[17]

According to these terms, Frank Waters is a visionary novelist whose mode of consciousness is mythic. He has a worldview that is as new as it is ancient and that has its source in mystical experience. His novels project a vision of reality as a whole, and, while he has devoted a lifetime to expanding his awareness of this totality, has explored Native American and Mesoamerican mythology, oriental mythology, and modern depth psychology (among other studies), it was an openness to spirit of place that prompted revelation. Thus when he was a boy of about ten, on a visit to his grandfather's gold mine in Cripple Creek, Colorado, he had an experience which might well have been the paradigm for later, fictionalized experiences of unity:

> Then suddenly it happened, the boy did not know how. All this dead stone became intensely, vibrantly alive. Playing on the dump one morning after he had washed the breakfast dishes, he happened to pick up a pinch. In the bright sunlight he saw with microscopic clarity the infinitesimal shapes and colors, the monstrous and miraculous complexity of that single thimbleful of sand. In that instant the world about him took on a new, great and terrifying meaning. Every stone, every enormous boulder fitted into a close-knit unity similar to the one in his sweaty palm. For the first time he saw their own queer and individual shapes, their subtle colors, knew their textures, felt their weight, their strain and stress. It was as if in one instant the whole mountain had become alive and known. [*The Colorado,* 22–23]

From some such core experience Waters developed his worldview. Whereas Faulkner, famously and vaguely, declared in his Nobel Prize acceptance speech that the human race will endure and prevail, Waters has shown why, in what circumstances. We will endure and prevail according to the degree of our unfolding consciousness of our role in "the universal plan . . . inherent in the beginning" (*Mexico Mystique,* 102). Although Waters's view of perception is of a numinous kind analogous to the individual experience, in Puritan tradition, of an unmediated encounter between man and God, human ego, will, and reasoning are—in contradistinction to that tradition in American literature—the major obstacles to fulfillment. Waters has learned from direct experience in the American West that Euro-Americans have a will to separate man and nature, which is treated as if it were an external object, and to dominate Native Americans, who have no such will and who regard man and nature as inseparable. Thus, while Waters admires human individuality in history and in moral action, he places no faith in conscious will and regards it, materialism, and excessive rationalism as the principal causes of modern tragedy. By perception he does not mean only what man perceives through the senses but also an intuitive knowledge of spiritual laws pervading and uniting mind and matter, an apperception. He envisions a universal plan which has nothing whatsoever to do with Judeo-Christian eschatology (the doctrine of last things such as death, judgment, heaven, and hell) or with our present conception of evolution as a process of accumulation. The unfolding of consciousness is ultimately, for him, the realization of one Absolute Consciousness, Irreducible Reality, an infinite existence underlying all forms, all changes, and manifesting itself "in us as we are in it" (*Mountain Dialogues,* 169). Far from being something new to be gained, the Universal Reality is realized when the objectifying tendency of the ego-centered personality, which identifies itself with objects, is dispelled.

The essence of Waters's vision as it is projected and developed in nine novels published between 1930 and 1971 may be summarized in three interlocking conceptual words: *unity, duality,* and *emergence.*[18]

UNITY

The entire universe manifests an inherent unity or wholeness, a hidden and creative order that expresses itself in human lives and in the material world. One cosmic power unites spirit and matter. The structure of man's psyche and that of the universe is the same, so that whatever happens in the microcosm happens in the macrocosm, and vice versa. This mysterious, organic, rhythmic, and dynamic force or energy, "an impersonal spirit of life, pervading and unifying every entity in nature—the living stone, the great breathing mountain, plant, bird, animal, and man" (*Pumpkin,* 65), is the one Universal Reality and the basis of the interrelationships of all life, including human kinship with lower forms of life. Myths about this immanent and transcendent unity were common among all the great civilizations which preceded our own. Parallel symbols for it are as various as the Self in Hindu philosophy, the Dharma-Kāya of Tibet's Mahayana Buddhism, the Taoist yin-yang mandala, the kachina of the Hopi Indians, and the winged serpent of both the Orphic Gnosis and Toltec-Aztec myths. Although the numinous realm of spiritual totality embraces and supersedes both Freud's personal unconscious and Jung's collective unconscious with its projections of archetypal thought forms, modern depth psychology offers a partial basis for understanding Universal Reality. So does Einstein's relativity theory, whereby time and space bend into a cosmic circle. And Christianity continues to symbolize unity through its doctrine of the transcendence of carnality by divinity. Therefore the concept of unity is continuous through the ages.

However, the separation of spirit and matter has been allowed to dominate the thinking of occidental civilization, producing a materialistic ideology, an overly rationalistic science, and an egocentric cult of individualism. The trend of occidental civilization is thus seen as against the evolutionary tide of nature, wherein all humankind must be recognized as one, and itself must recognize living relationship with the created universe. In spite of this trend there is hope for a meeting of West and East, modern and primal peoples, science and mysticism. The West's analytical mode of thought may be reconciled with the East's synthesizing process of meditative intuition. As we in the West discover "the potency of the living germ and cell to expand and multiply" and "the immense power of the material atom when released," we begin to approach the East, where "the smallest particle of organic and inorganic matter also is, or embodies, the infinite Consciousness and Power to Become" (*Mountain Dialogues,* 185). By a similar token, recent scientific discoveries in parapsychology and in the increasingly combined fields of physics, biology, and psychology are also leading the West toward the East's myths of unity. For instance, Jung's theory of synchronicity, which posits an *a*causal principle of reality, has been linked to physicist David Bohm's theory of an "implicate order" beyond the appearances of chaos. The concept of unity, in short, is very much in the forefront of philosophy today.[19]

All of Waters's visionary novels offer illustration of the concept. *The Lizard Woman* dramatizes the discovery of an earthly terrain shaped as a serpent biting its tail—an ancient symbol of cosmic unity. In *The Yogi of Cockroach Court* an individual is separated from humanity but in the moment of death realizes compassion and advances to experience of a universal Light. In *Pike's Peak* an individual perceives the unifying Self in nature but goes mad because he cannot realize it in his own, or "little," self. The hero of *The Man Who Killed the Deer* is separated from humanity and nature until he recovers relationship to the living universe. *People of the Valley* shows an individual who incarnates unity. And the protagonist of *The Woman at Otowi Crossing* emerges to an experience of totality just when the Atomic Age is bringing civilization and the planet to the verge of physical catastrophe.

DUALITY

The concept of duality lies at the very root of oriental philosophy and is perhaps best approached initially from the point of view of the Eastern mystics. When the Eastern mystics tell us that they experience all things and events as manifestations of a basic unity, this does not mean that they pronounce all things to be equal. They recognize the individuality of things, but at the same time they are aware that all differences and contrasts are relative within an all-embracing unity. The experience of transcending opposites makes one aware not only of the relativity of opposites but also of their polarity. Eastern mystics realize that good and bad, pleasure and pain, life and death, are not absolute experiences belonging to different categories, but are merely two sides of the same reality, extreme parts of a single whole. The notion that all opposites are polar means that they are interdependent, their conflict never resulting in the total victory of one side but in a manifestation of the interplay between the two sides. "In the East," according to Fritjof Capra, "a virtuous person is therefore not one who undertakes the impossible task of striving for the good and eliminating the bad, but rather one who is able to maintain a dynamic balance between good and bad."[20] This point about duality as a dynamic interplay between two extremes has been emphasized most extensively by the Chinese sages in their symbolism of the archetypal poles yin and yang, which together represent male and female sides of human nature: yin the female mode of consciousness, which can be described by words like *intuitive, religious,* or *mystical;* yang the male mode of consciousness, rational thinking. In many Eastern traditions the dynamic balance between male and female modes of consciousness is the principal aim of meditation. A fully realized human being is one who, in the words of Lao Tzu, "knows the masculine and keeps to the feminine."[21] According to Eastern mystics, the unity of such duality takes place on a higher plane—that is, in a higher dimension, in a four-dimensional world which transcends the three-dimensional world of everyday life.

Waters's concept of duality is quite similar to but not restricted to that in Eastern philosophy. It parallels (but until the mid-1940s was not directly influenced by) the Jungian notion of conscious and unconscious polarities, which must be reconciled if modern man is to find his soul. The polarities of cosmic duality—earth and sky, light and darkness, male and female, positive and negative, good and evil—are manifested in parts of the whole and find complements in the schisms that divide races and cultures and each one of us internally (rational versus intuitive, personal ego versus impersonal Self). The conflict between polarities induces a continuous change through movement, and it is movement that gives life to man and to the universe. There is interplay in everything: between time and space, between the dual aspects of matter as particles and as waves, between expanding and contracting epochs of geological evolution, between successive stages or "worlds" of human evolution, including the psychic interplay between conscious and unconscious mentation, and so on. The polarities in both nature and man are always inclined to move toward reconciliation, and the movement is toward new and higher forms, out of dynamic tension. That is the meaning of the quincunx archetype: four directional points are placed about a central point (as in the structure of pyramids, the Four Corners myth of an axial World Mountain, the Hindu myth of a metaphysical Mount Meru, and some representations of Christ on the Cross), for from the tensions of opposing points there evolves the central and centering human consciousness on the *way* to full self-realization.

Duality as an organizing principle in Waters's fiction and nonfiction is a continuous dialogue between polarized opposites. In *Mexico Mystique* the Mayan obsession with time is juxtaposed to the Aztec obsession with space. The negative vibrations of El Cuchillo in the Taos Valley of northern New Mexico are juxtaposed to the positive vibrations of Sacred Mountain: duality is the keynote to orchestration of *Mountain Dialogues* and will, there, move toward an astonishing exposition of East-West differences called "Jung and Maharshi—On the Nature and Meaning of Man."[22] Similarly, in the fiction there is dialogic interplay between people and place, between people of different races and cultures, and within characters themselves. Spirit of place can be negatively polarized as in *Yogi* or positively polarized as in *People* and *Deer*. The United States and its so-called Anglo characters are polarized to the masculine and the rational, whereas Mexico and its Indian and mestizo characters are polarized to the feminine and instinctive. In the nonfictional *Masked Gods,* by a similar token, the atom smasher of Euro-American science and aggressive materialism is opposed by the Indian drum, and this duality is a precursor of counterpointing in *Otowi,* whereby the Atomic Age and ancient America come into conflict, and ancient America, as it were, redeems the world, not as a victory of one side over the other but as a restoration of balance. The polarized characters in *Flight from Fiesta,* an old drunken Indian and a spoiled Anglo girl of ten, discover "common humanness" (102) and hence project a vision of racial and psychosexual reconciliation. The Anglo protagonist of *Pike's Peak* and the Anglo subject of the fictionalized biography, *To Possess the Land,* are dominated by their egoism but haunted by the repressed contents of the unconscious or by the "shadow" personality. And so forth.

Clearly, duality is a most unusual concept for those of us accustomed to either-or situations or to denial of the interrelationships of all phenomena. Of course, there is a certain aesthetic danger risked when a novelist uses psychoanalytical terms such as *repression, projection,* or *unconscious,* for there needs to be, in the words of one critic, "a critically important tension between doctrinal certainty and subjective skepticism."[23] Although Waters sometimes employs such terms in order to clarify a duality, he doesn't allow them to supplant his independent judgment or his vision of a dynamic reality in which words hold only relative significance.

Duality is not only an organizing principle but also a stance providing serenity of outlook on the passing parade of temporal events. If the conflict of opposites is eternal and yet moving toward reconciliation in a higher dimension, then the artist is in position to contemplate society and history from a timeless perspective that envisions their transitory and illusory nature. Compassion is called for—*Yogi,* for example, dramatizes what it means to separate life from the principles determining it—and timelessness must not be separated from time but seen as an eternal Now. The duality of life and death dissolves before such a stance. That is why, I think, the deaths of some of Waters's greatest characters—of Tai Ling in *Yogi,* of Maria del Valle in *People,* and of Helen Chalmers in *Otowi*—do not affect us as contrivances of plot or as special pleadings for the lives of saints but as a natural part of their lives and a containment of the future in the sense of transfiguration. The death of Maria del Valle is described in the concluding sentence fragments of *People:*

> A faint candle-lit darkness, and on the floor the shrouded shape of an old woman with gleaming spectacles of square gold. Like eyes of gold whose value could never be diminished by change, which could never be blinded by age and evil, or corroded by weather and misfortune. Steadily gleaming eyes that burned through time with a faith which could not be dammed, and with a gaze which saw neither the darkness of the day nor the brightness of the morrow, but behind these illusions the enduring reality that makes of one sunset a prelude to a sunrise brighter still. [201]

One recognizes here and there in American poetry and imaginative literature this kind of cosmic lift-off from weal and woe. It is the stance in some of Melville's greatest fiction, in the endings of *Moby-Dick* and *Billy Budd,* and in a number of the better poems in *Battle-Pieces:*

> *Wag the world how it will,*
> *Leaves must be green in Spring.*
> ["Malvern Hill"][24]

It is the stance explored by Eliot in the interplay of his *Four Quartets,* notably in the passage from "Burnt Norton" that conveys the stillness of God at the heart of all activity:

> At the still point of the turning world. Neither flesh
> nor fleshless;
> Neither from nor towards: at the still point, there
> the dance is. . . .[25]

And yet, I think, Waters's stance has not been surpassed, for its evocation of serenity and mythic harmony, in American letters.

EMERGENCE

The concept of Emergence is an original myth that points to something profound, namely that the processes of Creation are a continuous Genesis—one, and two, all that is created contains an aspect that is very close to and perhaps is what we would normally call mind or consciousness, except that there is no equivalent in English for the Sanskrit term *Chit:* that "consciousness" which is embodied in all entities of the universe in different degrees. If one thinks of an infinite, numinous power welling up from an underlying creative source and then considers *this* as evolution, one begins to grasp Waters's concept that evolution proceeds on psychic as well as physical levels. And if one then tries to set aside the theory that the present world is the final world and postulates instead that it is but an intermediate world in process of becoming, one also begins to visualize what a peak experience of Emergence might resemble. It would resemble the experience of highly evolved human types— shamans, yogis, seers, saints, and poets—or individuals such as Jesus and Siddhartha Gautama, the experience of totality being therein so full as to make coming worlds manifest.

Emergence may, however, be experienced by anyone, at any time, once the ego-fog has cleared. That there are ordinary human beings, nonprofessionals so to speak, who experience meaningful coincidences and exhibit un-usual powers of mind such as clairvoyance, precognition, and telepathy confirms the possibility of Emergence, though on a lower scale than that of a peak experience of the full creativity of the worldly planet and the universe. The point to emphasize in Waters's vision is that everyone's awareness may be increased. We exist already *in* a numinous world and have but to be awak-ened to the reality. In terms of Western psychology, the awakening arrives when the duality of consciousness and the unconscious is reconciled. In terms of Eastern teachings, what we in the Western world call mind or conscious-ness is really the unconscious, because it is not an objective observer but is in turn the object of the one ultimate observer, the Universal Consciousness. The word *timelessness* perhaps conveys these abstract terms more poetically, for the common experience of linear time as an illusion (as contrasted with the sense of past, present, and future as forming a whole) signals Emergence.

Myths of Emergence appear in both ancient Mesoamerican and South-western Indian cosmogeny. Waters gives them a psychological interpretation:

> According to Aztec myth, which in turn derived from the older Toltecs, there were four successive worlds, eras, or suns, each destroyed by a cataclysm. The first was a world of Earth, or dark matter, whose inhabitants were beyond re-demption. The second was a world of Air, of spirit destined to become incar-nate, its inhabitants being turned into animal forms. The third was that of Fire, from which only the birds escaped. The fourth was the world of Water, from which the fishes arrived. These four worlds were symbolized as a four-square mandala, or quincunx, with the Fifth World as a unifying center. Its symbol was man, in whom all the evolutionary movements of the preceding worlds were synthesized. Here then was the first appearance of man and the birth of spirituality, by which alone he could progress to further worlds. [*Pumpkin,* 57–58]

Waters interprets the new worlds as "periodic enlargements of consciousness" that "coincide with the cyclic changes dictated by the one cosmic power that governs the indivisible life of all mankind, all nature, the universe itself" (*Mountain Dialogues,* 237). Emergence as a psychological concept of evolu-tion is characterized by perception of dimensions, is accomplished at great cost, and is actualized as a way out of crisis in civilization. In spite of Waters's insistence that his own Emergence myth is wholly transcendental and not concerned with temporal conditions and changes on this planet, the fact that he expresses the myth in novels, which necessarily depict social and historical reality, will tempt many readers to speculate about their prophetical propensi-ties. People today are becoming gradually aware of time as a fourth dimen-sion spanning both past and future. People today are conscious of living at a historical verge when changes, almost inconceivable a mere generation ago, are announcing themselves in sexual attitudes, in awareness of ecological imbalances, and in political realignments. Are these evidence of vertical upsurges from deep within mankind? Since Emergence permits "intuition to speak to our inner selves" (*Pumpkin,* 72), it is a living myth that offers to world culture a form of sanctuary and a feeling of confidence.

Waters's visionary novels are dramatic revelations of the myth of Emergence. In the earlier novels the myth is recognizable in such conceptual terms as *self-realization* and *self-fulfillment*. The myth is most fully developed in *The Woman at Otowi Crossing*. But, as I shall argue in chapters to follow, all these novels in varying ways and degrees reveal a vision involving the three interlocking concepts of unity, duality, and emergence. The vision itself reveals to those who can respond to it freely—uncoerced by the ding-dong of doom in so many previous literary arrangements of reality—"a sunrise brighter still."

2

THE LIZARD WOMAN

AND THE EMERGENCE

OF THE DAWN MAN

IT IS A CRITICAL commonplace that Americans of European descent hold wavering loyalties to two different worlds and that the union of opposites is thus the very basis of an American outlook. We seek psychological and cultural meanings between the Old and New worlds, the past and the present, the self and society, the supernatural and nature. In literature, some of our writers are in dissent from the excessively affirmative brightness of the Everlasting Yea and shift our gaze to its dialectical alternative, the nay-saying rhetoric of a primal darkness in nature and in man. Whereas a Ralph Waldo Emerson or a Walt Whitman seem confident of man's place in the scheme of things, there are Americans in our imaginative literature who figure as persons displaced in time and space or in both. As Harry Levin has shown, Washington Irving's Rip Van Winkle is the American displaced in time; William Austin's Peter Rugg—from "Peter Rugg, the Missing Man" (1824)—is the American dislocated spatially, his story that of a man who set out for his destination years ago and finally arrived at Boston only to witness his ruined estate being auctioned off. The theme of the homeless man estranged from his time and place seems, Levin argues, a particularly American one, and inherent in estrangement is the yearning for a home to which—after a movement to, and sometimes a catastrophic quest to, a wilderness westward—a restless protagonist returns. This combination of wanderlust and nostalgia, moreover, is often expressed in the form of a journey to the end of night. If the spirit of this journey manifests itself in the dark imagery of nightmare—as it does in works as various as Edgar Allan Poe's *Narrative of Arthur Gordon Pym* (1838), Nathaniel Hawthorne's "Young Goodman Brown" (1835), Herman Melville's *Moby-Dick* (1851), and Eugene O'Neill's *Long Day's Journey into Night* (produced after his death in 1953)—we have urged upon us, and against the voice of the majority, the authoritative experience of the isolated self. Whereas our ethical sympathies adhere naturally to the bright side of life, where ambiguity and paradox need not apply, some of the greatest of American writers are appalled by the ambiguous and paradoxical mask of whiteness, as Melville was in the white whale by the shudder of solitude and the chill of empty space, or as Robert Frost was in the desert of the skies and the whiteness of snow:

> I have it in me so much nearer home
> To scare myself with my own desert places.

An anxious irony negotiates between the counterclaims of home and desert, favors experience over innocence, and frightens itself with landscape moods of silence and of desolation as a precondition of survival, illumination, and faith.[1]

Frank Waters's first novel, *The Lizard Woman* (published as *Fever Pitch* in 1930), is informed by this motif of a nightmare journey into desolation and its paradoxical illumination.[2] Written in 1925–1926, when Waters worked for a telephone company along the California-Baja California border, the novel was inspired by his firsthand acquaintance with the Great Sonoran Desert, summarized in *The Colorado* as "the end of a world" (81) with a fatal fascination that "exerts the most powerful and unbreakable hold of any landscape on earth" (82). Waters does more than evoke the spirit of the desert: it draws out of him an imaginary topography of myth. Thus *Lizard Woman* works on two levels: as a realistic report about a remote and desolate area and as an archetypal quest for the area's meaning at depth of spiritual import. It is an imaginary voyage more akin to *Moby-Dick* and to Joseph Conrad's *Heart of Darkness* (1898)—Melville's Pacific Ocean and Conrad's Congo having been truly experienced—than to such examples of the bookishly spooky and magically glaring as Samuel Taylor Coleridge's *Rime of the Ancient Mariner* and Poe's *Arthur Gordon Pym*. As an adumbration of a literary kind, *Lizard Woman* is the story of a protagonist's journey from the White House (part one) of home to the White Heart (part three) of a primordial and irreducible desert place and thence home again. The journey results in dislocation from history and society but also in a new sense of relationship to the universe.

Although all three of Waters's major concepts—unity, duality, and emergence—are presented in the novel, Waters himself, until 1984, opposed its republication.[3] Still somewhat reluctant, he that year permitted a small press in Texas to print an edition with the original title and a foreword explaining his reluctance, the difficulties he had encountered as an inexperienced young writer, the story of the book's conception, and his surprise at discovering in *Lizard Woman* a universal archetype that redeemed at least some of the faults. First, he explains, he had had no formal preparation as a writer: at the Colorado College he had majored in engineering and taken no courses in English or literature. "As a result," he remarks wryly, "most of us engineering students were unable to write an application for a job without copying a form letter" (vi). Second, he was learning his craft in the appalling conditions of an oven-hot "two-room shack . . . in El Centro" (v). Third, the experience of the desert compelled him to write, as though he had no choice in the matter.

> The novel was begun in [1925] when I was twenty-four years old and working as a telephone engineer in Imperial Valley, on the California-Baja California border. During my stay there I made a horseback trip down into the little-known desert interior of Lower California. After having lived all of my early years in the high Rockies of Colorado, I was unprepared for the vast sweep of sunstruck desert with its flat wastes, clumps of cacti, and barren parched-rock ranges. Its emotional impact was so profound, I was impelled to give voice to it with pencil and paper. [v]

Waters goes on to explain in the foreword how the desert's impact on his imagination assumed a mysterious and powerful form: "I began with a description of a remote desert valley enclosed by barren rocky mountains, around whose circular rim lay the semblance of a gigantic lizard with a woman's face meeting the end of her scaly tail" (vi). The universal meaning of this image, however, eluded him in 1925, and consequently he believed the narrative which blossomed from it to be a contrivance. Having begun his story with the "fantastic description" of the Lizard Woman, he confronted "the problem of inventing a beginning and an end to whatever story could enclose it," so the "enveloping narrative I contrived was an adventure story somewhat like the common pulp-paper Westerns, but told through a narrator as were many of Conrad's great stories of the sea" (vi). The narrative, he thought, was organized "arbitrarily," its dialogue "awkward," and he ended up with a story "of only two characters in an empty desert, to whom nothing dramatic happened" (vii). Only years later did he discover that *Lizard Woman* had "one redeeming virtue" (vii): a universal symbol had been projected from his own unconscious.

> Not until years later did I discover that I had unconsciously projected in my description of that imaginary desert valley of the Lizard Woman one of the oldest symbols known to mankind—the *uroboros*, the circle formed by a serpent biting its own tail. Its hieroglyph in ancient Egypt designated the universe embracing all heaven and earth. The modern psychologists C. G. Jung and Erich Neumann interpreted the *uroboros* as the symbol of primordial unity, enclosing the infinitude of all space and time; the Greek *pleroma*, the fullness of divine Creation. The serpent itself, linking the beginning and the end, symbolized timeless time. . . . It was all there, complete, although I had not known of it nor understood its meaning. [vii–viii]

"Excessively rationalistic and materialistic," Waters concludes, "we have stifled the intuitive truth of how closely we are linked to all nature, the earth, waters, and the stars above. The *uroboros,* to whomever it occurs as it did to me, offers the promise of universal unity that still lies within us waiting to be regained" (ix).

Waters's criticism of the novel, his discovery of the *uroboros* excepted, is too harsh. *Lizard Woman* is not an arbitrarily organized narrative but one coherent in structure and details.[4] The elements of "an adventure story somewhat like the common pulp-paper Westerns"—the search for gold, a fight that ends in a killing, and the like—do not make the dominant impression, for Waters transmutes all such elements by means of the alchemical art of ambiguity. Contrary to Waters's testimony about a story "of only two characters in an empty desert, to whom nothing dramatic happened," *Lizard Woman* reveals complex ironies of characterization based on human duality and thus foreshadows the techniques of his later novels. Finally, *Lizard Woman* is a psychological drama, its tensions not to be confined to mere illustration of the archetypal *uroboros*. Years ago, before Jungian psychology was properly understood, Frederick J. Hoffman warned that archetypes may "arrest the process of articulating psychic tensions" because "the archetypal process, by enlarging and depersonalizing the expressive experience, threatens to destroy both its individuality and its complexity."[5] Waters's novel, as I hope to show, converts the archetypal *uroboros* into the expressive experience. Its protagonist is that universal type of hero who is compelled to fight a dragon in order to be freed from "her" power and to retrieve a treasure. In psychological terms, this protagonist secures the "treasure" of knowledge and is liberated into a new world of consciousness. Although his experience estranges him from society, he has emerged into enlightenment and bears isolation's authority for the founding of a new cultural canon.

One evening on the edge of a desert four men gather in a border cabaret to discuss the character and experience of a young American engineer, Lee Marston, who cannot hear the discussion but can be seen near the balcony that overlooks a street riotous with cheap cantinas and bars. Eric Dane does most of the talking; to his listeners his words are like Marston himself, "infinitely sad, indefinitely aloof" (1), and the listeners see in Marston "a man whom time with both youth and age had passed unnoticed," his face "all serenity" reflecting "the calmness of one who has been drawn into the imperturbable serenity of earth and stars" (1). From this perception it is to be inferred that Dane, for reasons not yet disclosed, has been defending the thesis that human behavior is related to and affected by a spirit of place. Specifically, he regards Marston's present character as a mysterious outcome of the desert's "desolation" (2), of a "something, the very existent, intangible reality of the earth from which we emerged; something with the faint, dying echo of an immortal strain" which puts mere "facts" to rest before "the grip of power which existed before even man" (3).

The tension between "facts" and "desolation" will be explored and maintained throughout the novel. The facts are these: Marston has killed a man named Jim Horne and abandoned to her death the woman they both loved, Arvilla; greed and jealousy are assumed to be Marston's motives; but Horne's body cannot be found nor can the mysterious land of the Lizard Woman, where the events occurred; Marston, therefore, has not been brought to trial and is commonly regarded in the border district as "crazy" (135). Only Dane argues against judgment based on "facts." In his Conradian role of a secret sharer, he has absorbed from Marston a kind of mystical knowledge that reveals in its ambiguity that existence seems ephemeral but is really interrelated.

> In those barren solitudes he found something; and as its telling returns to me and I see him now, I know that his tale is not mine. And sometimes when the night draws about me close as the soft folds of a heated blanket and it is I who am alone, I feel that the tale is, after all, not alone his. For it partakes of those things beyond the reach of his understanding and ours. And yet, though he is again alone, he is not lonely; living in a maze of unreality which to me seems not always of his own making. His very solitude, it seems at times, plays for his ears its own music which not even I can understand. [6–7]

Just how much does Waters's handling of this passage owe to Conrad's *Heart of Darkness?* Dane's affiliation to Marston resembles Marlowe's to Kurtz, the nightmare of his choice. But, as we recall, Kurtz is a civilized white man who has regressed to savagery until nothing remains of his humanity but a dying cry of moral outrage, whereas Marston is a civilized white man who has grown from his experience of desolation. The narrator of *Lizard Woman,* unlike Conrad's Marlowe, has glimpsed, both in Marston and in himself, infinity, not naturalism's "brute within."[6] Where Conrad unmasks moral pretensions until we see the reality of the individual in society, Waters perceives a cosmic unity beyond the "maze of unreality" constituting worldly existence.[7] In short, Waters parted company with Conrad, and the parting is critically significant: if we see in Marston another Kurtz, another white man estranged from humanity, another lost soul, we overlook the musical, harmonizing "something" which Marston "found" and which makes him a stranger only to conventional, analytically minded society, not to essential humanity.[8]

As Dane's voice dissolves into an omniscient point of view, we are introduced to Arvilla, a mestiza, a part-Indian, part-Mexican dancing girl with "the face of a brown Madonna" (7). She is to be identified as the Dark Madonna of Mesoamerican myth, the goddess of earth and corn whom the Catholic Church renamed the Virgin of Guadalupe a decade after the Spanish Conquest.[9] She is also the Lizard Woman personified and wears "a heavy gold bracelet . . . beaten in the likeness of a lizard whose flaked tail was wrapped around her wrist and whose head was the face of a Mexican dancing girl" (11). Although there is undoubtedly an element of racial conflict in Arvilla's relationship with Marston, it is the serpent power of earth that is emphasized and that both attracts and repels the romantic young Marston. Since she, like the Lizard Woman, is an irreducible symbol, there is no cogency in the good-or-evil labels with which Marston attempts to tag her and which animate comic as well as tragic ironies throughout the story of the relationship. For instance, soon after meeting Arvilla, he purchases two well-groomed horses (emblematic of false pride in his masculinity) and foolishly imagines Arvilla as "clothed virgin-like in the lace of a white mantilla mounted only upon one of the two great roans ready for his hand to lead away" (24). Lured by the serpent power he cannot identify, Marston behaves as "a school boy on a vacation" (22), "a child who knows nothing" (24), "a small boy" (63) at the mercy since childhood of "fancies" (6) and "a dream richer than the gold of a summer sunset and as far away" (22). Viewed by Dane as "excessively romantic" (24) and "courtly" (28), Marston thinks of Arvilla as "his wife" (30, 45), and longs to possess her "in an ecstasy of bewilderment" (48), and, after love is made, he is infatuated with "her nude body gold as sand in the sun" (68). He deliberately tries to ignore what he knows about her, that she is a sometime prostitute with one goal in mind, namely, to rejoin her lover, the white prospector Horne, who has discovered gold but lacks what Marston can supply, an engineer's know-how and a box of chemicals with which to assay the find. The suppressed facts produce "doubts and fears" (67) about Arvilla's relationship with him, but the hidden, unconscious reason for these is the dramatized child-to-mother nature of his love, for he is dominated by and is dependent on his Madonna. What he does not know is this: she encompasses and incarnates the paradoxical duality of the creative principle—light and dark, sacred and secular, tender and cruel, vulnerable and ruthless, beautiful and loathsome—an all-inclusive and, above all, unconscious power of life and nature. "Arvilla of the night was of his dreams. She held all the alluring essence of something he had all but reached the night before. Arvilla of the day was another creature. She was of the desert, hard, unfathomable, inhuman, devoid of all feeling" (76).

The tragicomic subtleties of this "love" story are frequently impressive. For instance, not Marston's rifle but Arvilla's knife is the designated weapon of threat, notwithstanding the fact that Arvilla twice uses her knife for healing, once to open Marston's blisters, another time to remove a cactus thorn from Marston's horse. When his horses are dying of thirst, Arvilla dispatches them with her knife, and Marston is appalled. Thus, toward the novel's end, he is predisposed to believe that what Horne holds in his hand is a knife instead of what it is, a glass test tube associated (in a brilliant metaphor) with the "crucifix" (125) on which Horne will be, so to speak, sacrificed. Yet another of Marston's predispositions, this one played for comedy, is to rationalize his fear of women (i.e., of the dark aspect of the feminine unconscious) by dehumanizing them. Marston learns one night that he is to sleep beside Arvilla in the wickiup of an old Cocopah Indian woman whom he sees as "half human" (38), "an old witch" (40) with "yellow eyes . . . like two fangs" (41) and "whose hair hung like matted strands of decayed rope" (49). While this old crone lies down in one corner, Marston in another, Arvilla comes in silently, undresses in the dark, touches him and drops down beside him.

> He wanted to stretch out his hand; he trembled at the thought. He wanted to cry out, to tell her all things which oppressed him, to cry, "Arvilla, you are beautiful! Arvilla, hold me in your brown arms. Never, Arvilla, let me go back to men, to cities." Forever would he go with her across the expanse which lay like the soft moonlight before his eyes. The old woman spoke loudly, threshed about on the floor, lay quiet. A bead of perspiration gathered on his brow. He rose suddenly, paused a moment at the feet of the old woman as if he would damn her presence with a kick, and passed out of the shelter. [48]

The propriety of sexual restraint in the presence of a "witch" is surely to be commended, but the scene really functions not to ridicule Marston's behavior but further to expose the limitations of his awareness. Still subject to "men" and "cities," he cannot recognize that the old crone is but the alter ego of Arvilla, even though he has earlier observed them sitting together "looking on with the dull apathy of old women beyond reach of interest in common things" (39). To be granted love by Arvilla, *his* Lizard Woman, just as to be granted ecstatic vision later by *the* Lizard Woman, he must learn to balance the logic and one-sided rationality of patriarchal civilization with the world of instinct and to become—like Arvilla, the old crone, and Arvilla's burro—"a part of the desert" (51).

We are prepared for Marston to undergo a psychic change as "The White House" (part one), civilization and home, are left behind, and Marston and Arvilla enter "The Desert" (part two). Here Marston finds "scattered pieces of what might have been an old wagon . . . half buried, sticking out from the sand, and rotting in the sun" (63); and here, just before Marston and Arvilla make love, their spirits are united in the timeless presence of a land older than humanity in the evolutionary scale.

> Night with its royal serenity enveloped them in a mantle of silence. The mist and the darkness intermingled, were weighted by the smothering haze of heat and drifted upon them with the same ponderous presence of the rock cliffs. All the world, all that invisible lift of spirit which is the intangible presence of humanity, had drifted far away, back to the shores wherein lay like a dreamland of hushed words and faces of memory, the things which gave them life. The land, the vast sea of solitude, beat upon their senses like the silence of painted waves. They were adrift on a pictured mist, boundless, unfathomable, containing no limit of time or thought. As if they two alone watched from afar the dying reflection of their own unutterable thoughts struggling upon the black wall of a world beyond their comprehension. And then, as the stars fell out of what seemed a huge black box whose lid was suddenly snapped open, the voices of the desert burst out in a great clamor which died and blended with the song of earth and stars. [65–66]

The power of the land inherent in Arvilla is felt by Marston after the love-making: "He was in the first sweeping current of a power which forever transcends all limits of time and space, which beyond all understanding gives to a woman something beyond even her own unfathomable gift of comprehension" (68). Precisely at the midpoint of the novel Marston begins to change: Arvilla's "mirrored dry strength of the desert, inflexible, ruthless, determinate . . . the expression of her spirit overflowed into his," and "he understood in her the unbrooding silence which had engulfed him" (78). Significantly, the rhetoric of these passages not only opposes understanding and comprehension to engulfing, envelopment, and walling-in (images with the negative connotation of restraint and death) but also, paradoxically (here and elsewhere in the text), makes knowledge dependent on enclosure by night, silence, Arvilla's brown arms, and the circular Lizard Woman (images with the positive connotation of wholeness, fullness of life, and reconciliation). Later, at the moment of Marston's vision of the Lizard Woman, he is said indeed to have attained "knowledge" (99). Then and thereafter he appropriates for consciousness that which previously was in the unconscious, beyond the ordinary rational order of understanding. But this appropriation, signifying emergence to a level of increased awareness, still leaves Lee Marston with fear of envelopment, and his story will continue to explore the death-life ambiguity of that image.

Marston's quest, as we have seen it thus far, may be summarized as a recovery of lost contents experienced in land and in sex as reunion of self and nature, with discovery of his own duality providing the bridge toward unity. The pattern is threefold: (1) departure from the "white" world of reason and technology in order to encounter the unknown instinctive life recalled from childhood as being a world of wonder, not terror; (2) partial breakdown of rational defenses as these are threatened by nature in her terrifying aspects; (3) protection and aid by nature in her nurturing aspects and growth of a new consciousness of relationship to nature, initiating but not completing assimilation of the cosmic wholeness beyond duality. Ironically, as the power of Marston's consciousness waxes, the power of Arvilla's unconscious wanes. She becomes the submissive, adoring, vulnerable woman of his dreams just as he gains strength from her and from the desert. In a revealing episode Marston uses his box of chemicals to test a water hole for arsenic poisoning and sees Arvilla's eyes "intent upon him, subservient, devouring, devotional" (89). He who has all along felt threatened by envelopment easily mistakes her devouring look. Just before the episode she has seemed to him "the embodiment of all evil" (87). Now, failing to realize that Arvilla loves him, he feels repulsed by her gaze and is reminded that Arvilla and the almost-forgotten Horne require his box of chemicals to satisfy their greed for gold. Once again the novel achieves focus by means of ambiguity, for Marston could have recalled, but didn't, that gold is to be associated not just negatively to lucre but also positively to the golden bracelet (emblem of the Lizard Woman), to Arvilla's skin, and to the sunny land of his dreams. Even as he becomes the dominant partner in a scene requiring of him some survival skills—and in the psychology of symbols ego-consciousness is masculine—he loses touch with his feelings and ignores Arvilla's plea at the end of part two, "Be with me. I am afraid!" (96).

"The White Heart" (part three) opens with Dane's commentary on Marston's vision of the Lizard Woman. Marston had "felt as though he were squatting in the position of an ancient sun-worshipper . . . at the very hour of creation," staring at the "sterile whiteness of a sea within a sea," feeling "the very manifestation of all Nature" seep into his soul and fill "the void to completeness" (98–99).

> And standing there alone in that immensity of creation and alone in the presence of God, he bowed his will to an omnipotent power of nature. He felt that it was as though the spot had never known the presence of a Creator. As though the very mountains seemed like a signet ring of God himself flung on that spot and preserving forever the enclosed space from Creation. [100]

Fear of enclosure has become interfused with the appallingly wonderful whiteness of the Lizard Woman, which carries a host of associations: the pale horse in Scripture, the albatross that bedeviled the Ancient Mariner, the engulfing glitter of Antarctic snow and ice at the conclusion of Poe's *Arthur Gordon Pym,* and the prehistoric white whale of Melville's imaginary voyage. It is the essence of the white heart of the land of the Lizard Woman to be, like Moby-Dick, utterly unique and beyond reduction into categories; she is neither good nor evil, though her whiteness carries the connotation of faith. And this symbolization is striking, because the imagery of the Bible from Genesis to the Apocalypse presupposes a primal darkness, a void that God shaped by creating light and dividing night from day, whereas Waters's image of primordial chaos envisions a different order of events, nonbiblical and apparently Amerindian in origin. It is the Lizard Woman "who made the world from rock" (93), "who had created the world for God at His Command" and "then in the very throes of conception . . . flung herself down and begged Him to leave her this one spot of untouched chaos" (102). She is thus to be identified as the Great Mother Goddess who was the central mythological figure in the ancient world before the emergence in the Levant of the patriarchal deity of the hieratic states.[10] Waters's version of the myth, moreover, does more than reaffirm the priority of the female principle of the cosmos: the Lizard Woman is *left over* from Creation, akin to the sun, and a residue of primal whiteness. The psychological implication of this cosmology is that there is psychic energy stored up for continuance of creative evolution in mankind's expanding consciousness.[11] I shall return to this idea presently.

Marston, we are told, rose to his feet and "felt the knowledge and heritage

of all mankind seep and fuse itself into his soul and transmit itself to his understanding" (99). Arvilla's spirit saves him from "stark madness" (100); that
is, *his* Lizard Woman, being mortal, invigorates the loyalty to home just
when the claim of desert threatens to overwhelm an American protagonist estranged from time. He, too, being mortal continues to project upon her his
fear of the unconscious (Waters here anticipates a major theme of *Pike's
Peak*) and proceeds toward the encounter with Horne. As we might expect,
given his earlier predisposition to dehumanize people who threaten him,
Marston considers as subhuman the lonely prospector who lives in a cave, resembles a rabbit, speaks in squeals and shrieks, and is companioned with liz-
ards, Gila monsters, toads and scorpions. When Marston observes Arvilla
"naked to the waist . . . lying across Horne's lap" while Horne is "playing
with her" (117), they become "far removed from his understanding" (118),
and he is utterly disgusted when Horne kisses his boots and kneels before him
"like a pietist before a priest" (130). The result is that curiously American
reaction bred by wilderness experience—violence. Acting in what he thinks is
self-defense, Marston strikes Horne with a piece of rock and kills him. Then
he knocks Arvilla to the ground, leaps for the burro, and heads for home and
civilization, linking Arvilla's last-minute declaration of love to "the taunting
cruelty of the dread figure" (132) of the Lizard Woman.

The denouement to this melodramatic ending is given by Dane in the last
chapter. Marston was found on the desert ten miles from the border town.
Arvilla had followed him "as if at last she had found one path without a turn,
without a thought for gold" (134) but died after reaching the first range of
hills. Recapitulating a verdict he has pronounced from the beginning, Dane
claims that "something, a real inexorable embodiment of that omnipotent
structure of creation which existed before God created man, filled his soul
with a force he was powerless to stem" (135). Dane asks his listeners to
"forget the damned, blind facts" and be "charitable" (135) to a man who, like
himself, has heard the voice of solitude and become a stranger to the world.

Commenting on the dubious honesty of characters in *The Merchant of
Venice,* William Empson notes how irony in a subdued sense requires of an
audience "a generous skepticism which can believe at once that people are
and are not guilty" and also believe that they have "still lingering in their
minds the way they would have preserved their self-respect if they had acted
differently."[12] *Lizard Woman,* I think, requires a generous skepticism. If
Marston is guilty, why is he "indefinitely aloof," his face "all serenity" reflecting "the calmness of one who has been drawn into the imperturbable serenity
of earth and stars"? One answer to this question, perhaps, is that a narrative

involving guilt for a crime puts mystical generalizations to a severe test. Unlike Emerson, Waters does not commute easily between self and the Over-Soul. But a better answer to the question, I believe, is that Marston is a kind of tragic hero.

Tragedy is an affirmation of man's importance and nobility, and a tragic ending needs to be explained as the result of human wills in conflict with each other or with fate. If a hero has been subjected to nature's indifferent laws and thus exonerated from full human responsibility for his deeds, he may represent a case history rather than a tragedy in the classical sense. Are we to believe, then, that the Lizard Woman stirred herself to crush a fly? If so, the sound of Marston's suffering reaches us faintly, like that of a stranger whom we cannot hope to comfort in spite of Dane's plea on his behalf. Or, on the other hand, did Marston suffer the consequences of his tragic blindness with respect to Arvilla's love yet *also,* in the Promethean cast, steal something away from the Lizard Woman that gives him enough self-respect to recognize error and to move the human spirit forward? "In those barren solitudes," Dane insists without irony, "he found something," and we know what he found: detachment, serenity, calmness. So this "something" has positive connotations, as does solitude, a condition to be opposed to loneliness. Marston has found something *beyond* the destructive component in the Lizard Woman, in Arvilla, in himself, and in the White House of society that participates in the White Heart of nature. His discovery is then beyond guilt, for a potential in nature has been activated in him and made available to reality.

A perceptive English scholar, Tony Tanner, has argued that American literature exhibits a "wondering vision" that leads us out of history and society into a static, though receptive, state of suspension in front of sheer nature. The Transcendentalists, relying on fervent but vague generalizations about the unlimited self, wanted, so this argument goes, to relieve us of active will and conscious thought, reabsorb us into nature, and give prestige to "the crystalline fragments of momentary experience."[13] The "seeing individual eye" is stressed in Emerson, Thoreau, and Whitman, even in Hemingway, and a hero such as Mark Twain's Huckleberry Finn "seems to have a distant origin, a remote destination, and to move inside a halo of isolation and loneliness." The result is resilience and resourcefulness but also confinement, like that of a trapped animal, and an increasingly desperate feeling of alienation in which one seeks to be restored to "a sense of the miraculousness as well as the gratuitousness of the stuff around us."[14]

Waters belongs to this tradition—if it is a tradition—of wonder, but he demonstrates in his very first novel that wonder is based not on a state of suspension but on a principle of reciprocity between the physical and psychic worlds. The hero, Marston, has not reached a dead end but lives in serene expectation of renewed life. Herein lies the relevance of the myth of the Lizard Woman as leftover Creation. Whereas in the occidental ranges of mythological thought and imagery, the ground of being is normally personified as a Creator, of whom Man is a creature turned inward in order to establish a means of relationship with God, the supreme aim of oriental mythology, as Joseph Campbell sees it, is "to render . . . an experience that goes beyond: of identity with that Being of beings which is both immanent and transcendent."[15] This observation points up the originality of Waters's vision, at least from an occidental and American perspective, and helps to explain Marston's serenity as a self-transcendence compatible with tragic folly and the guilty consequences. No momentary miracle of relationship with God, experienced but lapsed into disillusionment, has manifested itself. Marston's experience of identity with the Lizard Woman has put him in possession of a knowledge that sets him free within the cosmic order, though not within the human.

Critical inquiry into *Lizard Woman* along psychological lines, using especially the studies of C. G. Jung and Erich Neumann on the archetypal image of the *uroboros* or Great Mother, seems fruitful in view of Waters's subsequent accord with "Jungian" themes, expressed in both fiction and nonfiction. Neumann contends that an archetypal image such as the *uroboros* is "constitutionally present in every human being."[16] Accordingly, the fate of modern man is enacted in stages within the world of interior human experience. It follows that the hero of this psychic drama, though he may seem an outsider to culture, is really an insider or Great Individual—shaman, prophet, poet—whose momentary uprising of consciousness creates a new cultural canon in accordance with his illuminated revelation. Neumann's name for this hero is "the dawn man."[17] Because the ego tends to dissolve back into unconsciousness, that is, regress to childhood, the *uroboros* is an emblem of death. When, however, the *uroboros* is experienced as paradise, all-sustaining and all-containing, it symbolizes "the nativity of the ego, and of the dawn of consciousness, the coming of light."[18] A creative principle is at work from the beginning. Ego-consciousness, which on that account is associated with light and sun symbols, then recognizes, fears, and resists as its enemy that dark aspect of the *uroboros,* or the unconscious, which would dominate and destroy the developing ego. As Neumann describes this resistance, "ego development leads to a stage in which the Great Mother no longer appears as friendly and good, but becomes the ego's enemy, the Terrible Mother."[19] Fearing possession by this feminine uroboric dragon, "either with effeminacy and castration, by being transformed into her, or with madness and death," the masculine ego-consciousness "recognizes this destructive tendency as being not just a hostile intent of the unconscious, but as part of itself" in order "to incorporate it, to digest and assimilate it, in other words, to make it conscious."[20] An individual grows when the Great Mother assumes a human, personal form—a real woman or the soul—and becomes the feminine component in personality, to which the ego relates itself and by means of which, in effect, it transcends its own mortality and is liberated "to create a new spiritual world of human culture in the likeness of the divine."[21]

The dawn man of this myth of emergent consciousness brings light but also suffers in various ways. Having discovered the duality of the *uroboros*—Terrible Mother and Good Mother, a maddening enchantress and a bringer of wisdom, voluptuous harlot and inviolable virgin, immemorially old and eternally young—the hero breaks up "the unbearable white radiance of primordial light"[22] and establishes the Good Mother in the conscious world as a value but largely excludes the Terrible Mother from the conscious world, with the result in our culture of a loss of contact with the unconscious, of an exhausting isolation in himself, or of an eruption into violence.

The story of Lee Marston of *Lizard Woman* reveals, albeit unconsciously on Waters's part, the emergence of the dawn man. Marston's past consists of childhood's involuntary, pleasurable dreams about the unknown. His quest takes him toward the uroboric world of the unconscious, symbolized by the desert continuously analogous to the sea, water being the unconscious element. He is both attracted to and repelled by Arvilla, personification of the *uroboros,* struggles against her dominance, and breaks through to an increase of conscious knowledge, a strengthening of the will, and a capacity for voluntary action—hallmarks of ego-consciousness. However, the nebulous power of attraction hitherto exerted by the unconscious (the desert, Arvilla) crystallizes into a negative quality of the inimical (Lizard Woman and Arvilla as Terrible Mother). The death of his horses seems to reveal a destructive policy of the unconscious which Marston resists. Sexuality seems to him an "evil" disintegrative force, even though he is attracted to Arvilla as a conjuration of humanity from the dragon shape which distorts humanity and her. Although Marston recognizes Arvilla/desert/Lizard Woman as part of himself, that is, assimilates unconscious elements into consciousness, his ego, being predisposed to give value to the Good Mother and to exclude the Terrible Mother, loses touch with the unconscious and resorts to violence. Lee Marston suffers guilt *and* emerges into consciousness, expresses sadness *and* serenity, loses innocence *and* gains an experience of cosmic unity. The power of the Lizard Woman as dragon-mother has been held in check, and Marston's rebirth within her total Being as the uroboric Great Mother, symbol of both perfection and chaos, has authorized him, through the medium of Eric Dane, to tell a story of the dawn.

The validity of psychological interpretation of mythology remains open to question. Nevertheless, the correlation between Neumann's "history" of an archetype with *The Lizard Woman* is evidence of Waters's imaginative depth. A powerful and—as it turns out—universal vision illuminates his fiction from the beginning, not merely an idea of transpersonal psychology nor a didactic impulse to illustrate the wonder of psychic landscape. The preoccupying concepts of unity, duality, and emergence will acquire consciously philosophical dimensions in Waters's later fiction and nonfiction, but they originate in his imagination.

3

THE YOGI OF

COCKROACH COURT:

AN AMERICAN BOOK

OF THE DEAD

READERS ACCUSTOMED TO a benevolent spirit of place in Waters's novels are sometimes surprised to discover a negative spirit in his second novel, *The Yogi of Cockroach Court* (written largely in 1927). This is not to say that the novel as a whole lacks positive vision, but that its affirmation is achieved out of and because of the materials of a dark and illusory environment. The psychic landscape of the city of Mexicali, where Waters lived for a while from 1925 through 1927, evidently possessed a presence that projected itself into his mind and affected his spiritual state, perhaps inducing a crucial adjustment to a morally bleak atmosphere in the form of a search for a positive statement of values.[1]

According to Charles Adams of the University of Nevada, Las Vegas, students recognize similarities between Las Vegas and the Mexicali in Waters's novel. Both cities sell illusions, condone the dark side of behavior, and are populated by strangers.[2] They are, I would add, "instant cities"[3] of the New West that have sprouted in response to transitory economic factors such as, in Las Vegas, legalized gambling, and, in Mexicali, the growing of cotton in the delta of the Colorado River. As a spiritual landscape the vitality of the fictionalized Mexicali is ephemeral, its inhabitants anxious to go nowhere along a repetitive horizontal plane. The search for permanence, for an ethic of relationship along a vertical, supramundane plane of investigation, manifests itself as the alternative to the world of Cockroach Court, a microcosm of the modern wasteland. The novel's four main characters—Barby, Guadalupe, Sal, and Tai Ling—lead isolated lives on the horizontal plane. The potential for self-realization on the vertical plane flickers in all of them, but only Tai Ling, an old Chinese shopkeeper, makes a consciously directed effort to attain Nirvana, an ego-transcending psychological state of Enlightenment. The novel is structured so as to reveal its meaning at a culminating point when, as the central figure, Tai Ling, is dying, his meditations bring him an archetypal visualization of Light and realization of at least some of the Buddhahood or divine qualities which, he believes, are latent in every human being.

It is essential to the novel that Tai Ling is a Buddhist who practices the meditative discipline of yoga. He is not, as Daryl Grider correctly observes, a Charlie Chan: "his Buddhism and yogic discipline, unlike Chan's Confucianism, are not cosmetic . . . not intended merely to add a dash of exotica to the story, but rather are intrinsic to its meaning."[4] The question is bound to arise as to why Waters, who is not a Buddhist and has never practiced yogic meditation, would commit his imagination to the internal development of such a maverick character. Grider proposes, and I believe he is right, that Waters's own mystical experience of reality has led him to seek out, for his own clarification, "accounts of similar experiences in a number of different sources."[5] One of these clarifying sources has been Buddhism, specifically Mahayana Buddhism as explained by W. Y. Evans-Wentz in a number of remarkable books about later scriptures (Tantra) from Tibet. The two of his books most relevant to *Yogi* are *The Tibetan Book of the Dead* (1927) and *Tibetan Yoga and Secret Doctrines* (1935). In a note appended to his novel Waters acknowledges that he drew upon *Tibetan Yoga and Secret Doctrines* as a source of "yogic precepts quoted and paraphrased" (277).[6] *The Tibetan Book of the Dead* is not so acknowledged. Nevertheless, I think, it is this book, containing the *Bardo Thödol* (which Evans-Wentz somewhat misleadingly names a "Book of the Dead") and his lengthy introduction, which, if it is not a direct source for *Yogi,* yet provides us with an understanding of its archetypal vision. It is in *The Tibetan Book of the Dead* that we discover the archetype of death as the supreme moment of vision and rebirth.[7] Since a similar archetype controls the meaning of Waters's novel, it is not farfetched to approach *The Yogi of Cockroach Court* as an "American Book of the Dead."

This critical approach calls for a prefatory summary of Mahayana Buddhism and of *The Tibetan Book of the Dead.* For the former, I shall draw upon the observations of Lama Anagarika Govinda in his book *Foundations of Tibetan Mysticism;* for the latter, I shall draw upon Govinda, Evans-Wentz, and Jung's "Psychological Commentary" on the text.

According to Govinda, the Buddha who is worshipped is not the historical personality of the man Siddhartha Gautama but the embodiment of the highest spiritual qualities such as love, compassion, sympathetic joy, and equanimity. It is, therefore, not the man Gautama who was raised to the status of a god but the divine which was recognized as a possibility of human realization. "Thereby the divine did not become less in value, but more," Govinda declares, "because from a mere abstraction it became a living reality, from something that was only believed, it became something that could be experienced" as "a rising from a plane of lesser to a plane of greater reality." Therefore the Buddhas and Bodhisattvas are not merely personifications of abstract principles but "prototypes of those states of highest knowledge, wisdom, and harmony which have been realized in humanity and will ever have to be realized again and again." The teachers of Mahayana ("the Great Vehicle"), recognizing the danger of dwelling in mere abstractions, were never tired of emphasizing that these Buddhas—whether historically concrete beings or timeless archetypes of the human mind—"are not allegories of transcendental perfections or of unattainable ideals, but visible symbols and experiences of spiritual completeness in human form." The Buddhahood that a yogi seeks has this meaning of the spiritually complete, and the aim of the search "cannot be achieved through building up convictions, ideals, and aims based on reasoning, but only through conscious penetration of those levels of mind which cannot be reached or influenced by logical arguments or discursive thought." Such penetration and transformation "is only possible through the compelling power of vision, whose primordial images or 'archetypes' are the formative principles of our mind." One may object, Govinda continues, that such visions are purely subjective and therefore nothing ultimate. The subjectivity of inner visions, however, does not diminish their "reality-value," because the visions "are symbols, in which the highest knowledge and the noblest endeavour of the human mind are embodied." Their visualization, moreover, is not of "an independent or separately existing external world." The external world and his inner world are for the Buddhist only two sides of the same fabric. That is why the essence of Tantrism is "invariably of a mystic nature, i.e., trying to establish the *inner* relationships of things: the parallelism of microcosm and macrocosm, mind and universe, ritual and reality, the world of matter and the world of spirit." If the yogi remains attached to his ego, the inner connections between dynamic forces are disturbed. Such a partial view "can only be eliminated by a total vision or an experience of the whole, which combines all aspects in the unity of a higher dimension." In meditation, a total vision, "unsullied by thoughts and mental representations, undivided by discriminations, desires, and aversions" effects "indescribable and inexplicable happiness." But this joy does not separate the yogi from life. On the contrary, to recognize and transform the dynamic forces of the universe, which are not different from those of one's own mind, is "not only for one's own good, but for that of all living beings."[8]

The point, where *Yogi* is concerned, is that Tai Ling, a Buddhist, has the conscious desire to penetrate to a direct awareness of reality and, since he is a yogi, anticipates that his purposeful efforts will establish the inner relations of things, or the ideal state of Buddhahood. If we think of him as a sinner who is seeking salvation in an after-life heaven called Nirvana, we miss the mark. What he seeks is spiritual completeness in this life and for the sake of life. He is no fool, in this respect at least, and his aspirations to become a prototype of those states of highest knowledge, wisdom, and harmony which have to be realized in humanity are to be accounted admirable and noble. Ironies abound in this story of a yogi who is trapped in the world of illusions, but Tai Ling invites not our scorn or disapprobation but tragic pity. In the end, when he has begun to approach a total vision, his triumph is hard-earned and quite wonderful, even though by his own reckoning on the scale of perfection he has fallen short of his goal and will be reincarnated to continue progress in another life. True, he has not finally been liberated from the cycle of birth and death called the Wandering (samsara). He has, however, glimpsed the Light that is a sense symbol of Nirvana. There's victory in that glimpse—not only a victory for him but also a victory on behalf of the poor, benighted denizens of Cockroach Court.

The Tibetan Book of the Dead is meant to be a guide for a dead man during the period of his *Bardo* existence, symbolically described as an intermediate state of forty-nine days' duration between death and rebirth. The book is also a guide in the realm of creative vision: its visions, as Govinda explains, "are neither primitive folklore nor theological speculations" but are concerned "with the visible projections or reflexes of inner processes, experiences, and states of mind, produced in the creative phase of meditation." Thus the book is "for the living, to prepare them, not only for the dangers of death, but to give them an opportunity to make use of the great possibilities which offer themselves in the moment of relinquishing the body—either for a better rebirth or for final liberation."[9] The book teaches, in a metaphorical sense as well as a moral one, that we must die to our past and to our ego in order to realize the full meaning of our existence as human beings. To experience what the text refers to as "the Radiance of the Clear Light of Pure

Reality"[10] is, however, said to be vouchsafed during the actual process of dying, provided that the dying person's consciousness is weaned away from the dictates of reason and from the supremacy of egohood. One must be ripe for the liberated state. As is commonly the case, the dying person still feels the pull of samsara, the phenomenal universe, and is drawn away from Nirvana. This failure, if it can be so called, is caused by karmic illusions, defined by Jung as "illusions which result from the psychic residua of previous existences."[11] The law of consequences then takes effect, so that the dead person faces reincarnation into a new life which shall bear him nearer to his final goal, a knowledge in which the knower is one with the known.

The Tibetan Book of the Dead purports to treat rationally of the whole cycle of existence from death to rebirth. It projects a vision of, as Evans-Wentz asserts, "the most essential laws of nature affecting human life."[12] *Yogi,* as we shall see, projects a similar vision.

Barby is a mestizo orphan, part Mexican-Indian, part Yankee, taken in to be sheltered by Tai Ling, who actually prefers self-sufficiency to fellowship. Tai Ling's noninvolvement—"Compassion flooded his heart; he let it ebb" (33)—is a partial cause of Barby's growth to early manhood with "a terrifying sense of his persistent isolation" (32). Barby's isolation is also caused by marginated social status and its attendant feelings of fear, shame, and resentment. Fearing exposure of his inferiority, he seeks to maintain appearances at all costs: "And always his warped pride suffered from the unforgivable; not the act, but that others had seen it" (140). Like the archetypal *pícaro* of Spanish picaresque novels of the sixteenth and seventeenth centuries, Barby exhibits a failed identity, its condition of loneliness inseparable from the fear of love.[13] When he meets Guadalupe, a "percentage girl" at a cabaret, he momentarily glimpses "like a star, a meaning to his life" but is too cut off from "the deep flow of human communion" (34) to surrender egohood to love. Instead of experiencing in sex "the last fusion and the last dissolution" (55–56), he sees Guadalupe as means to another end: "through her he possessed the world" (60). He uses analytical and surveillance techniques to take possession of the secrets of her past. When she escapes from his "imprisonment" (81), he arrives at an emotional dead end:

> The taste of his freedom went sour. Again his nerves seemed to screw themselves up into a knot. He forgot his intricate schemes for revenge, and began to be deathly afraid lest some day he come upon her unaware. Dreading the possibility of meeting her on the street with Sal, of seeing her in the cabaret, he ventured out warily. A sudden step behind him on the street, a voice in his ear, and he whirled around as if suddenly detected in a shameful act. Not to be seen

by her first! It grew to be his one concern. Convincing himself that she was planning to circumvent him by the last monstrous ignominy of casually coming upon him, he grew to look for her with a consuming fear of detection. [141–42]

Barby's final stage is insanity. Hired to smuggle laborers into California, he crashes a truck laden with illegal cargo through a police barricade and feels, just before dying, the "joy of complete victory, the madness of unrestrained power" (241). His kinship to "world dictators" (230) is underlined—too heavily, I think. But negative words for Barby such as *victory, power,* and *master* effectively produce positive meanings when used for Tai Ling, the master of yoga who seeks psychological power in order to attain a victory over ego-identity.

Guadalupe is portrayed more sympathetically than Barby, though ultimately to the same effect—a dead end. At the beginning of the novel, she is a young Mexican-Indian with an appeal about her of "something fresh and tragic" (19); in the epilogue, she is a professional artiste and promiscuous lesbian who pretends to an innocence long lost and plays with people's lives as she once toyed with clay mice. Her words, "Life is simple . . . when you know exactly what you want" (275), conclude the novel on a chilling note.

Readers who question—or marvel at—Waters's audacity in 1927 in portraying a lesbian would probably agree that he is equally audacious in permitting a female character to experience sexual orgasm, hardly a prominent feature of American fiction until recently (in 1973, for example, in Erica Jong's *Fear of Flying*). Waters's description of Guadalupe's ecstasy conceals no heavy irony: "Abruptly the woman touched her; a terrible, exquisite and convulsing pleasure possessed her. There was no darkness, no thought, nothing but this mounting wave of ecstatic pleasure that bore her swiftly to a crest. She screamed out—a great sigh, fell back into a trough of glorious lethargy, and closed her eyes" (187). Waters's attitude toward Guadalupe is often sympathetic, and that includes her discovery of homosexual inclination and expression of sexual freedom *before* the loss of innocence. She is symbolically associated to the Aztec goddess of earth, corn, and rain, Tonantzin, renamed the Virgin of Guadalupe after the Conquest of Mexico. As a personification of Tonantzin, the Guadalupe of the novel is part of everything that is "timeless and indestructible" (18) with a "peculiar impersonality" (48) that keeps her intact when strangers seek to subdue her. This unimpaired quality of character, even though it becomes hardened isolation, retains some dignity and is linked to her rebelliousness, for, if we accept the premise that female passivity articulates defeat in male-dominated society, her active revolt against Barby and others earns a positive construction. That her "climax of self-realization" (185) *is* sexual, as contrasted to Tai Ling's cerebral self-realization, imposes the negative limitation: sexuality is not *the* alternative to materialism and may in fact prove an extension of its illusions, as happens in the novel's epilogue. If we focus too much attention on Guadalupe's lesbianism, we may overlook her illusionism. By the same token, if we focus too much attention on sexual perversion, we may overlook the degree to which male-dominated society helps to engender materialistic motives and sexual orientation to the masculine component in personality. Waters gives Guadalupe a narrative voice which "escapes" male assumptions and challenges the muddled yin-yang dialectic of Tai Ling's "principles of nature" (190), whereby females allegedly must accept final subjugation by males.[14] In the final analysis, she defeats herself.

Orphaned when her village in the sierras was plundered during a Mexican revolution, Guadalupe spends childhood on an American reservation, at the mission school in the care of a nun, Sister Teresa. One night when Guadalupe is ill, Sister Teresa molests her with "horrible, nervous, outlaw hands" (82), then tells the girl that the crime is "nothing but a dream" (82). In one racial and historical irony, there is truth to the pretense: the Catholic conquest of the Indians did not eradicate worship of the Dark Madonna of the Tepeyac, to the girl "a stronger god" (82) who gives her a vitality and individuality lacking in "the decadent Cocopahs, Mojaves and Yumas about her" (83). Thus, after Sister Teresa dies, Guadalupe coldly watches the lowering of the coffin but opens her eyes "to the mountains on the edge of another world . . . covered with a dark blue mantle and dotted with specks of light, like toasted maize grains, by the bright morning sun" and feels "free" (87). This vision of the Earth Mother, while it separates Guadalupe from Catholicism, is ironically qualified by the imagery of sunlight. When the Sun Father is present, the duality of sun (male principle) and of earth (female principle) is fused into wholeness, but when the duality is unbalanced through the absence of the sun, Guadalupe remains in bondage to the earth, which is to say to the dark unconscious without control of fear and desire.[15] Having left the reservation and also service at a boardinghouse whose owner tries to rape her, she escapes to the border town only to fall as if transfixed—it being night—into the clutches of an old woman, Oakie, "monster of secret desire and nameless fear" (106), whose repulsiveness contains "the germ of attraction which held her prisoner" (178). Now the girl who had previously been victimized by homosexual molestation is unconsciously participating in depravity. Following her affair with Barby, Guadalupe rationalizes as integrative love her lust for the lesbian, Peña, whose name in Spanish connotes the hardness of rock and the exclusiveness of a club. In Peña's mouth, Guadalupe believes, "the cloying nullity of dark night had been [banished]; it became instead a prolongation of her intense and living day" (187).[16] Peña, we are told, "fused her whole life and set the course of her future—that secret light of longing which had banished forever the cloying nullity of dark night" (206). Clearly, the imagery of fusion here differs in kind from that of "the last fusion" (55) whereby male-female duality is transcended: Guadalupe's interiorizing of fusion to her own ego is but slightly disguised behind reference to an exterior "other." Her belief that she is "at last wholly herself" (188) is subverted by her separateness in any relationship, and her "secret light of longing" is identifiable as the sexual heat of her own masculine ego. Far from being liberated into the light of consciousness, she has regressed to the confinement of the dark unconscious.

Sal is an American percentage girl whose helpless sinking into alcoholism and prostitution is, unlike Guadalupe's slide into corruption, foreknown. Least prominent of the main characters, Sal is the most pathetic of them because she is the most intuitive, a Cassandra whose understanding of causality leaves her with few illusions. She senses her doom in the negative spirit of the desert:

> You're just sittin' at the window watchin' them wrinkled up old hills shinin' away in moonlight and sunlight till you don't know which it is. Then it happened—sure as shootin', sure as God made little green monkeys. Them hills would begin puffin' up like balloons till you thought they'd bust. Why, you could feel your head puffin' up till you had to hold it from explodin' too. Nuts we were. Goin' plumb nuts. And me that was in a good house once in Kansas City with pretty curtains on the window, yellow roses and all, and a streetcar clangin' by outside. The conductor always waved. [49]

Her "profound knowledge of all human frailties" has "opened her eyes to the irremediable follies and the inexorable price of her misspent youth," but she has depended on "luck" (219) to delay arrival at her final destination—a prostitute's crib on Cockroach Court. As the epitome of "all the poor little fish and human cucarachas" (259) in the world, she is most in need of the pity and compassion symbolized in Tai Ling's effigy of the Bodhisattva, equated by Tai Ling to "her own people's Bodhisattva known as Jesus" (224). However, when desperation drives Sal to Tai Ling's shop, she screams at the sight of the effigy, to her but "a horrible, leering, heathen idol" (223), and flees from the one man who might have comforted her.

Everything in *Yogi* depends on what Tai Ling might have done and did not do and on how he recognizes his principled separation from humanity and affirms solidarity with it before his death. Like Axel Heyst in Conrad's *Victory,* Tai Ling has sought moral self-sufficiency and tried to ignore the human worth of those who intrude upon his privacy.[17] Like the reasoning protagonist of Sophocles's *Oedipus Rex,* Tai Ling thinks he has avoided his fate, only to know himself at last as "his own barrier" (193). The sign for his shop, the Lamp Awake, is emblematic of his tragic flaw: the letters for a state of wakefulness have faded, leaving "La Lampara . . ." as a marker of something missing in his character, soon revealed by his choice to be "a lamp unto himself" (26) in renunciation of "this world of ignorance" (25) so flagrantly present in the Plaza de las Cucarachas, where he lives.

Tai Ling's aspirations for a vertical leap from ignorance to bliss are constantly thwarted by a well-meaning but sluggish conscience. Soon after arriving at Cockroach Court, he is employed by Mendoza, "a young, flashily dressed Mexican, a former pimp" (34), who uses the shop as a front for an opium den. When Tai Ling recognizes the evil inherent in selling illusions, he quits business, but neither Mendoza nor Chino Juan, a rival, credit his "principles" (38). As the narrative begins, Mendoza talks a reluctant Tai Ling into once more using the cellar of his shop for criminal purposes, this time as an overnight stop for Chinese laborers to be smuggled across the border. This involvement Tai Ling tries to square with his conscience by using the proceeds to open a cantina named the Sun of May and to give it outright to Barby as a wedding present. Why would a yogi who detests materialism, who seeks the sun of illumination through meditation, and who fears a karmic rebirth think that the Sun of May, a spurious symbol of rebirth, will be well-managed by Barby or that Barby and Guadalupe intend to get married, unless his own capacity for thought is darkened by sentimental illusions? Why would he give a phonograph to Guadalupe, knowing she will dance to its music, absorbed in her body, when he practices yoga in order to forget the body, unless his fleshly instincts customarily prevail over his spiritual aspirations? In sum, whatever Tai Ling does to effect a common good involves him in a pattern of evil. Gradually he perceives that the source of evil lies within, especially when he fails to gain "the utter tranquillity and complete objectiveness" (143–44) required for the final stage of yogic mediation. So he tries to make amends. First, he permits his essentially compassionate nature to operate in the field of life:

> He no longer kept aloof upstairs as if they did not exist, but went downstairs to administer to his frightened, wretched compatriots as helplessly caught as he. He spoke simple words of kindliness, chafed their cramped and knotted knees, salved torn patches of skin, gave them hot tea—all to the end that they and he might derive from their common brotherhood a minimum of good out of the evil enclosing them. [144]

He is making moral progress, of course, but his wish to derive a good from acts of compassion points to an egocentricity and an inadequacy in the situation. Second, he quits the smuggling business, knowing that to do so may result in the sacrifice of his life, as it does in fact. But other lives will be lost as well. Barby replaces him as a smuggler and dies. Nor can Tai Ling resist the temptation to run his old rival, Chino Juan, out of business, so that self-sacrifice (leaving Mendoza, practicing yoga) is again qualified by self-interest. Chino Juan burns down Tai Ling's cantina. A tong war erupts, resulting in various killings. Tai Ling hides in his cellar, is crushed beneath a collapsed beam, and is deep in meditation when police close in to finish him off with a bomb.

There are two crucial scenes in the cellar. The first, which I shall call the recognition scene, occurs when Tai Ling unequivocally understands how he has separated himself from life and compassionately affirms solidarity with humanity. "How," he asks himself, "could he have separated life from the principles which guided it; ignored the fusion that already existed if one could only see it?" (259). This thought is then joined with feeling:

> He thought of all the poor little fish and human cucarachas, the blind beggar at the corner, all the men betrayed, the mothers who had lost their sons, all the misery and sadness, ignorance and loneliness throughout the world. The old man wept. He wept because he no longer felt separate; because he too was a part of all the misery that ever existed. [259–60]

He is no longer trying to make amends. He is not seeking forgiveness. He is recognizing the interrelatedness of life—a recognition that brings him to a new and higher level of development but still leaves him, where higher consciousness is concerned, characterized by a sadness which is the longing for light.[18]

The second scene, which I shall call the death scene, occurs when Tai Ling is deep in meditation, unaware of the police who are in the room above the cellar and are preparing to throw a bomb into it. Here is the scene in its entirety:

> There had been the cellar and the tiny glow of the guttering candle, and that which came to know itself freed from the illusion of this space that cramped it and this time that flickered around it.
>
> This knowledge, knowing itself composed so largely of physical sensations and stimuli, then knew itself a knowledge which detached itself from all this sensory phenomena; knew now neither the darkness nor the silence into which it retreated.
>
> Yet again this knowledge began to know itself known. It knew itself known as another complex compound of perceptions, cognitions, reasonings, memory, reflections.
>
> And gradually the knower separated from the known with another curious

certainty of detachment. In a boundless, timeless void, the knower observed the known give birth to the knowledge. The knowledge that included, impenetrated and connected the known and the knower. All in a vast and aching void.

But now the observer began to be observed. The knower itself became another known. And no sooner did the new knower know the known, than it too became observed by a new observer.

So through the immeasurable, timeless void the observer pursued the observed, and becoming the observed was itself pursued by the observer.

And now suddenly in the unfathomable darkness, the quintessential silence of the illimitable void, there exploded light. An explosion of silent, radiant light. An explosion of transcendental bliss.

There was no longer separation of observer and observed. The knower, the known and the knowledge merged together and knew itself one.

There was but one consciousness that in radiant light, in transcendental bliss, became identical with the immeasurable and timeless void. As it was identical with every microcosmic reflection of the void in its illusionary boundaries of space and time and matter.

So that this consciousness being aware of its nature of the void, was also aware of its nature in the illusion of space, of time, of matter. It was aware again of the cellar cluttered with debris and falling earth, of the pale morning light flooding it, and of the figures bent over it. [261–62]

The external "action" of the scene is the explosion of the bomb. Waters has timed this explosion to coincide with Tai Ling's self-transcending death, the "explosion of silent, radiant light." Thomas J. Lyon objects that this daring, ironic tour-de-force may be too neatly contrived.[19] It is nonetheless consistent with the archetype in *The Tibetan Book of the Dead* whereby the moment of death is perceived as the moment of greatest illumination. The light of the bomb is an objective correlative for Tai Ling's experience, but the radiance connotes, and "transcendental bliss" confirms, a spiritual success. That is to say, the irony does not work to all sides. It is ironic that the world of Cockroach Court fails to understand Tai Ling, and it is even more ironic that Tai Ling until the recognition scene has failed to understand himself. In the death scene he does attain knowledge, is truly an enlightened yogi. The scene illustrates what Evans-Wentz writes in *Tibetan Yoga and Secret Doctrines:* "*yoga* is the practical means whereby the human mind is enabled to realize the illusory character of sense perceptions and objects of the phenomenal world, and, also, of the concept of the self as a thing separable from all other selves."[20]

One might easily object to an illustrational bent in the scene. In Eliot's *Four Quartets,* so this argument might go, mystical philosophy is conveyed in personal, sensuous language, whereas Waters's language is impersonal, rarely imagistic (light being the prime image), and full of esoteric concepts (such as "void" and "consciousness"). I myself, after several readings of *Yogi,* considered the impersonality of the scene, if not exactly a flaw, then an effect of the recalcitrance of the materials. I could perceive the difficulty of representing a disciplined yogi's thoughts, from which the samsaric illusions of the senses would necessarily have to be excluded. I knew that the term *yoga* means a "yoking together," and so it seemed appropriate for Tai Ling to be, as he is, fusing dualities at a very high plane of awareness indeed, no less than a perception of Absolute Consciousness pervading and at the same time "observing" the character's unconscious mind. This, after all, is Waters's familiar concept of unity, and Tai Ling's experience of unity comes close to expressing the concept of emergence.

On a closer reading, however, I realized that the impersonality of the scene is itself the metaphor not only for the yogi's mental state but also for karma. Karma is the East's impersonal concept for a law of universal moral order. Karma dictates Tai Ling's destiny in the death scene, much as the West's personalized concept of agents of retributive justice guides characters known to us from Greek and Shakespearean drama. Waters deliberately adopts an impersonal language, perhaps in order to make us wince at the nebulous presence of immutable laws governing the whole cosmos.

This reading of the death scene redirects attention to the novel as a visionary work of art. By which criteria are we judging the success or failure of characters in *Yogi,* if not by the consequences of their intentions and acts? What Evans-Wentz in *Tibetan Yoga and Secret Doctrines* says about the law of karma is relevant here:

> That man and all man's faculties are the result of causes our scientists grant, but save for a very few of the greatest of them, like [T. H.] Huxley and William James, they have not as yet grasped, as the Oriental thinker has long ago, that man is man and just the kind of man that he is because he is the result of an apparently interminable concatenation of causes with a history which goes back for unknown millions of years. In a biological sense, man is to-day literally the heir of all the ages; and, as a direct outcome of how he wills and acts now, so shall his future status be in his evolutionary progression here on this planet.[21]

Measured before the magnitude of this concept the achievement of Tai Ling represents considerable psychological progress, even though he has accumulated too much bad karma to have more than a glimpse of the Light, after which he will descend—according to the pattern set forth in *The Tibetan Book of the Dead*—to rebirth. The other characters remain in thrall to their biological inheritance, to their environment, and to their individual karma, unable to will and act as Tai Ling has done.[22] They are failures, but failures in an evolutionary process rather than in a merely social and sexual sphere.

From the perspective of universal laws, the whole world is Cockroach Court. And this is the perspective from which Waters envisions his material.

The Yogi of Cockroach Court is largely a work of the 1920s. With the Jazz Age and Prohibition setting the tempo for action, the strain of living in a materialistic, modernizing world is dramatized as an immersion—characteristic of American fiction of the period—in violence, crime, sexuality, and decadence. Social protest is another characteristic of the period, its associated theme of human solidarity announced for *Yogi* by an epigraph presumably composed by the revolutionary Mexican muralist Diego Rivera.[23] Certainly a passion for emancipation from bondage surges through the thoughts of the main characters in the novel. Moreover, Waters seems to share with his literary contemporaries an old American ideal of forging a new consciousness to meet cultural crisis. There is immersion in that crisis; set against it is what Malcolm Bradbury (following Leo Marx) has called "the metaphor of the alternative, the silent, still universe . . . which could be held to restore a sense of direction and give an equipoise and luminosity to art."[24] Bradbury has in mind the initiation into the big woods in Faulkner and the green image of the enravaged American dream in F. Scott Fitzgerald. Although Waters's alternative metaphor is a yogi's search for Absolute Consciousness in the universe and himself rather than, merely, an improved social awareness, the author is no less modern than his contemporaries in sounding the period's experimental tone. Tai Ling represents an active principle at work in the universe, an authentic symbol of possibility in relation to the future. Waters's depth of preoccupation sets him apart from many of his contemporaries.

Waters's essays on literature show him preoccupied with fiction that reveals universal order as a cause-and-effect relationship. Two of these essays are pertinent here, "Relationships and the Novel," published in *The Writer* in 1943, and "Visions of the Good: What Literature Affirms and How," a lecture presented in 1986 at a writers' conference in Winona, Minnesota.[25] In the 1943 essay Waters rejects adherence to orthodox form and declares the main function of the novel to be "to reveal the relationship between man and his surrounding universe" (105). This relationship is "continually increasing, expanding" in a revolutionary world wherein modern man "finds himself alone in a vaster space with the debris of all his former securities, comforts and beliefs tumbling about him" (106). When the artist catches the "vital inter-connectedness" of characters, or that between people and the conditions of their place and time, "this relation builds up its own inherent, proper form" (107). Waters illustrates his theme with George Stewart's *Storm,* a novel that reveals the cause-and-effect relationship between a force of nature and the people and things affected by its destructive passage. *Storm* is thus for him a "significant" novel because it reveals "a relation to something pertinent in all our lives which we have formerly ignored as nebulous and abstract" (107). Something as impersonal yet as alive as a force of nature fulfills the "essential purpose" (105) of a novel, truly universalizing its meaning. In other words, for Waters, our connection to the universe, not exclusively the traditional interplay of character and society, is the ultimate concern of the novelist.

In the 1986 lecture Waters defines the function of literature in its higher forms above entertainment and escape as visionary and prophetic, "something that reveals the purpose of our existence, gives us a vision of our potential creativity, and helps to raise our level of consciousness." Literature is both "a repository of the past" and a "glimpse, as it were, of something beyond our temporal existence," a vision "which affirms or suggests that the world and man, matter and spirit, are one, and that some strange power helps to direct the course of our lives." Waters sees this vision reflected in myths of all races, in the plays of William Shakespeare, in the novels of Fyodor Dostoyevsky, D. H. Lawrence, Faulkner, and Isak Dinesen, and in "America's greatest novel," *Moby-Dick*. Visionary works of literature "possess the common quality of awakening in us a sense of something transcendental somewhere 'out there' beyond us or 'in here' within us." But in what literary manner is the transcendental communicated? Specifically, it is communicated as "the nebulous influence of fate, destiny, nemesis, karma, whatever we call it." This influence can be personalized, as in the Fates of Greek mythology, objectified, as in Moby-Dick, or impersonalized, as in the East's concept of karma, but its essence is "that every intent and action causes eventually a compensating effect." Representation of the influence is a perception of a "law of universal moral order which guides our continual 'becoming' . . . and our development to a higher level of consciousness. . . ." Because intuitive awareness of a purposive law guiding our existence "lies in each of us," the higher forms of literature and myth can bring that law's influence to "conscious recognition."

The ideas in *Yogi* are compatible with a theory of literature which thus accommodates both occidental and oriental myths of "becoming." The West's scientific idea of evolution, suggested by the word *destiny,* is analogous to the East's psychological idea of evolution, suggested by the word *karma.* Both destiny and karma project into a work of literature an influence that reveals a sense of a universal moral order connecting the microcosm "in us" and the macrocosm "out there." In *Yogi* Waters has drawn upon the East's concept of karma for thematic purposes—it is culture-specific for a Chinese protagonist—

but has yielded nothing by way of a scientific stance toward his material. What he has yielded, however, is the West's habitual sense of a historical return to divinity. If evolution has so far taken place unconsciously on the physical plane, and if destiny is in process of becoming consciously achieved, one task of literature begins with the exposition of man's distance in his normal secular life from the universal order of which he is a living part. But the West and the East have approached such a task from different mythological perspectives. In the West, the prevalent myth has been that man was removed from the divine through a historical event, so that he will be led back to the divine through another historical event, whereas in the East the prevalent myth has been that man has been blocked from reunion with the divine by psychological darkness or displacement, so that psychology—the practice of yoga—will be his vehicle of return. Psychological orientation leads toward recognition of unity beyond the duality of matter and spirit. An individual's awakening requires no outside reference or authorized community, because the mystery and power are both immanent and transcendent.[26] So it is that in *Yogi* the apparent failure of Tai Ling to attain to reunion with the divine is but a moment of arrest during a progressive evolution for the direction of which he is responsible, given his own inherent limits. The death scene affirms a process that is ultimately progress. Although multitudes will suffer and die during the unfoldment of human destiny, every life contributes to the foundation of progress, and, because every life is thus connected to every other life, one can only feel compassion for those who are struggling on the way.

Waters seems to have developed early his stance toward the spectacle of the world. The uroboric archetype in *Lizard Woman* is an objectified influence of destiny and universal order. When the protagonist, Lee Marston, is depicted as serenely detached and infinitely sad, a spatial cosmology is interposed between him in his realized mythic role (a timeless universal activated within him due to the psychic influence of the Lizard Woman) and ego-identity. He has wrenched control of his destiny away from the unconscious directing force personified in Arvilla and has reached an emergent stage of consciousness. Marston, however, is not ready to engage his will to collaborate in the transcendent task of evolution. Tai Ling, in contrast to Marston, not only makes a conscious effort to achieve a fully evolved state of being within universal order, but also understands that he is subject to an impersonalized influence of destiny, which he knows as karma, a map of past and future. Of the other characters only Sal is intuitively aware of causality and of her distance from reunion with divinity. Barby and Guadalupe might have been liberated from themselves by the fusion of love but remain imprisoned by unconscious instincts. And, of course, Tai Ling is not unlike them. He is the yogi *of* Cockroach Court, still partially ego-trapped, hence condemned to an undesired karmic return and future strivings for conscious enlargement. Although in his eyes failure to achieve Nirvana is a catastrophe, he is, from Waters's perspective, on his way—the Bodhisattva Way, the way of "one whose being is enlightenment."

In *The Colorado,* Waters describes his Mexicali experiences in terms of a search for a stance. A "boy," persona for himself in his early twenties, has drunkenly stumbled over the corpse of a murdered prostitute:

> He is not frightened, for his youthful innocence has clothed him in an armor invulnerable against harm. He is too drunk to feel horror, pity, anger, responsibility, or even to listen to that philosophy of acceptance which would have told him that in the tide of life perpetually swelling against mankind's frontiers death means little. [310]

The nature of this "philosophy of acceptance" as a view of human destiny has already been revealed in a prior passage describing Mexicali's underworld:

> The underworld, moving slowly and cautiously like a snake, begins to circulate. The professional gamblers, the dealers and the bartenders. The hundreds of half-naked prostitutes in their scuffed, colored slippers and sweat-blotched shifts. The thousand sateen-coated, sibilant Chinese. The horrible beggars crawling from the gutters with the ground crickets and the cockroaches. The brutal-faced mestizos, chollos, criollos, coyotes and cross-breeds. All the rateros, the pimps, the petty criminals and refugees of both countries, all the drunk and dissolute, the marihuana addicts and the hop-heads, the damned and diseased of this greatest slum in the whole basin—all those who by their labor and the prostitution of their lives forever lay the invisible foundation of progress, and make of each frontier the strangest, cruelest, most pitiful and most alive spot on earth. [309]

Nothing in the paragraph has prepared us for the sudden detached calm of "the invisible foundation of progress." With this phrase the spectacle of the world of Mexicali, which is the world of *Yogi,* dissolves into evolutionary perspective and into the posture of compassion. The point of view of eternity, always potentially available, presupposes the synthesis and interrelationship of all dualities, if one could but see it—Waters's philosophical stance in a nutshell.

Waters's stance toward the yogi is for the most part ironic, the allegiance qualified. Tai Ling, deluded by duality, has isolated himself from humanity. As the implied author—a presence in narrative fiction who affects the production of meaning, who is not the protagonist but rather the inventor of the protagonist, along with everything else in the narrative[27]—Waters is not fully allied with Tai Ling until the recognition scene, and even in it he holds his protagonist at an appropriate distance, Tai Ling being immobilized at the point of death and unable to dispense with bad karma. Tai Ling can grasp intellectually the idea of a light to come to a world of darkness, can spell out the common goal of attainment to what Waters calls in *Masked Gods* "the spiritual selfhood of the Buddha, of Jesus" (223), but his individual karma remains a debt to be paid.

The idea of death as a struggle at a decisive moment brings to death a particularly excruciating sense of significance. The dying person, seen as psychologically ripe for a reversal of the aims and intentions of the conscious mind, may augment a previously limited consciousness and even experience illumination for the first time. But karma has its catch-22, as we can formulate from notes appended by Evans-Wentz to *The Tibetan Book of the Dead:*

> One of the Doctrines peculiar to Northern Buddhism is that spiritual emancipation, even Buddhahood, may be won instantaneously. . . . But here again success implies very unusual proficiency in *yoga,* as well as much accumulated merit, or good *karma,* on the part of the devotee.[28]

> In the realm of the Clear Light . . . the mentality of a person dying momentarily enjoys a condition of balance, or perfect equilibrium, and of oneness. Owing to the unfamiliarity with such a state, which is an ecstatic state of non-ego, of subliminal consciousness, the consciousness-principle of the average human being lacks the power to function in it; *karmic* propensities becloud the consciousness-principle with thoughts of personality, of individualized being, of dualism, and, losing equilibrium, the consciousness-principle falls away from the Clear Light. It is the ideation of ego, of self, which prevents the realization of *Nirvana* . . . and so the Wheel of Life continues to turn.[29]

If a lack of yogic proficiency and of merit doesn't catch the dying person in the spokes of the life-death cycle, then a final-second loss of equilibrium will. The yogi must be able to function in a state of transcendental bliss. In spite of lofty, manly, and heroic aspirations, the yogi may be pressed into future incarnations. The death of Tai Ling is to be interpreted according to these formulae. He has never reached the final stage of yogic meditation. He has accumulated too much bad karma. Whatever transcendental bliss presents itself, it is nonfunctional: the death scene is the beginning of the after-death state called the *Bardo.* At the supreme moment, Tai Ling enters the *Bardo* state, exactly what he didn't want.

The Yogi of Cockroach Court doesn't flinch from depicting karmic repetition along the horizontal plane of mundane consciousness. Life on this order is like the cantina where Guadalupe and Sal dance: named Las Quince

Letras ("the Fifteen Letters"), it repeats its own number. The "bonds" (33) to one's racial past are almost inescapable tendencies; thus, for example, Tai Ling experiences nostalgia for romantic Chinese songs. And there are the inherited tendencies of duality. The characters of Barby and Guadalupe are encoded with a more or less instinctive will to dominate and a more or less habitual ignorance. This motif of heredity is especially evident in the novel's prologue. "So brightly blazed the sun upon the dunes and down the curving beach, so tranquilly dozed the village under its ragged palms, that only the rising wind marked September's ominous departure" (3): so begins the novel. Soon there arrives from the Sea of Cortez the *Flying Fish,* skippered by a Yankee known only as El Borracho ("the drunkard"). Is this wind identifiable with (in the words of Jung's commentary on *The Tibetan Book of the Dead*), "the fierce wind of *karma,* which whirls the dead man along until he comes to the 'womb-door' "?[30] Such a gloss at least fits the narrative context. El Borracho, Barby's father, has lived a life of "futility" (5) destined to repeat itself in the son. When we learn that fish are for Tai Ling a symbol of sentient beings living in illusion, the *Flying Fish* may be perceived as foreshadowing Barby's inherent tendency to illusion. But the rising storm suggests impending change in the tide of life. Thus what seems to be a repeating life-death cycle is really open to change. Barby will almost drown in the tide, but he finds "sanctuary" (20) in Tai Ling's shop,—in the place where release from the karmic cycle and progress along the vertical plane of consciousness are being actively sought.

In Buddhist philosophy, birth and death are not phenomena that happen only once in human life. Accordingly, to be born a human being is a privilege because the "Bardo of Life,"[31] as it is perhaps properly called, offers the rare opportunity of liberation, through one's own decisive effort, from death's illusory nature. *The Tibetan Book of the Dead* is addressed to initiates and reveals the secret that life has dominion over the realm of death. *The Yogi of Cockroach Court* is obviously not a book of initiation and instruction. But I have described it as an American Book of the Dead because it dramatizes a decisive effort to experience the radiance of supramundane reality in unfathomable darkness, even while the world *as* Cockroach Court squanders the privilege of life. Like *The Tibetan Book of the Dead, Yogi* has a vision which is apparently of archetypal origin. Like devotees of Mahayana Buddhism, Waters represents the world from the point of view of the mystery of eternity itself. He proposes in *Yogi* the attitude that all is to be accepted with compassion in a world that is always evolving according to august and austere moral laws.

PIKE'S PEAK:

THE SEARCH FOR THE

SUPREME UNIVERSE

PIKE'S PEAK, published in 1971, is a 743-page novel rewritten from a 1500-page trilogy of the 1930s—*The Wild Earth's Nobility* (1935), *Below Grass Roots* (1937), and *The Dust within the Rock* (1940). Although the new novel shortens the trilogy by half and in other ways offers a revised text, in essence *Pike's Peak* differs but little from the trilogy, the materials of which are brought into improved focus. The trilogy has been transformed out of its own ground, like the butter hidden in cream.[1]

The 1971 edition of *Pike's Peak* was subtitled by the publishers *A Family Saga: An Epic Journey of the American Soul* and the 1987 reprint of that edition *A Mining Saga.* There are, to be sure, elements of saga or epic in this long novel. The time span is impressive: *Pike's Peak* is the story of the Joseph Rogier family, which lives at the base of the 14,000-foot mountain near Colorado Springs for three generations, from the 1870s through world war and depression. Rogier's unpretentious house on the edge of the prairies pens up a crowd of women and children dependent on his success as an architectural engineer and builder, and the novel's scope is enlarged through the narratives of Rogier's daughter, Ona, son-in-law, Jonathan Cable, and grandson, March Cable. Stories of pioneer settlement in the West conjure up expectations of vast horizons and fabulous deeds, and this novel about gold mining, the first

American novel of its kind, meets the demand: Cripple Creek in the Pike's Peak region was once the world's most productive source of gold.

An epic depicts a people's whole way of life, and more people in the West were involved in mining and in the building of cities than were ever involved in Indian fighting and cattle ranching. The story of Joseph Rogier is, in fact, a paradigm of Euro-American history in its New World inflections on the frontier. Historical experiences of exile, conquest, and colonization, of dreams of a better life, of faith in mechanical progress, and of belief in the atomic individual's unchurched and immediate access to the revelations of God are gathered here at the heart of the continent where the peak is a beacon of promise and a numinous source, like Melville's white whale. If it is true that the identity of the American people was formed on the frontier, then Rogier's quest for durable selfhood is a pointedly historical one—epic, too, in the tradition of *The Divine Comedy* and *Moby-Dick*. The important thematic passages in *Pike's Peak* involve us in Rogier's search for the meaning of life in the mountain. In these passages Waters most nearly appropriates for poetic purposes the epic convention of interaction between men and gods—for the peak is Rogier's god.

Epic qualifications notwithstanding, *Pike's Peak* is a novel. Moreover, where genre is concerned, it is the kind of novel that has the vision of tragedy. For tragedy, which is the inevitable result of taking a complete view of the human situation, makes the richness and beauty of life depend on a balance. The basic tenet of this worldview is that all life is maintained by observance of the natural order—that is, perception that what goes on in one sphere affects what goes on in other spheres. Both Greek and Shakespearean literary tragedy reveal that a disorder in the human system is symbolically paralleled by a disorder in the social system, these in turn by a disorder in nature. The core of tragedy's idea of order is the sacredness of the bonds which hold human beings together and establish a balance in their lives and between them and the natural order.[2] To say, then, that *Pike's Peak* reveals a tragic vision is to call attention to ideas of disorder and of order represented in the action and to levels of tone, especially to the presence of tragic irony. On the surface, *Pike's Peak* is a regional history stocked with what might be called documentation of mining. Actually, mining is but a metaphor for psychological excavations. When Joseph Rogier succumbs to gold fever, it is not gold he is seeking in the depths of the earth. It is no less than the secret of the supreme universe that he seeks, which is to say the secret of himself in relation to nature. The narrative of that search is a tragic one precisely because Rogier's mind is disordered, out of balance within itself and thus out of tune with the very object of his heart's desire.

Tragic irony controls those passages in which Rogier expresses his belief that the supreme universe is embodied in the Peak, outside himself, whereas it is clear that he is projecting upon the Peak the archetypal contents of his own unconscious mind. When he finally realizes that he has been mining in the wrong place, that the source of faith is immanently in himself, we are being given a climactic recognition scene toward which the action of the novel has been directed since the first chapter, when a young Rogier ponders the secret of the Peak and envies the wild Indians who seem to possess that secret already. Although in his old age Rogier recognizes his mistake and how ruinous it has been, financially and emotionally, for his family, he cannot relinquish the idea of encountering his God, as it were face to face, like a Job. This is perhaps the greatest thing about Rogier, that he does not doubt that the supreme universe is the totality of opposites. Still, he himself cannot, as if pulling a switch, bring intuition into balance with reason, thereby integrating personality in relation to itself, to society, to the land, and ultimately to the universe. His granitic will, the stuff of heroes of the American West in their excessively masculine obsession about dominance, continues to separate him from the feminine softness of adobe, Waters's symbol of the powers of the unconscious wherein Indians and Mexicans recall their allegiance to Mother Earth. And so Rogier goes completely mad. Singlehandedly he tries to dig a tunnel from his garden toward the Peak, toward "the brightness and the glory, the incandescent mystery of that secret and immortal Self" (615).[3] When the tunnel collapses upon him, he is injured and not long afterward dies. The tragic pity of this failure is underscored by the career of March Cable: having begun by repeating Rogier's error of seeking for the supreme universe, for "Self," in the earth, March directs the quest inward and is rewarded by a hope engendered by the evolutionary perspective of Emergence— "all humanity streaming out from its common womb of the unconscious, beginning its slow climb into the light and freedom of consciousness" (718). It is the reconciliation of this psychological duality which lights the way to unity and order.

The way of reconciliation is also dramatized in the possibility of racial harmony, as between whites and Indians. Considered as a tragedy, *Pike's Peak* shoulders the burden of the history of America and its West, a tragic awareness opening up on two fronts: that of the attempt of pioneers to comprehend the land psychically, failing which comprehension they then subdue it to European and eastern American patterns; and that of encounter with the Indian, whose enduring presence, often historically regarded as an obstacle to progress and respectability, in reality undermines all notions of a heroic Manifest Destiny. Although Waters does not sentimentalize his portraits of

the Indian—some are barbaric and some are naive, like the rich Osage chief-
tain who drinks water from a toilet bowl at the Broadmoor Hotel—*Pike's
Peak* keeps focus on Indian atonement with the spirit of the land. It is this fusion which puzzles Rogier. Ona, however, is initiated into it. When she is pre-
pubescent, hungry Indians invade the Rogier kitchen to steal utensils and to
demand pancakes. One young Indian, impressed by Ona's "indomitable silence and stony face" (23), swings her toward the stove:

> Suddenly, with one hand, he pulled up her calico dress and on the next slow
> swing pressed her naked bottom against the hot iron of the stove. It all hap-
> pened instantly and at once. She could feel the sharp pain of the burn on her
> right buttock, the faint odor of singeing white flesh; and at the same time the
> steady fixed stare of his black eyes into her own, a stare that seemed to pene-
> trate so deep into her that for an instant they became one. [24]

The penetration of eyes becomes an explicitly sexual metaphor as Ona begins
menstruation. The scene foreshadows her mature attraction to the part-
Indian Jonathan Cable, whom she will marry in spite of her mother's objections to having a "red niggah in the house" (183).

Rogier himself is not burdened by the psychosis of racial prejudice. A
Southerner by birth, he is fond of the black slaves who raised him. And, at
first, he is not possessed by a will to conquer the land:

> It was a great land, long as time and wide as the imagination, with the rhythm
> of its own being. Always conscious of a sense of uplift, Rogier looked down as
> if from great height upon the slow evolution of his kind from their cenozoic
> ooze. He could see them crawling upon the slimy land, slinking into the
> steamy jungle as he had seen men vanishing into the half-light of the Carolina
> swamps, then emerging slowly out upon the wide grassy lowlands of the
> Mississippi basin. Always westward and upward until they stood at last upon
> this great arid plateau fronted by lofty mountains raised like a pulpit before
> which they could shout their everlasting queries at the empty sky above. This
> was the end of their hegira! Not a land new and raw to be molded at their will,
> but one so old it had outlived the forests imbedded in the limestone cliffs just
> west of town. A land to be lived with, not conquered. [35]

Evolution is quickly narrowed to the theme of westward migration and
mingled into Rogier's personal sense of "hegira," or separation from a spiritual home, but his own gift of rhythm here suggests accommodation to the
rhythm of the land. Gradually, however, Rogier accumulates the psychological dynamite that will explode into gold fever: a feeling of alienation from nature and God; a powerful and deadly desire to return to the womb of the
earth and to cut himself off from the roots of life; and envy of the financial

success of a former hired man, Stratton, the "Midas of the Rockies" who discovers the richest gold mine in the world.[4] Rogier's soliloquies become claustrophobic, like underground caverns festooned with exotic images projected from his unconscious upon the Peak:

> Rogier, however else anyone knew him, was a man for whom time had stopped. The flowing linear stream of time—what an illusion it really was! Time was a great still pool, an element as basic as earth and air, water and fire, in which life developed at its own immeasurable pace to its own degree of fulfillment. Time! What did it mean to him now? In that invisible, immeasurable, impalpable pool both he and the Peak had been rooted for aeons to confront at last the meaning of their inner selves. Rogier kept staring at it in moonlight and in sunlight, as its dual faces of benign motherliness and masculine malignity combined into an enigmatic mask which he now recognized for what it was. In geological time it had stood there, a monstrous volcano belching fire and smoke upon a world that had sunk beneath forgotten seas. It had stood there in orogenic time, a lofty snow-crowned peak looking down upon a virgin continent yet unraped by greedy man. Through the quick gasp of a century it had remained inviolable while lesser prophets, robed in silver, had been gutted of their riches. . . . For he also was a growth within that immovable, immeasurable, deep pool of time, as old as the Peak itself. And now at last in their moment of truth and fruition they faced each other like two adversaries bound together in a common selfhood. Over them both a common golden sun rose and set. Through both their flesh ran the veins of liquid golden life, pulsating to the same diastolic and systolic beat. And in each of them glowed the reflection of the one great sun, the golden sun that was the heart of all. Gold! A great gold heart embodied in the depths of that extinct volcano whose remnant was the puny Peak. A heart whose beat was in rhythm with his own; whose meaning, if he could but fathom it, would illumine for him the secret of his existence which had seemed so alien to this mortal earth. Of course he would reach it, if he had to blast the whole dom top off the Peak and dig by hand down to the convergence of its golden veins in the heart that lay beneath! For time, the human illusion of flowing time, no longer existed. He had been born for this, geological eras, biological ages ago. Born as an incipient mammal to grow into an individual egohood only to seek and to find at last that universal self which combined within it both himself and the massive Peak whose granite armor he was meant to pierce. [311–12]

If this interior monologue reveals madness, it is still the madness of a brilliant man with scientific, moral, and religious insight. Only certain phrases betray the madness: "rooted for aeons to confront at last," "faced each other like two adversaries," "to grow into an individual egohood," and the like. For Rogier's mind is overthrown by faulty logic that has its implied source in solipsism, egomania, and anthropomorphism. This builder whose analytical skill allows him to measure things wants the "immeasurable" (the word is repeated three times) to yield itself in his own image—even if he has to blast "the whole dom top off." The unbalanced mind induces an absurdly aggressive image of the destruction of nature, but the tragedy is that his own mind is being destroyed. The gloss on this ironic soliloquy is provided when Rogier realizes his mistake: "The great snowy Peak was . . . like himself, a material shell, a transient symbol" (658).[5]

But it is one thing to recognize that an object in nature is a transient symbol of a supreme universe and another thing to claim for the discovery a designification of nature.[6] Are we to interpret *Pike's Peak* as the drawing of a line between self and nature, with nature a meaningless external force which refuses to be assimilated in consciousness? Is Rogier falsely infusing nature with meaning? Or, if self and nature are meaningfully coeternal, does *Pike's Peak* represent validation of the search for the supreme universe, while, as I believe, exposing the tragedy of mind inherent in the way Rogier set about it?

Three decades intervened between completion of *The Dust within the Rock* in 1938 and of *Pike's Peak* in 1969. During this period Waters's art achieved maturity, and his knowledge of history, religion, psychology, and modern science expanded to produce major works of fiction and nonfiction. Insights into the profoundly universal meanings of Indian ceremonialism found expression in *Masked Gods* (1950) and were confirmed and deepened in *Book of the Hopi* (1963) and in *Pumpkin Seed Point* (1969). These same three decades, of course, had witnessed world war, the Atomic Age, and the H-bomb, seen the beginnings of a "conquest" of space, and marked the rise of the United States to a position of world dominance. To Waters, these were but the latest manifestations of a materialistic and overly rationalistic civilization which for untold centuries had been obsessed with the subjugation of nature and which was now headed at accelerated pace toward self-destruction. His trilogy of novels in the 1930s had already foreseen the shape and cause of the tragedy and highlighted it by means of a contrast between two views of nature, the Euro-American and the Indian. To the world in 1969, the message of the trilogy would have seemed more relevant than ever.

A contrast of white and dark-skinned races and cultures is nothing new to the modern era. Often regarded as a contrast between "advanced" and "primitive" peoples, it juxtaposes values of people who live in close harmony with nature and of people who have sacrificed emotional spontaneity for the privileges of scientific and industrial society, as if the inner resources of man were a fixed economy in which advances in one direction must entail sacrifices in another.[7] D. H. Lawrence had even attempted to rehabilitate the Quetzalcoatl myth as a response to the ills of modern society.[8] But Waters, who from firsthand experience can scout the applicability of such terms as *advanced* and *primitive,* has something new to say *with* the contrast between races and cultures, and it is this: instinct and reason are to be reconciled on the intuitive level of increased awareness, a reconciliation with an ethic of relationship with the living universe and with all races of humanity. That is the note sounded in *Pike's Peak,* a novel that rejects the dualistic thinking of the modern world—self and object, man and nature, mind and matter—and imaginatively conveys the idea of a complementary origin of dualities in a supreme universe. *Pike's Peak* is a masterpiece of "deep-structure" revelation.

The essay "Two Views of Nature," included as a chapter in *Pumpkin Seed Point,* helps to show what Waters was thinking when he wrote *Pike's Peak.*[9] Man has learned to distinguish himself from the rest of nature but holds two views of his relationship to it, which I shall call the sacred and the materialistic views. The sacred view retains an obligation to the dictates of the unconscious which embodies the primordial past and is the only religious source of the feeling of interrelationship between man and nature. The materialistic view, on the other hand, insists on the separation of man and nature, ignores the unconscious, and seeks to subdue nature. The sacred view, associated with Indians and animism, stems from a long religious tradition of belief that Creation is imbued with one consciousness and infused with one power, of which everything in the universe is an embodied part. The materialistic view, associated with Euro-Americans and pragmatism, balks at the notion of a living universe in which everything, however embryonically conscious, is meaningfully or spiritually evolving. Whereas the materialistic view of nature has produced untold social and technical benefits, paradoxically it has also produced spiritual impoverishment and its destructive consequences.

Waters prefers the sacred view of nature. Every land, he declares in the essay, has its own spirit of place. It follows that each entity in nature not only has an outer physical form but also an inner spiritual force, an all-pervading, impersonal spirit of life. At first glance this seems to be a mystical premise without scientific basis, yet Einstein's mass-energy equation, by removing the distinction of matter and energy, admits the principle of "life" into the image of electrical fields unified by the attraction of their opposite polarities. Whether *life* is then a term that includes psychical along with physical energy is debatable, but, as we shall see at the conclusion of this chapter, the debate is in the forefront of theoretical physics and other sciences today.

Whatever the American spirit of place is or was, its effects were experienced as, for the most part, beneficient by Indians and, for the most part, inimical by Euro-Americans. In "Two Views of Nature," Waters visualizes the wilderness through Indian eyes:

> How wonderful it must have been, this ancient and unknown America, this new and promising Fourth World, when man first saw it through Indian eyes! So glistening fresh with the dawn's dew upon it. So pristinely pure, so virginly naked in its beauty. How enchantingly diverse the land was with range upon range of snowcapped mountains, shimmering deserts lying below the level of the seas that gnawed at its shores, arctic tundras merging into illimitable plains of waving grass, rising into high-level plateaus, and sinking again into fetid tropical jungles. All teeming with life in every form, tiny plants and dense forests, birds, reptiles and insects, and countless animals of many unique species now extinct, like the buffalo whose vast herds blackened the tawny plains. A land with its own great spirit of place, its own brooding destiny hovering over it with invisible wings. [*Pumpkin,* 63]

The theme of an untouched virgin land vitalized by some secret source of virtue and power in the universe is a familiar one in American literature.[10] Emerson and Thoreau elaborated upon the theme; the very wildness of the American wilderness nourished Thoreau's rejection of civilization. Melville, whose attitude toward nature was ambiguous, sometimes saw paradisiacal innocence as an attraction of the wilderness, as in his celebrated image of the White Steed of the Prairies in chapter 42 of *Moby-Dick:* "A most imperial and archangelical apparition of that unfallen, western world, which to the eyes of the old trappers and hunters revived the glories of those primeval times when Adam walked majestic as a god, bluff-bowed and fearless as this mighty steed."[11] But Waters in the passage just cited is not promoting a nostalgia for lost innocence or a program of recovery from quiet desperation. He is apotheosizing the aliveness of nature, granting to nature the first function of mythology, which is to arouse the feeling of awe before the mystery of Creation. The forms of nature have names but they are not acted upon by Indian eyes—or by verbs—as if they are objects. The sacred view of nature springs from belief that there are ultimately no separate, discrete "objects" but an indivisible whole.

The materialistic view of nature also springs from a long religious tradition. Waters traces it to Genesis 1:28, "Be fruitful and multiply, and replenish the earth, and subdue it." Created in God's own image and divinely commanded to subdue the earth, man in the Judeo-Christian mythology is created apart from nature. Hence, Waters surmises, "in this view of the dualism of man and nature perhaps lies the real beginning of human tragedy in the Western Hemisphere," for the "Christian-European white race, from its first discovery of this pristine New World of the red race, regarded it as one vast new treasure house of inanimate nature that existed solely to be exploited for the material welfare of man" (*Pumpkin,* 66–67). The materialistic view has had three tragic consequences. First, subjugation of the land has caused irremediable damage to earth, air, and water. Second, because Indians were often viewed as part of that nature inimical to the white man and an embodiment of evil, they were virtually exterminated. Third, the conquerors of the New World, especially in North America, repressed inner nature—consisting of unconscious forces and instinctual drives—and the repression has produced a tragically disordered personality:

> Our own minds and bodies became the battleground of man against nature, man against God, and man against himself, divided into two warring selves: reason and instinct, the conscious and the unconscious. [*Pumpkin,* 69]

Social, economic, political, and technological expedients cannot remedy this disorder, yet the remedy lies within the mind, if we open it to "all the voices, shapes, and symbols through which intuition speaks to our inner selves" (*Pumpkin,* 72).

The tragedy of Joseph Rogier is essentially of the kind described as the materialistic view of nature. His feeling of exile torments him and has personal and representative significance. When his father gambled away his plantation, the boy Joseph was exiled from home. With the triumph of a materialistic North in the Civil War, young Rogier could not feel rooted in the new nation. Above all, though, he is a religious exile—an *existential* exile, if we are to describe his condition with a term made philosophically fashionable in the 1950s. Like Captain Ahab, his distant prototype in the literature of the United States, Rogier wants to break through the masks of appearance to the true meaning of his existence—with a vengeance: "He had no doubt of his own desire. To tear apart the very earth, to thrust his hand into its living flesh, and like an Aztec priest to hold up its heart to the eyes of eternity as proof of his mastery, his fitness to proffer homage to the greater mastery" (*Nobility,* 263). Although this passage is omitted from *Pike's Peak,* Rogier's tragic flaw is at least partially hubristic, its origin in a materialistic view of nature which translates religious quest into the language of conquest. At this juncture, his tragedy is a representative one: his own mind and body are the battleground of man against nature, man against God, and man against himself, divided into two selves, reason and instinct, the conscious and the unconscious. Rogier represents Christian-European civilization as Waters describes it in "Two Views of Nature." Where Rogier's projection of "evil" upon the Peak, his adversary, is concerned, he represents that universal type of mankind that reveals itself whenever a scapegoat psychology is at work and the excluded contents of personality are transferred to the outside world, experienced there as an object, and destructively discharged upon it. In sum,

Rogier represents the split personality of any society or civilization in which a one-sided consciousness feels the "exiled" side increase its pressure until madness brings down the roof, as in a collapsing mine.[12]

Literary tragedy perceives order beyond disorder. *Pike's Peak* reveals the disengaged, "other" side of Rogier's mind as the unconscious and represents it in Indian characters and in their ceremonies, which engage it. At least some of the pioneers have powers of intuition to combine instinct and reason into a whole personality. Rogier has these powers but fails to achieve integration. Ona has them and becomes integrated. But it is March Cable's narrative that best counterpoints order against disorder. It is his destiny to resolve the conflicting duality of an Anglo-Indian heritage. Influenced by his grandfather, he pursues an education in engineering, finds it sterile, leaves college without a degree, and, after wandering for years in Mexico, feels confirmed in the sacred view of nature. By the end of the novel, he has rejected a career in mining and begun to consider new studies in depth psychology. In the remarkable dialogue which concludes the novel, March repudiates bondage to either pole of his duality. Neither his grandfather's granite nor his father's adobe will do—neither rational consciousness nor the unconscious—and even the umbilical cord binding him to his mother and to the earth must, he realizes, be severed. Although the seat and source of faith in the unconscious, it is not the ultimate source, for him, of a supreme universe. He must search for that mystery at the point of intersection between consciousness and the unconscious, between masculine and feminine, heaven and earth. This way there is hope for a "cable" between worlds.

Pike's Peak begins when Rogier sees the mountain looming before him "like something risen from the depths of dreamless sleep to the horizon of wakeful consciousness, without clear outline yet embodying the substance of a hope and a meaning that seemed strangely familiar as it was vague" (1). It ends when March Cable stares at the mountain "as if at an imperishable monument to a faith he had finally surmounted," and a circle is closed, with a significant difference:

> And now silence spoke with the voice that outspeaks all. Listening, he saw it before him, like something risen from the depths of dreamless sleep to the horizon of wakeful consciousness, without clear outline yet embodying the substance of a hope and meaning that seemed strangely familiar as it was vague. Toward it he began his long and resolute journey. [743]

Close analysis of these framework passages shows that a difference between Rogier and March Cable has been concealed in the use of pronouns and their antecedents. The *it* in "Listening, he saw it before him" ambiguously refers to *silence, voice,* and the Peak (understood). Whereas Rogier experiences only visual space between himself and an object, March Cable closes the gap by fusing the object with the voice of silence, which is the voice of the living land. He feels resolutely at home with an unmanifest knowledge that transcends transient symbols. He begins his journey, *his* search for the supreme universe, toward "it," also an ambiguous reference to "substance of a hope and meaning" and to the Peak (understood). The Peak almost disappears, in grammatical effect. Rogier thought of it as an object and put his faith in it. March Cable, who has learned to link outer object with inner being, perceives not an object but an intersection of the total mind, something personal and conscious being filled from the impersonal depths of the unconscious.

The difference between Rogier and March Cable should not obscure their similarity: both infuse nature with meaning. Rogier is not merely or all the time a typically rational, analytical, despotically willful man. He is gifted with intuition and mystical insight and surreptitiously self-tutored in such esoteric books as the *Upanishads* and *Bhagavad-Gita.* He grasps, intellectually at least, concepts of nonlinear time and of a phenomenal world floating in a cosmic consciousness, which he identifies, in accordance with oriental mythology, as Self (capital S). He is, as tragedy requires, a high personage, with the qualification that the tragic action of this novel is largely private and hidden from public view. So what really is the nature of this hero's flaw, if, like all mystics and the greatest creative minds, he denies time's reality and seeks the depths? The answer to the question lies not in what he knows but in the way he knows it; or, to be more precise, in the degree to which he entrusts his fate to an egocentric epistemology. What he knows—that nature is infused with meaning—is not false. How he knows what he knows has a blind side. For March Cable knows, as Rogier only suspects in lucid moments, that the object of mystical union, being ineffable, cannot be translated into symbols. Designation of the Peak as the divine power can only have a relative reality, and, because the unknown reality cannot become an object of knowledge, there is only silence. Moreover, March Cable adheres to the hermetic dictum that links the microcosm with the macrocosm, nature with man, and the observer with the observed. Not a full-fledged mystic, Rogier seeks reality outside himself as seeker. Thus he yearns for kinship with nature yet surrenders to an attitude of exploitative power over nature. As a partial mystic, Rogier never doubts that humanity intersects with a living universe. The true mystic March Cable, though, lives psychologically in the intersecting mode of creation, letting go of and dying to each moment and therefore living in the timeless present.[13]

There is no question that Rogier's search is for something more than gold, that it is for the supreme universe itself, for unity, and that it is psychologically doomed from the start. There is also no question that he is mad at least some of the time and that he is wrong as long as he is mad. Significantly, because he is a representative man, the society he lives in is also psychologically doomed, also mad. Rogier's brother-in-law, Tom Hines, abandons family and loses himself in the mountains. A few lonely prospectors such as Stratton strike it rich—and remain lonely. The smug inhabitants of "Little London" hardly fit a description of a well-ordered society.[14] Restricting itself to the surface of life, this unbalanced society is as unfitted for Rogier, who seeks life's depths, as he for it. The same is true of Ona, Jonathan Cable, March Cable and the composer, Boné: all are misfits who at best indicate some well-ordered society of the future. Therefore, to call attention to the relationship between Rogier and society is to expect complex levels of tone in *Pike's Peak*. Although irony reveals many of Rogier's thoughts and actions as mad, there are occasions when his humanity and wisdom exist apart from madness, and from these occasions almost all the ironies have been lifted. Rogier's is not the wisdom of the fool. It is the intelligence, the nobility, and the dignity of a gifted man. It follows that his search for the supreme universe is a manifestation of his wisdom, a wisdom too devout for falsity.

His reflections on the Peak as a sacred mountain are a case in point:

> He found his own feelings duplicated by reverence accorded other sacred mountains in the world—Popocatepetl in Mexico, Cotopaxi and Capac Urcu in the Andes of South America, Kilimanjaro of Africa, Fujiyama in Japan, Olympus in Greece, colossal upthrusts of the Himalayas in Asia. From time immemorial the root races of every continent, the black, the brown, the yellow, the red, and the white, had made pilgrimages to these great sacred mountains, as had the Indians to Pike's Peak, with votive offerings, prayer, song, and dance. Rogier had come to believe it was a matter of rhythm. For the spirit-of-place of each continent, each land, vibrated to a different, indigenous rhythm. And only by attuning himself to this vibratory quality of his motherland could man release the dammed up power of creation within him. [127–28]

These reflections may have a base in scientific possibility as well as in religious authority. The "vibratory quality" of earth is physically attributable to radioactivity, to electromagnetism, or to solar energy flowing in and through, especially, high rocky mountains. If psychic energy is locked within the human mind as physical energy is locked within the atom, then a fusion of mind and matter that releases energy potentials is not inconceivable, given what our nuclear age already knows about releasing atomic energy's power. Strange as it may seem, too, Rogier's underlying belief in a Universal Mind pervading all forms of life cannot be dismissed as quixotic madness induced by readings in esoteric texts.[15] His quest to surmount earthly existence has indeed been universally associated with mountain worship (or with monuments such as pyramids and Gothic cathedrals which carry out the mountain theme of spiritual aspiration). If there is an influence or quintessence that gives sacredness to mountains, then, according to Evans-Wentz, the devotee tries to share in it by partaking of its flesh and blood, as if it were a divinity incarnate; and this eucharistic ceremony, acceptable in ancient and modern cultures as an accession to grace, is suggested when Rogier affirms that the Peak "was a living body like his own, the rock strata of its skeleton fleshed with earth, its veins watered by spring and stream; and in whose deep and hidden heart glowed the golden sun of life" (128).[16] That this divine source, uniting physical and psychic realms as two aspects of a transcendental, supreme universe, is viewed in *Pike's Peak* as an archetype projected from Rogier's unconscious does not mean that his vision quest in itself calls for a cure. His feelings are genuine and profound. The Peak, for him, is really the wild earth's nobility, to acknowledge which is to obey the laws of one's own nature, "the only self-fulfillment, the only true success" (111). He is really brave, his determination unconditional, even when the Peak takes on "the inimical aspect of the great devouring cosmic serpent itself" (274), for he knows "that there comes to every man in that one long evolutionary life no more interrupted by death than by sleep the time when he must fight through to the life of his own inner being and so make the turn into the greater life of which he was an ultimate part" (296). In short, Rogier's heroic search for the supreme universe imposes admiration even though his idée fixe intervenes to disgrace him.

His reflections on timelessness are also wise. In one scene, he comes out of his shell and, motivated by an unspoken love for his young grandson, reveals the essence of his philosophy: time and space converge in man himself, effecting reconciliation of humanity in one organic, endlessly evolving, creative whole. All ironies have departed from the scene, which begins when Rogier playfully asks March, " 'Do you know who I am?' " and March, for whom the question of identity is uppermost, listens respectfully as a white-haired old man, before whom is a piece of onionskin paper, pounds a drafting board with his fist. The sudden orator, Rogier, continues:

> "I'm the great eunuch, the wind between the worlds, the frost of glacial epochs yet to come. I'm the maker of seas, the destroyer of mountains, the biggest joke of Eternity and the invisible hand of Infinity. Time—they call me Time—a great worm crawling through Chaos eating up worlds to come. I'm Time, boy, whose other name is Space, the unmeasured and measureless, the great un-

created without beginning and end, the nothing from which is created the all. If I can be shrunken to here"—he jabbed a pencil-point on the paper—"I can also expand to everywhere, just as I can be both now and always. Call me whatever you want. Divide me with clocks and calendars, fence me off with foot-rulers and surveying lines, and I vanish into the nameless One I am." [526]

Illustrating his theme, Rogier stacks up a column of wooden blocks reaching almost to the lofty ceiling of his shop and then commands March to climb a ladder and place on top of the pillar the sheet of onionskin punctuated with the pencil point. That paper, he then explains, represents all the time of existence of all mankind, whereas the pillar represents all of geological time on earth. Momentarily Rogier's madness creeps into the explanation but is expelled by wisdom:

"I reckon you're catchin' on now to what a man might find out if he could sink a shaft to the bottom of that column, to the beginning of time, eh? Why, he's likely to discover that he's had all his work for nothing! All that time, the whole dom column, is condensed in that piece of paper on top; in a pencil-point marked on it; right in himself, by Jove! " He tapped his head. "And the reason is, like I told you before, he's the Beginning and the End which meet like the ends of a great circle." [528]

As if to bend together the top and bottom of the pillar, Rogier stretches his hands, the pillar topples down, and he is sent sprawling. A bit of slapstick relieves a scene in which Rogier, sane, is in earnest.

Waters, too, is in earnest. The reconciling symbol of a cosmic circle, the *uroboros,* had appeared in *The Lizard Woman,* its significance later corroborated by relativity theory and by Jung's theory of the collective unconscious whereby a supreme space-time continuum exists in the mind and links the past with the future, without beginning or end. Waters envisions the circle in terms of the myth of Emergence, "evolution of man physiologically and psychologically, his perception of time as another spatial dimension, his correlation of the unconscious and conscious, and the final reconciliation of his own psyche with that of the cosmos—the ultimate meaning of life for all mankind as well as for individual man" (*Masked Gods,* 437). Elsewhere, in his essay on "Time," he notes two aspects of supreme space-time: space is "here" and "everywhere," time is "now" and "always" (*Pumpkin,* 105).

Pike's Peak, it can now be asserted, does not invalidate the search for the supreme universe, even though human tragedy in the Western Hemisphere is revealed in a separation of man and nature.

It remains to be indicated that the vision of Waters in *Pike's Peak* has, so far, proven prophetic of the direction of scientific thought today.

Two complementary modes of thinking are counterpointed in *Pike's Peak*. Considered dualistic, but interpenetrating and balanced when recognized as intersecting, they are the rational-analytical-verbal-linear-masculine mode and the intuitive-holistic-nonverbal-nonlinear-feminine mode, or the poles of reason and intuition. Although the duality and complementarity of the two poles were recognized in many ancient forms of philosophical, religious, and psychological endeavor, the scientific recognition that they operate physiologically is new and restores to intuitive processes their dignity. Our most recent evolutionary accretion, the analytical activities of the left pole or hemisphere of the human brain, has tended to obscure awareness of the functions of the intuitive right hemisphere, which in our ancestors must have been the principal means of perceiving the world. Indeed, as Carl Sagan has speculated, intuition may actually be the more competent mode, "our highly prized rational and analytical abilities . . . localized in the 'other' brain—the one that was not fully competent to do intuitive thinking."[17] Mere critical thinking, without creative and intuitive insights, is sterile and doomed. The solving of complex problems requires the activity of both hemispheres and their collaboration through the corpus callosum (the bundle of nerve fibers which is the principal cabling between hemispheres).

Access to a timeless reality, significantly dramatized as possible by characters in *Pike's Peak,* has also been found, in recent studies of the psychology of consciousness, to be an available mind function. There is no process in the external world which directly gives rise to time experience. Time, as Robert Ornstein observes, "exists in itself" and not in "how it relates to hours."[18] In his opinion, to open one's consciousness to awareness of a timeless interconnectedness of life is not an especially esoteric or "mystic" privilege but, rather, a granting of personal permission to shift from an analytic world containing separate, discrete objects and persons.[19]

The principle of interconnectedness as involving three ideas—unity, harmony, and mutual respect—is now seen by neuropsychologists as their revolutionary discovery of the brain's architecture. The brain is not hierarchical but heterarchical; that is, it is an organization of autonomous units serving in specialized capacities on different levels of a system yet working toward common goals. Thus, while complex work involving millions of neurons and billions of synapses takes place at a level that proceeds effectively without our conscious intervention, consciousness itself is freed to concentrate on the priorities of the moment and to expand awareness. Evolution has avoided an inflexible, hierarchical, command-control organization of the brain and instead has emphasized integration of independent units. The lower-level cognitive centers form higher-order ones.[20] Thus, recent mind-brain research strongly tends to confirm Waters's evolutionary view of a reconciliation of instinct and reason on a higher level of increased consciousness.

The hemispheric brain, the subjective and nonlinear realm of time, and the emergence of increased awareness are, then, fields of contemporary scientific discovery anticipated in the creative mythology of Frank Waters in *Pike's Peak* which, we recall, originated in the 1930s. But what is science saying about the novel's central theme, the search for a supreme universe combining physical and psychic energies, the pencil point of a human consciousness perceived as the place of entry for connecting mind meaningfully to nature?

Science has changed its whole understanding of the universe, as a field of energy and not simply as a materialistic, mechanistic model. This new understanding has opened physics, biology, and psychology to the spiritual dimension of reality and to mysticism. Currently, in fact, there is a movement to reconcile science and mysticism, seeing remarkable similarities between Western science and the wisdom traditions of Greece and the East.[21] Although philosophy since Kant dismisses nature from its concerns and has given up on the search for the "deep structure" of things, science has made the quest for unity its province. The reconciliation of self and object, man and nature, mind and matter, inner microcosm and outer macrocosm is a possible scientific consequence. Mysticism proposes that the universe originates in consciousness. At its most subtle and inward point, physical energy and psychic energy become indistinguishable yet are but the expression of something beyond themselves, in which they are rooted and reconciled. Science, while not quite ready to concede mysticism's proposal about a Universal Mind, Atman, or Self, has nevertheless reached the stage where there is perceived a hidden order at work beneath the seeming chaos of the particles of matter described by quantum mechanics. If there is an ultimate formative principle that operates in an organismlike universe, a unity and wholeness whatever its name, then mind and matter derive from the same source ground. Physical and psychic then become two aspects of something which is only separable in thought, not in reality, and it follows that what man is, is a clue to the universe.

From the examples, to follow, of the work of Jung, Prigogine, and Bohm, it is evident that a scientific movement in the direction of mysticism is indeed active, its basic assumption being that the universe is unfolding according to a hidden, dynamic, and enfolded order. Jung's collective unconscious exists in an objective, enfolded form, its archetypes unfolding their projections into attention, clothed in the images and symbols of a particular culture. If something such as an archetype thus partakes of movement yet stands outside it, then the way in which things happen together suggests arrangements of causally unrelated events which have the same or similar meaning. Jung and physicist Wolfgang Pauli gave to such meaningful coincidences the term *synchronicity,* an acausal unfoldment with its wellspring in a total enfolded order manifesting itself in both mind and matter. Another example from current science concerns the work of Ilya Prigogine, Nobel Prize-winning chemist and author of *Order out of Chaos: Man's New Dialogue with Nature* (1984). Concentrated in thermodynamics, his work, as summarized by philosopher Renée Weber, "teaches that living systems can to some degree escape entropy through their capacity for self-organization; in them a higher order not predicted by entropy can emerge out of the dead end of chaos."[22] The idea of matter as alive—responsive, relational, and self-modifying in response to the activities of other matter—points to a constant creativity in nature, an eternal unfolding of the universe's potential from an all-encompassing background. So finally, the philosophy of David Bohm, one of the world's foremost theoretical physicists, links up with the work of Jung and the others. Bohm's *Wholeness and the Implicate Order* (1980) proposes that in that background's inward recesses both matter and consciousness have their source. When one considers all visible, "explicate" matter, what is going on in the full depth of one moment of time can be said to contain active information, at an "unconscious" level, of a subtle dimension, an "implicate order." Bohm postulates that human consciousness unfolds from the same implicate order as does matter. One can no longer claim that consciousness is one thing and matter is another. Man, in short, is enfolded in a total wholeness and unity of the universe.

Pike's Peak envisions the reality of this supreme universe, a mystery made manifest by means, not of rational analysis, but of "intuition of the living moment" (732).

5

PASTORAL, MYTH, AND

HUMANITY IN

PEOPLE OF THE VALLEY

SOME OF THE crucial words in *People of the Valley* are *faith, fulfillment, truth, reality, enduring,* and *inward*—in opposition to *progress, illusion,* and *outside*. Their philosophical import is usually transmitted implicitly through character, event, and imagery, but the discourse of the implied author or narrator sometimes brings the words themselves into explicit display. Thus it is said of Maria del Valle, the novel's protagonist, that she "believed in fulfillment instead of progress," fulfillment defined as "individual evolution" requiring "time and patience," progress defined as being "in haste to move mass" and hence "admit[ing] neither" (134).[1] We are told that "faith is not a concept" and "not a form" but "baptism in the one living mystery of ever-flowing life" (177) and that Maria's eyes "burned through time with a faith" and "a gaze which saw neither the darkness of the day nor the brightness of the morrow, but behind these illusions the enduring reality" (201). A similar idea is expressed in relation to the passage of seasons:

> It all went on outside her as it went on in memory inside, changing but change-less, and thus an illusion. What remained was their common core. It was the reality she pondered. . . . At times her steady gaze seemed turned inward—as if it had rounded the earth only to return to the duplicate within her. [117]

The words form a nexus of meaning that calls for discussion prior to critical examination of the whole text.

The dominant Western tradition of thought on the subject of faith is that it is belief in various propositions beyond the scope of human knowledge. But there is another tradition: faith conceived as a personal encounter with a divine mystery, which does not require propositions on the authority of God nor demand a human will to treat as certain a proposition which is felt not to be true. Faith can mean simply a mode of putative knowledge or awareness, with the reality of the divine assumed as a manifest fact. As our experience reveals a familiar, settled environment that has become intelligible to us, we may attribute significance to recognizable patterns of interrelationship, as between an individual, a place, and the physical universe, with an all-encompassing situation of significance interpreted as one's being in the presence of the divine and within the sphere of an ongoing divine purpose. According to John Hick, a philosopher of religion,

> the primary religious perception, or basic act of religious interpretation, is not to be described as either a reasoned conclusion or an unreasoned hunch that there is a God. It is, putatively, an apprehension of the divine presence within the believer's human experience. It is not an inference to a general truth, but a "divine"-human encounter, a mediated meeting with the living God.[2]

Faith as personal encounter holds out no requirement for self-transcendence. It is, rather, the inward realization of an enduring reality or truth being fulfilled in us and for us. If not the dominant Western tradition, this way of thinking about faith, fulfillment, and reality is still well within Christian boundaries and is also not incompatible with mysticism and with Eastern philosophies inasmuch as it brings the mystery of life within the standard cognitive ranges of knowing and believing.

All of Waters's works of fiction and nonfiction affirm as a faith, in this cognitive sense, the all-encompassing, integrated unity and wholeness of the universe. The macrocosm is duplicated within the microcosm. Psychic landscape, or the spirit of place, is a point of entry into a numinous world where encounter occurs. Here, for example, is one of Waters's recent statements about unity:

> The earth is not inanimate. It is a living entity, the mother of all life, our Mother Earth. All her children are alive—the living stones, the great breathing mountains, plants and trees, as well as birds and animals and man. All united in one harmonious whole. Whatever happens to one affects the others and subtly changes the pattern of the whole. For all these living entities, like man,

possess not only an outer physical form, but an inner spiritual component. [*The Colorado*, preface to the 1984 ed., xiii]

To attribute significant aliveness to all entities is, for Waters, to have realized the numinous by living within it, and *being within*—one of his favorite locutions[3]—means not to leave the world by means of a transcendent impulse but to become awakened and emerge in relationship to the world in all its detailed and numinous particulars. This emergence, moreover, is not to be confused with cultural primitivism, an attitude which elevates the values of instinct and lowers or pretends to dispose of the values of reason. Emergence outlines a universal point of view in which familiar dualisms are harmonized with evolutionary development. Even though a fragmented perception, one that lurks on the outside of entities and interposes conscious will and ego between itself and nature, threatens to dominate nature, there is a place for rational ingredients of the mind as long as these are balanced with instinctive, unconscious ingredients. When, indeed, the material "progress" of a complex, industrialized, and technological civilization dominates living entities, the land as well as man, life is impoverished to sterility. On the other hand, should the instincts win out over the conscious ego in the struggle for domination, man disintegrates morally and psychologically. The emergent sense of being within is actually an ongoing reconciliation of the polarized powers, for, if we are not separated from the living entities of the numinous world, then conscious mentation and human culture participate in all that endures.[4]

Waters's fusion of seemingly disparate entities such as nature and culture is remarkably calm and derives from poetic vision. *People of the Valley*, which he has called "the poem of the earth in action,"[5] offers many examples of such fusion, among them the following:

Dawn-dusk drew the charcoal outline of a hut on the mountainside. Then the dirty gray light of day, like a soiled brush, thrust through the pines and smeared it with drabness. [21]

It was day, and the rising sun marked her time on its dial. [22]

A rainbow brilliantly colored as a Chihuahua serape hung over the shoulder of the sky. [77]

Little javelins of sunlight struck the opposite wall of the mountains, were deflected back by cliff and rock, or fell split and broken down the water-gashed hillsides. The air grew luminous with spears and arrows of gold. Pine needles glistened metallically. Micaceous rocks glittered like cut diamonds. . . . Far off, a window glass gleamed crystal. [138]

> The little stream played its arpeggio on the rocks. A deer bounded over a string
> of logs, its quick hoofs striking a pizzicato. [199]

If human culture, as activity or artifact, were here merely endowments of an inanimate nature, these examples might represent that artistic relaxation called the "pathetic fallacy." Waters's major premise, however, that the earth is not inanimate, creates a legitimate logic of its own: the spiritual component of all entities permits figures of interchange an inseparable energy.

Waters's novels show as a major concern the dichotomy between seeking faith and being within. Both Tai Ling in *Yogi* and Joseph Rogier in *Pike's Peak* consciously seek the numinous world, and their fulfillment or emergence is blocked by this ego-tainted procedure. Both March Cable in *Pike's Peak* and Martiniano in *Deer* abandon seeking as a conscious act of the will and find a way to fulfillment in intuition of the living moment. Neither Lee Marston in *Lizard Woman* nor Helen Chalmers in *Otowi* is consciously seeking the revelation of timeless mystery that each finds. Unlike these characters, Maria in *People* neither seeks nor finds the mystery; being within it, she also incarnates it. The secret of her power over the people, we are told, is "complete freedom from self which alone makes possible complete creative power" (183), and her unobstructed faith in timeless essence signals her transfiguration into a redemptive personality. The novel's last sentence (already partially quoted) asserts that her steadily gleaming eyes

> burned through time with a faith which could not be dammed, and with a gaze
> which saw neither the darkness of the day nor the brightness of the morrow,
> but behind these illusions the enduring reality that makes of one sunset a pre-
> lude to a sunrise brighter still. [201]

Maria's being within dissolves distinctions of past, present, and future into a dynamically evolving reality. Significantly, the trope for the myth of Emergence is sunrise, the moment in this creative mythology when union of the dark, feminine, earthbound, unconscious principle with the light, masculine, solar, conscious principle presages increased awareness of a greater life. The union of these principles in future has, in fact, already been accomplished in Maria: earth and sun, water and fire meet in her. "Her blood," we are told, "became water, wine, fire" (37). Maria is thus the vessel of the Holy Spirit, an indigenous parallel to Virgin Mary, who, in effect, releases the signs of faith to those who receive and respond to them of themselves, uncoerced by mythologies which would place the radiance of divinity aloft rather than in the mythogenetic zone of the human heart.

The main constants in *People* are Maria and the beautiful blue valley with which she is identified. She acquires knowledge through a process of accretion, but her birthright and source of faith is the eternal earth:

> One miniature hand was closed upon a bit of dirt. It was her birthright, Doña Maria never let it go. [25]

Although she lives for ninety years, her inner essence endures unchanged: "She was immune from all but the ultimate destruction of her inessential outer shell" (123). Maria, therefore, inasmuch as she represents a constant, is not a dramatic character in the usual sense. There are no changes of heart, only vicissitudes to be suffered; no epiphanies to be attained, only articles of faith to be tested and passed along to others. Maria's heart is not in conflict with itself, and this situation presents Waters with a major problem in the dramatization of his materials. He solves it thematically by drawing upon the resources of a traditional literary genre, the pastoral. Another problem faced by Waters is how to indicate more of the truth about Maria than she, an illiterate Mexican-Indian, might be expected to know. Waters solves this problem omnisciently by defining Maria against a background of communal code and ceremony, by giving her a force of silence behind her words and acts, and by consistently revealing her in a mythical dimension whereby she wears a mask larger than life. As a result of such solutions, *People of the Valley* is not only an elegant but also a unique contribution to American and world literature, one that combines pastoral and myth—the one a traditional genre, the other a summoning forth of the Goddess Mother of the universe, through whom pours a continuous act of self-giving and a guidance to the light beyond dark—yet does so without stripping a female protagonist of her individual humanity.

What is the pastoral?[6] We had best ponder this question at once because, in the modern world, emotional investment in rural life can be hazardous to ideals. A writer who wishes to celebrate an ideal of harmony embodied in nature and in people who once lived or still are living close to nature may end up escaping from complex society and its problems, and such a confinement in space and time may deliquesce into a pool of nostalgia and sentimentality. When pastoral is not escapist, it seems an acceptance of defeat, that is, modern society's defeat of cherished values accrued in the land. Yet I say *seems* because the conflict between the machine of civilization and the garden of nature only projects a social myth in the pejorative sense, so that a defeat on social and political grounds may actually not decide the issues raised by the pastoral, which may have more to do with a feeling on various levels, including the creative level of myth, than with beleaguered ideals. For instance, pastoral may align itself with comedy, as it does in Faulkner's *Light in August,* and can function to maintain sanity and human perspective in regard to complex problems.[7] Or—I speculate with a glance toward *People of the Valley*—pastoral's evocation of some feeling of wholeness in rural life may serve as host to myth's evocation of the mystery and order of the universe. Indeed, if pastoral has the ability to move us honestly, the power may be due to its projection of calmness, as if from a numinous source. That is my own view, and there is support for it, as I shall presently show, but pastoral is usually not considered in terms of its mythic, religious, and psychological accommodations.

The usual critical view is that the pastoral ideal and social reality are irreconcilable and that pastoral fables, at least since the Industrial Revolution made its presence ominous in England and in the United States, are documentaries of an insoluble dilemma. George Eliot, for example, after completing *Adam Bede* (1859), perhaps the earliest important English novel to deal largely and realistically with humble rural life, declared, "I have arrived at faith in the past, but not at faith in the present."[8] She had envisioned a rural order distant in time and space from an industrialized urban world. As a modern landscape of power and alienation encroached upon "innocent" regions, she could rebuke the values of the "present" by setting in contrast to them a life of harmony existing in an actual past and in a believable setting, sequestered and concrete but immobilized, withdrawn from complexity. Her "faith in the past" or in the stability of a remote rural microcosm is a state of mind opposed to and by "the present," a state of mind evidently demanding capitulation to industrialized, technological, urban civilization. And, of course, neither George Eliot nor Thomas Hardy nor D. H. Lawrence capitulated: if there was no way back to society, there might be a way out. But loopholes for the soul now seem to be closed, because nothing in the idyllic garden seems capable of resisting the sudden and implacable machine. According to Leo Marx, the machine is *in* the garden to stay:

> The power of these fables to move us derives from the magnitude of the protean conflict figured by the machine's increasing domination of the visible world. This recurrent metaphor of contradiction makes vivid, as no other figure does, the bearing of public events upon private lives. It discloses that our inherited symbols of order and beauty have been divested of meaning. It compels us to recognize that the aspirations once represented by the symbol of an ideal landscape have not, and probably cannot, be embodied in our traditional

institutions. It means that an inspiriting vision of a human community has been reduced to a token of individual survival.[9]

In a preindustrialized world such as the England of Shakespeare, a pastoral fable such as *The Tempest* resolves the contradiction of nature and society through a pattern of journey and return: overly civilized people remove themselves to nature, which has the benefit of simplicity as well as the caveat of pure instinct and Original Sin, and then return to society with a chastened Art, which is man's power over the created world and over himself. But in an industrialized world, implied or present in such American classics as *Huckleberry Finn* and *The Great Gatsby,* one either repudiates society and lights out for new territory or yearns wistfully for an innocence lost. Marx concludes, "The resolutions of our pastoral fables are unsatisfactory because the old symbol of reconciliation is obsolete."[10] Thus pastoral, in his view, "helps to mask the real problems of an industrial civilization."[11]

I have summarized the usual critical view of the pastoral because it helps to explain why modern literature in this mode can and often does reflect the reality of a loss and defeat of a social microcosm, rural life. Yet if attention is shifted from sociopolitical reality to an enduring reality in nature itself, the pastoral doesn't mask the real problems of modern society but perceives them for what they are—an illusion. The greatness of Robert Frost's pastoral art, for example, has been attributed by John F. Lynen to its evocation of "a world of archetypes, or ideas."[12] Frost's rural New England "will always at first appear to involve an escape from the world as we know it, but actually it is an exploration upstream, past the city with its riverside factories and shipping, on against the current of time and change to the clear waters of the source."[13] This, I think, is an eloquent statement in defense not only of the universality of Frost's regional poetry but also of the pastoral genre, for it is capable of moving beyond metaphors of contradiction—the machine in the garden—to a heightened conviction of the mystery in nature and in man, who is a part of nature. Moreover, I would add, pastoral does not need to be rooted in a Judeo-Christian mythology that divests nature of grace, nor, to press the point, in Western science's mythology that divests nature of spirit. And is the old symbol of reconciliation, as between nature and society, truly obsolete? It is, if one is reduced to "sociological" thinking about literature: the machine spares few gardens, not even, now, the moon. On the other hand, reconciliation is always possible in the mythological thinking about literature. In fact, the journey-and-return pattern in *The Tempest* (and in Shakespeare's mature comedies as well) is but a variation of an archetypal pattern: the hero or author-surrogate goes on a journey from the world of outward forms to an eternal source and returns to the world with the message of life renewed.[14] No machine can dominate the inexhaustible source of life nor prevent a human point of view from springing up in relationship to it.

The land and people of the remote Mora valley in northern New Mexico formed the inspiration for *People of the Valley*.[15] But when Waters moved to Mora in 1936 to live there off and on for two years before he settled in Taos in 1938, he brought with him vivid impressions of the rise, elsewhere in the American West, of a new technological civilization of which Boulder Dam on the Colorado was the symbol. While it was being constructed on the bed of the river in 1932, he had seen the dam, had even marveled at it, but had sensed something monstrous in the proceedings. He recalls the scene, as follows, in *The Colorado:*

> I stood on the bed of the river. The vast chasm seemed a slit through earth and time alike. The rank smell of Mesozoic ooze and primeval muck filled the air. Thousands of pale lights, like newly lit stars, shone on the heights of the cliffs. Down below grunted and growled prehistoric monsters—great brute dinosaurs with massive bellies, with long necks like the brontosaurus, and with armored hides thick as those of the stegosaurus. They were steam shovels and cranes feeding on the muck, a ton at a gulp. In a steady file other monsters rumbled down, stopping just long enough to shift gears while their bodies were filled with a single avalanche, then racing backward without turning around. [339]

These images of an inhuman and insatiable force omit its meaning. But when Waters describes a dam in *People,* at one point a manuscript entitled "Dam in the Mountains" (Tanner, 42), he uses the consciousness of Maria del Valle to spell out, at first whimsically but later symbolically, that the machine of Progress, of which the dam is symbol, ultimately means spiritual death:

> So this Máquina, this monster, labored to give birth to a dam there. . . .
> Steam shovels squatted in the fields, careful attendants to feed it. Great trucks rolled down and up the long macadam bringing more supplies. The Mofres' little powerhouse was being built to warm and light it. Shops and a tool house became its nursery. A long mess hall and bunkhouse spewed nurses in dirty denim. The old inn held its doctors, filling with engineers and construction bosses and vapid wives to gawk at its souvenirs and bewail its lack of plumbing.
> All waiting, like the people, to see born this child of progress, this new dam of the Máquina.
> Ay de mi! Nature travails alone in the thicket, being hardy and not to be denied. But the machinery of progress needs much attention; it has no faith; anything may break down. [180]

Later, Waters enlarges upon the metaphorical meaning of the dam when Maria, like an aged Demeter companioned with a young Persephone, imparts her wisdom to Piedad, her granddaughter:

"There is no dam but, in the end, is wrong; the dam of stone which would obstruct the flow of water, the dam of harsh morality which would retard too long the flow of life. But this flow must be sanctified by your faith in it or it is equally wrong." [194]

Maria condemns the dam on psychological grounds, viewing it as any obstruction, retardation, or repression that is excessive in domination of the elemental, unconscious, and evolving flow of life. Her condemnation is not shrill, nor has imagery of the dam been presented as a conventional obscenity, nor has Waters (through Maria) denied to the machine of Progress its power to bring social benefits. The issue has simply been elevated from a social to a spiritual plane: the machine represents an excessively rationalistic, materialistic civilization that produces an impoverishment of life, whereas the way of the people who derive faith from their relationship to the land rejoins them to the archetypal mother's creativity.

The people of *People of the Valley* are Mexican-Indian. Despite an overlaying topsoil of Christianity, the meaning of their lives stems directly from the land, possession of which is to them an alien concept. Waters is careful and precise in portraying the history and ways of these unspoiled, uneducated, and unsophisticated people whose lives are pregnant with the universal values that spring from specific fact: his stance toward the people is both affectionate and detached, neither condescending nor overly protective, and he doesn't exploit them as a comical proletariat. In brief, Waters's people are descended from colonists who in the seventeenth century pushed northward from Mexico along the Chihuahua Trail and established settlements in the mountainous region between Santa Fe and Taos and between the Rio Grande and the Sangre de Cristo mountains. The settlement pattern was determined by two considerations: conversion of the Indians and the availability of water. Because Indian villages had also been located near the best water supplies, the Mexican colonists often lived close to people whose presence on the land goes back for untold centuries; and the resulting mixture of races in an extremely isolated region produced a people with a powerful sense of community and with an equally powerful regard for personal independence. In most respects the culture was and is of a type found throughout Latin America: people are aligned to the family as the principal unit and to the father as the principal authority, and it is difficult for adults of either sex to maintain self-respect unless they are united (not always in wedlock) and have children. Yet personalism permits one's idiosyncrasies and intensity of being to become the bases of assessment rather than status or roles, and customs are not always binding. Therefore it is quite possible for an unmarried woman to attain to some special authority based on the people's perception of her wisdom or unusual powers (for instance, as a *curandera* or healer). Because Maria del Valle is precisely such a character, this particular point is worth emphasis, for Waters has drawn her portrait from life: she is a distinct type of quick-thinking, wisely speaking Hispanic (here, Mexican-Indian) woman revered for her knowledge in villages from northern New Mexico to the Strait of Magellan.[16]

The plot of *People* shows two alien cultures, that of the Mexican-Indians and that of the Euro-Americans (Anglos or gringos in the regional parlance), gradually coming into conflict during the span of a century. The crisis is reached in the 1930s, when the American government undertakes to construct a dam in order to control periodic floods in the valley. Ironically, this progressive plan that seems to be for the benefit of the people will really require the eviction of the people from ancestral lands. The people miss the irony; Maria does not. She tries to stall the government's plan long enough for the people to recognize the necessity of their way of life, and how the new ways will destroy it, but in the end, when the dam is built, Maria can save her people only by sending them to another valley she has secured for them.

Although Maria is naturally gifted, she has to learn to become a leader, and much of the plot is devoted to this process of learning. Maria's mother, a Picuris Pueblo Indian, dies in childbirth, leaving the infant to be found and raised by two old Mexican goatherds. These "philosophers" (26, 29) try to divine correlations between the patterns in goat skulls and those of the moon and stars. Even though they try to deceive people with their prophecies, Maria sees through the deceptions. Yet she still founds her life of wisdom on the core of truth in their teachings, namely the interrelationship of macrocosm and microcosm. "The great dome of the midnight skies, and the dome of the earth rounding from horizon to horizon: both forever repeated with the triangles and squares of stars . . . upon the lesser, miniature skulls of beast and man" (29). Unwittingly, the goatherds also provide her with a lesson in the dangers of abstracting life from its inner reality. Having fortified their mountain home with a rampart of stones, they are drowned as a flood breaks it down. Maria then lives in a hut high in the mountains until she is fifteen, at which age "the goat girl" (34) visits the village of Santa Gertrudes, where she is enchanted by the sound of a gringo soldier's music box. Mistaking the "master" (37) of the box for the "master of the song" (38) of sexual desire, she has a casual affair with the soldier and soon gives birth to a child, Teodosio.

She has learned "that there are some things one cannot escape" (37) such as "harvest and fulfillment" (41). She has not yet learned that the "power of the blood" must be joined to the "power of the mind" (127) to produce detachment from the "valley of illusion" (135).

At eighteen she moves from her hut to live with Onesimo, a young muleteer and religious fanatic "like a martyr tied to a cross and searching the heavens for an echo of his faith" (47). Institutionalized Christianity is, to her, a "meaningless outward form" (52) of "incomprehensible ritual" (53), but Onesimo wants their newborn child, Niña, to have a legally sanctioned name. Maria agrees to marry him. The padre of the local church, however, refuses to perform the ceremony because Onesimo is, one, poor, and, two, a member of an outlawed sect, the Penitentes. Maria has now been meanly instructed in the economic and political considerations of a secularized institution. She respects, though, the symbolic meaning of the death and resurrection of Christ inasmuch as the mythic pattern repeats the seasonal one of the earth. Yet when Onesimo dies in the Penitentes' reenactment of the Crucifixion, she is sure that faith does not come from a search for self-transcendence in "pitilessly empty" (66) heavens but from being within "the power of the earth below" (50). It is her faith in the earth which pulls her through years of poverty and the people's distrust of her as an unwed, single woman with a penchant for producing children from chance encounters with nameless men. Hoarding seeds of grain, she sells them to improvident farmers; collecting herbs, she becomes respected as a *curandera;* consulting goat skulls, she gains a reputation as a fortune-teller. By the age of fifty she is for the people a feared and respected figure of authority who has added to her native and growing sagacity a shrewd comprehension of Anglo civilization's economic, legal, and political machinery. She sees to it that her children are legally named and thus entitled to possess their lands under the jurisdiction of the United States. Her one weakness is pity for a lonely old miser, Don Fulgencio, who wants to marry her. Suspecting that he wants to gain control of her property and its water rights, she nevertheless goes through the ceremony, and, after the wedding, he ignores her. She returns to her hut on the mountainside, but not before Don Fulgencio's sister has given her gold pieces from a buried box. Presently a flood drives Maria and the people into Santa Gertrudes for shelter. Seeing Don Fulgencio protecting his box of buried gold, she attempts to save him, but he knocks her unconscious with a shovel, dislodging all her teeth save one. He is drowned; she, recovered, leads the people to the safety of high ground, a foreshadowing of her later role as their protector and savior.

At eighty she first hears of the dam. Suspecting fraud, she learns that

Don Fulgencio had been in league with the Mofres (the Murphy brothers from Ireland) to control all water rights in the valley and to profit from sales of water and electricity after construction of the dam. Whereas most of the people have lost to Don Fulgencio land they never knew they owned, Maria, educated in the ways of an alien culture, refuses to sell hers. But she must prepare the people to defend the values by which they have endured. She revives old customs, dispossesses of his land her own son Antonio in order to demonstrate the meaning of homelessness, and gets herself arrested for rallying the people to their faith. When it comes to a vote at a water district meeting, Maria is not even present except as the people's "common conscience, the invisible and invincible backbone of their solidarity" (154). The people refuse to sell their land; they believe that Maria has led them to victory. She is not deceived. For the next ten years, her tactics only delay the inevitable construction of the dam, time enough for her to prepare Piedad as her successor and to set aside land for the people in another valley. When the government has the land appraised and condemned, Maria advises the people to accept payment only in gold and silver and to bury the coins according to custom. Some of the people, ignoring her advice, squander government checks in a city forty miles away and become destitute and angry. The Mofres' store is burned down. But on the final day, when the people are evicted, most of them have their buried coins available for starting a new life, to which Piedad leads them while Maria, dying, remains behind in her hut. Placing pieces of gold on her blind eyes and wrapping herself in an old burnt-orange blanket that has been with her since infancy, she dies just before the valley is to be inundated, converted into a lake behind the new dam.

Considered as a pastoral novel, *People* might be little more than a melodrama of social and political protest, a New Mexican *Grapes of Wrath*. It is curious, however, that Waters distributes moral responsibility about evenly between the opposed forces of machine and garden. At first, the encroachment of the modern world, like the gringo soldier's music box, is nonthreatening. Perhaps an allusion to "Bishop Lamy's new church" (33) hints at something sinister to come, especially if the historical Lamy is regarded as an empire builder instead of as the saintly hero of Willa Cather's *Death Comes for the Archbishop*. But the corrupt padre who refuses to marry Maria and Onesimo seems almost inoffensive when the violence of the Penitentes seizes the foreground of attention. Gradually, of course, technology comes into or near the valley—a railroad, rattling tin automobiles, the dam in all its component parts—and a bank and new courthouse in Santa Gertrudes certainly represent legal, political, and monetary systems foreign to the people of the valley. But, again, the agents of the machine, impersonal as they may be, seem relatively nonviolent; the police never fire a shot. By contrast, the garden is rife with violence: the natural violence of floods, self-mutilations by Penitentes, Don Fulgencio's assault on Maria, the burning of the Mofres' store. And some of the people are themselves corrupt: a midwife tries to extract from Maria information about the gringo soldier in order to blackmail him; Don Fulgencio and the county recorder, Sanchez, make fraudulent land deals; the shopkeeper, Pierre Fortier, tricks Teodosio into surrendering Maria's valuable burnt-orange blanket from Chimayó. If, then, savagery and a transient regard for gentleness and mercy characterize the people of this garden, the coming of the machine almost appears as, in the long run, a civilized necessity, like Prospero's control of Caliban in *The Tempest*. Even Maria admits before Don Eliseo, an educated and fair-minded judge, "I do not oppose the dam, new customs, a new vision of life," and she acknowledges the possibility of "benefits" (166). Perhaps, we might think, the defeat and dispossession of the people are just an inevitable continuation of American history on the frontier, a sad but somehow justified implementation of Frederick Jackson Turner's celebrated hypothesis about social regeneration as the outgrowth of unbridled liberty and opportunism on the frontier. We might think, too, that the people's removal to a new land is adequate compensation, albeit an unsatisfactory artistic resolution of a pastoral fable.

The creative mythology of *People* refutes this ideological way of thinking. Maria is a mythical character with an authority that allows her to exist in time and space and, simultaneously, to transcend time and space. The events of her life interact with both social reality and a reality of a higher order.

The novel's implied author or narrator establishes a point of view that preserves Maria's mythical dimension within a realistically bucolic frame.[17] There is no incompatibility between his discourse and her story. As her ally, he tells of, and her actions show, the mystery of ever-flowing life as an enduring reality beyond the illusions of time. This alliance with the inward and essential character of Maria permits him to portray humorously but without condescension the outward and inessential aspects of her character. She is wise but illiterate, occasionally benevolent and compassionate, more often a wild, promiscuous, cruel, and dictatorial crone with a cigarette clamped by her single remaining tooth and with a voice like a low rumble or hiss. She is indifferent to the naming of five bastard children until she understands the legal ramifications of this neglect: Teodosio, described as "a listless, loose mouthed man with his fly unbuttoned" (85), is named by the midwife; Niña is generic; Antonio de la Vega is identified because he watches the cow in the pasture; and Refugio Montes, because his father took refuge in the mountains! These details do not disturb Maria in her mythical dimension.

The point of view of the implied author also functions to invest the valley with symbolic meaning. Synonymous with Maria del Valle, it is a landscape of Mother Earth with the Goddess Mother herself seated at its hub. A third function of the implied author's point of view is to resolve the contradictions between nature and culture. The archetypal pattern of journey to a sacred source and return to the world is completed in and through him. He has, as it were, come to a pastoral center from a modern, complex culture that is fragmented and spiritually impoverished, and he offers, by way of return, the message of revitalization. Maria is virtually identical with nature.

> Her powerful and primitive features, timeless with sorrow and fecundity, are savage and enduring as if cut out of rock: a rock beaten, smashed and worn by waves but still jutting into the promontory beak of nose, high cheekbones and solid jaw into the surge of life. The eyes are small and black and bright, the eyes of a hawk. Only the dark, red-brown flesh of her seamed and sagging cheeks appears touched and worn by time—but still timeless and enduring as the red-brown earth forever furrowed by the plow. [9–10]

Her cheeks are "two seasoned piñon knots," and she stands "straight as a pine" (12). On the day of her death, as she squats against a hillside rock, she and her rebozo, outward manifestations of her life, are blending back into a natural world from which she sprang:

> The sun poked through the fir above her and shone on hair gray and rumpled as the dead moss she leaned against. Her dirty black rebozo seemed streaked and rusty as the oxidized iron in the rock. She wiggled a bare toe in the green grass. A beetle crawled across her leg. [196]

Maria is likened to the natural world through imagery, but she also is associated with ritual and folk observances that resonate with a history extending to Neolithic times and beyond. On the Day of St. John the Baptist, she immerses herself in an icy stream in order to "be immersed in the one living mystery, the waters of life" (176), a baptismal ritual of obvious antiquity. When she lies down to die, she places gold coins over her eyes, and this practice is a partial survival of the ancient and widespread custom of burying all a man's valuables with him in order that he may pay a toll for being ferried to the land of the dead and that he might not return as a ghost to haunt his home vicinity.[18] Maria's divination from goat skulls is an especially striking example of a ritual performed by shamans, augurs, and astrologers from early times. In fact, the Bronze Age civilization of the Shang centered around bone divination. According to F. David Peat, "The pattern of cracks, together with their interpretation, formed an 'acausal parallelism' with events in nature and society, so that the microcosm of the act of divination formed a mirror in which were reflected the patterns of the macrocosm."[19] Such synchronicity is still sought today in the remote mountains of China but has also been reported from the American Southwest.[20] All these examples of archaic survivals in *People* have the artistic effect of identifying Maria with the constant and enduring, making her a symbol of uttermost beginnings.

Maria as a symbol of uttermost beginnings presupposes that she be born an orphan, the Divine Child in whom *the* origin first was and from whom everything is springing up, the archetype representing, according to Karl Kerényi, "the divine principle of the universe at the moment of its first manifestation."[21] Like the archetype of the Divine Child, who comes into being from the womb of Mother Earth, Maria is associated with boundless water and with the imagery of sunrise and is equipped with all the powers of nature to be invincible, which is to say, in Jung's words, "a wholeness which embraces the very depths of Nature."[22] Accordingly, she should be expected to unite pairs of opposites—the Divine Child has an androgynous character for this reason—and to be self-contained, without a master, a divine presence uniting male and female, time and eternity. Maria fulfills this expectation. In her, traditionally masculine and feminine characteristics merge, the powers of mind and blood, of leadership and fecundity, of Father Sun and Mother Earth. Thus, when the men of Mora want to know Maria's opinion about the proposed dam but fear to approach her, they are described as "satellites swarming around a common sun, but at a respectful distance lest they be scorched" (13). With the cigarette she always holds or demands from men, she appropriates a sort of phallic symbol of authority.[23] She also learns that waiting for a master is futile. "Like the land," we are told, "she had been fruitful and enduring, ever waiting for a master" (157), but her partners, from the gringo soldier to the impotent Don Fulgencio, cannot dominate a primal being who is, mythologically considered, antecedent to the division of sex.

Maria's authority, then, is ultimately cosmic, and she focuses it in herself at the mythic center of the universe. This "centering" of a character is, in fact, a significant aspect of all of Waters's novels, as I shall argue at the conclusion of this study. The creative energy of the universe is symbolized in such a character, as Campbell explains:

The effect of the successful adventure of the hero is the unlocking and release again of the flow of life into the body of the world. . . . The torrent pours from an invisible source, the point of entry being the center of the symbolic circle of the universe, the Immovable Spot of the Buddha legend, around which the world may be said to revolve. . . . The tree of life, i.e., the universe itself, grows from this point. . . . Again, the figure may be that of the cosmic man or woman (for example the Buddha himself, or the dancing Hindu goddess Kali) seated or standing on this spot, or even fixed to the tree (Attis, Jesus, Wotan); for the hero as the incarnation of God is himself the navel of the world, the umbilical point through which the energies of eternity break into time. Thus the World Navel is the symbol of the continuous creation: the mystery of the maintenance of the world through that continuous miracle of vivification which wells within all things.[24]

Such an Immovable Spot, World Navel, tree, or axial rock (in the Navajo mythology explored by Waters in *Masked Gods* the world axis is "the Rock-Around-Which-Moving-Was-Done")[25] appears in *People* as Maria herself, as her hut, and as the 9,000-foot crag from which she looks down upon the valley. She is "a rock beaten, smashed and worn by waves but still jutting into the promontory beak of nose" (9). She lives where "jutting cliffs" mark the "handle" of the "curving bow" (19) of the blue valley to the north and to the south, thus at the hub of the two "crescent" (180) shapes, symbols of birth and death (i.e., the waxing and waning moon) at her command.[26] When Maria goes to church, "all this sound and smell and movement beat vainly, like waves, against the jutting altar" (53)—vainly, because she is herself the shrine or altar at the inexhaustible point of creation. Once, when she is looking at her hut, her "eyes saw it in time as well as in space, saw it as the point of a completed circle" (116), presently identified as "the point of her completed circle" (123). It is she who is the center of the symbolic circle of the universe; it is she who is the figure of the cosmic woman through whom pours the mystery which changes yet is changeless.

The most down-to-earth symbol of Maria's authority is, however, the humble burnt-orange blanket to which there are recurrent references. It belongs to her mother and is said to bring "life and color" (21). It is taken momentarily away from Maria by an art dealer who vaguely apprehends its magic: "His mouth watered when he saw it glowing in the sunlight, felt its weave and wonderful softness" (120). It gives Maria strength in time of decision: "wrapping herself in the soft burnt-orange blanket . . . she was philosophizing" (134). As she prepares herself to die, she wraps herself in it. Over the years abused and ignored, it, like Maria herself, comes to stand for the integrity and continuity of her life. Its burnt-orange color suggests the creative solar power that covers the earth. Above all, it is a symbol of law. When

Judge Eliseo, representig the Court, visits Maria, he declares, " 'In me you see a personal man robed with the impersonal authority' " (164), but Maria's blanket robes her with the authority of a law that is not secular but divine. Like the Prophet of the Koran, who wrapped himself in a blanket when he uttered divine verses, Maria attests to a reality which endures, whatever the mantle, blanket or flesh, of the passing world of phenomenality.

The female protagonist of *People* is not in conflict with herself nor, for the most part, with her people. Living as a single woman, until her fifties, in a Mexican-Indian community, where matriarchy is the exception, not the rule, Maria is isolated, both feared and revered, and only when the people believe that she has triumphed over the government in the matter of the dam do they "almost" call her "Santa Maria" (159). The primary conflict in the novel is the conventional pastoral one between a rural way of life and a complex modern culture, with its dominating technology. Maria and the people, it would seem, are defeated by the machine of progress. There then opens up a disillusioning prospect for human survival. Can the enduring nature of earth and of people organically attuned with it be communicated in a positive manner? The evidence of *People* is affirmative: a conflict that cannot be resolved satisfactorily at the social level has been shifted to the province of myth, which opposes constants to a world of flux. In Maria del Valle, Waters symbolizes a correlation with earth and its attendant archetype, the Goddess Mother of the universe, the Eternal Feminine.

At this juncture a critical problem in the characterization of a female protagonist arises. Whereas oneness with the Eternal Feminine affirms the endurance of humanity, stress may fall on fertility and instinct as being fundamentally better than any aspect of culture and mind. Such an emphasis defines cultural primitivism and makes sexist stereotyping of women and minority figures highly probable. The white male novelist who produces an affirmative type in a woman who also happens to be an Indian risks losing sight of her individuality; his creation remains "other," separated from the human community by gender and race. One doubts that Waters even foresaw this problem—but he solves it. Seeing all entities as an inseparable unity of mind and matter, he disposes of the philosophical separation of "male" mind and "female" matter. In fact, Maria represents the androgynous ideal.[27] It is true that she is at least partially identified with the power of the blood and wholly with the flow of life, and these identifications, taken out of psychological and religious context and placed in a sexual one, could be misinterpreted. But the stress in *People* lies not on the biological role of a woman in assuring continuity of the race but on self-fulfillment and emergence within a numinous world, thus quite emphatically on a woman's (or any person's) individuality. Still, as an "object" of veneration, Maria may seem to some readers to live outside the meaningful life and to be engulfed by all she symbolizes. That view, I contend, is invalidated by one's experience in reading the novel: Maria is a flesh-and-blood female character, a complex human being who assumes an authoritative role for the good of her family and people, who is wise yet simple and illiterate, sometimes uncertain about herself and superstitious, often lonely and vulnerable, with a forthright and dignified bearing and with a heart that silently bleeds.

The stereotype of "the indestructible woman" in works by Faulkner, Hemingway, and Steinbeck has been thoroughly and judiciously examined by the feminist critic Mimi Gladstein.[28] She agrees, as I do, with the dictum of Carolyn Heilbrun that the "male-fantasy novel" forms "the mainstream of U.S. fiction . . . [and a] refusal to allow full humanity to women,"[29] although Heilbrun, I would add, sees Nathaniel Hawthorne's Hester Prynne in *The Scarlet Letter* as an exceptional characterization that has left no descendants.[30] Frank Waters, the one major white male American novelist whose characterizations of women in *People* and in *Otowi* meet the most exacting criteria for full humanity, has been overlooked by feminist critics. He is not primitivistic, psychically imbalanced, or misogynous, as Faulkner, Hemingway, and Steinbeck are said to be. The contrast can, I hope, emerge as fairly obvious when we examine quotations from three contemporaneous novels, Faulkner's *Hamlet* (1940), Steinbeck's *Grapes of Wrath* (1939), and Waters's *People of the Valley* (written in 1939; published in 1941).

Faulkner's idea of a superhuman earth goddess is Eula Varner. His initial description of her, when she is not yet thirteen years old, dwells on her sexuality and fertility to the exclusion of all else:

> On the contrary, her entire appearance suggested some symbology out of the old Dionysic times—honey in sunlight and bursting grapes, the writhen bleeding of the crushed fecundated vine beneath the hard rapacious trampling goat-hoof. She seemed to be not a living integer of her contemporary scene, but rather to exist in a teeming vacuum in which her days followed one another as though behind sound-proof glass, where she seemed to listen in sullen bemusement, with a weary wisdom heired of all mammalian maturity, to the enlarging of her own organs.[31]

The pomposity of this passage is surpassed only by its puerility.

Steinbeck's idea of an enduring woman is Ma Joad. She is a steadfast, serene earth goddess in an early description:

Her hazel eyes seemed to have experienced all possible tragedy and to have mounted pain and suffering like steps into a high calm and a superhuman understanding. She seemed to know, to accept, to welcome her position. . . . And since old Tom and the children could not know hurt or fear unless she acknowledged hurt or fear, she had practiced denying them in herself. And since, when a joyful thing happened, they looked to see whether joy was on her, it was her habit to build up laughter out of inadequate materials. But better than joy was calm. Imperturbability could be depended upon. And from her great and humble position in the family she had taken dignity and a clean calm beauty. From her position as healer, her hands had grown sure and cool and quiet; from her position as arbiter she had become as remote and faultless in judgment as a goddess.[32]

The sentimentality of this passage, the giving of more emotion to the facts than they may deserve, can perhaps be forgiven in the light of Ma Joad's real suffering: she has been uprooted and has endured a series of deaths and hardships, starvation, harassment, and a hostile society. Indeed, as Gladstein has observed, Ma's characterization transcends the mythic. Steinbeck, however, like Faulkner, limits his regard for women to their role as perpetuators of the species, as in the scene when Ma tries to share with her daughter, Rose of Sharon, a woman's experience:

And Ma went on, "They's a time of change, an' when that comes, dyin' is a piece of all dyin', and bearin' is a piece of all bearin', an' bearin' an' dyin' is two pieces of the same thing. An' then things ain't lonely any more. An' then a hurt don't hurt so bad, 'cause it ain't a lonely hurt no more, Rosasharn. I wisht I could tell you so you'd know, but I can't." And her voice was so soft, so full of love, that tears crowded into Rose of Sharon's eyes, and flowed over her eyes and blinded her.[33]

Touched, Rose of Sharon will now submit to her lot, as assigned by Steinbeck, to be another mindless universal.

Waters's handling of a similar scene is significantly different. Sixteen-year-old Piedad has come to spend the winter with her grandmother:

At night they crouched together before the fire. A white-bearded storm shook the hut and blew his frosty breath down the chimney. Piedad shivered, drew close to Maria.

"Mi abuela, my grandmother Doña Maria," she asked, "why is it that children call the frightening boogie man whom none have ever seen 'El Abuelo'—a grandfather? Surely you frighten me not at all."

"My child," replied Maria. "To youth, age is incomprehensible. To ignorance, wisdom is frightening. So that El Abuelo having age represents the learning which the ignorant child fears. Now that is wrong. But even grownups have it. They possess learning and knowledge, and still fear the wisdom which they have not attained. We must all learn to be unafraid of the dark, the child of learning, the man of wisdom. Hence we shall all reach the true maturity which is eternal youth."

The fire writhed into a heap. Piedad threw on another stick. The flames uncoiled, rose up and shook like snakes. The resin rattled. The glare outlined pinkly the rows of goat and ram skulls on the rafters.

"Doña Maria," spoke the girl again, "it is said by all that by skulls and herbs you could read stars and weather, foretell good crops and misfortune, the future of man. Why is it you use them no more?"

Maria sighed. "Ay de mi, child! For many years I have ceased to read them. They were helpful in those days of my youth when like you I mistrusted the unseen trail ahead. It is true I had a knowledge of the signs and the events they portend. But not wisdom—the wisdom to perceive the future in each moment, in each stone and blade of grass. The past also.

"It is like this. A child looks at life as a wolf at the trail of his quarry. He has no sense of the past, only a hunger to devour the future. Thus, to pursue it with success, he soon stops and raises his head. He sniffs the wind. He observes the signs—even those on goat skulls. He listens to all the world around him.

"Now, you understand, he is at middle age. Having memory, he can see part of the trail behind him as well as the present he treads. But still the future winds unseen before him, up toward the cliff top shrouded in mist. He reaches it. Pues! That dreaded and hungered for future is no more than the present which resembles the past. They are all one. His fears were nought, his predictions useless.

"Entiende, muchacha? I will say it again for your simple ears.

"Life is a great white stone. You, a child, stare at it and see only one side. You walk slowly around it. You see other sides, each different in shape and pattern, rough or smooth. You are confused; you forget that it is the same great white stone. But finally you have walked around it, stared at all of it at once from the hillside above. Verdad! Then you see it: how it has many different sides and shapes and patterns, some smooth, some rough, but still the one great white stone: how all these sides merge into one another, indistinguishable: the past into the present, the present into the future, the future again into the past.

"Hola! They are all the same. With wisdom who knows one from the other? There is no time, which is but an illusion for imperfect eyes. There is only the complete, rounded moment, which contains all."

And Maria, with gray filmed eyes which saw more, clouded, than when they had been bright, reached blindly for her little sack of tobacco. "Ay de mi! Often I hear steps outside. I look up to see a man in the doorway. It might be Onesimo as he was called, a certain gringo soldado, Don Fulgencio himself, dead these many years. No! It would not surprise me if he were any of these. There are shapes of men less alive than shadows of men. So do even I confuse what has been and will be again with what is."

Thus in her wisdom she taught that winter the lessons which must be learned by each alone, and did not see the incomprehension in the girl's sleepy eyes. [157–59]

Maria's intuitive wisdom comes from a deeper source than Ma Joad's purely physical cycle of birth and death. Piedad does not represent an occasion for instruction in a sex role and some implied necessity of submission to it. On the contrary—and significantly for those of us who take seriously the sexism of American literature—Maria feels called upon to impart, as the essence of her life experience, the message of individual evolution through stages of perception. Of course, since Maria's faith cannot be taught except in parables or learned except through personal growth and experience, Piedad, unlike Rose of Sharon, comprehends nothing. There is something mushy in Steinbeck's handling of the scene, but not in Waters's. Moreover, there is something bordering on impertinence in the way Ma Joad speaks. It is as if Steinbeck has invested so much fantasy in creating an earth goddess that he can't question her infallibility. Maria, by contrast, humbly confesses to doubts, fears, and confusions. Waters succeeds here and elsewhere in *People* in bringing his female protagonist fully and individually alive as a complex, fallible human being.

Maria's humanity bleeds to a prick. One detail must here suffice to reveal her world of feeling. It appears in the scene after Onesimo's crucifixion. His empty shoes are delivered to Maria, who has been to this Jesus both nurturing mother, as befits her name, and lover:

> The sudden meaning of their appalling emptiness stabbed her like a knife. It carved out her heart and bowels and mind. She stood more empty than the shoes, one hand clawing at her face, holding her breast, then pressing against her belly.
> Teodosio and Niña were gulping goat's milk from wooden spoons. Maria bent down to her own bowl, and lifted a hair from the milk with her forefinger. Suddenly she straightened. With a fearful howl she flung open the door and rushed out into the night. [68]

It is one human hair, one thread, but it is enough. By such a tiny thread, Waters is showing us, the whole fabric of passionate humanity is knit together.

6

THE ALLEGORY OF

EMERGENCE IN

THE MAN WHO KILLED THE DEER

THE MAN WHO KILLED THE DEER (1942) is a remarkable example of Waters's archetypal imagination at work. Thirty years after the novel's publication he still vividly recalled how it all began:

> From the day I wrote the first page—in ink on a manuscript that was later destroyed—the novel seemed not of my doing. I remember that fall morning in Taos, sitting in front of the fireplace in the big room above the garage in back of Tony Lujan's house just inside the reservation. The story did not have to be contrived; it unfolded, like a flower, its own inherent pattern. The words came easily, unbidden, as the flow of ink from my old, red Parker. I don't mean to imply that it was anything like 'automatic writing,' whatever that is. Simply that it seemed impelled by the unconscious rather than by rational consciousness.
>
> There seems to be some validity for this statement. The novel has been used as a subject for a master's thesis at the Colorado State University, interpreted from the viewpoint of Jungian depth-psychology. A similar approach has been taken in a *Tesi di Laures* prepared for the University of Genoa, Italy. At the time I wrote the novel, however, I had not read Jung.
>
> What seemed to touch off the book were two incidents. I had strayed into the county courthouse where a hearing was being given an Indian for killing a deer out of season in the Carson National Forest. A few mornings later, when I was bending over the washbowl to shave, I envisioned reflected in the water three figures evidently discussing the incident and who bore striking resem-

blances to the old, blanketed governor of Taos Pueblo, Pascual Martinez in his Forest Service boots and whipcord, and Ralph Myers, the Indian trader. Right then the idea of the novel presented itself, and after washing the breakfast dishes I sat down to write it.[1]

If, as I surmise, the idea of the novel is implied in its title, Waters had begun by striking into a Paleolithic stratum of world mythology, that of a covenant between men and animals, suggesting a sacramental relationship of hunter and hunted beast, an experience in the psychological dimension of their being one and the same. In the words of Campbell, "The beast to be slaughtered is interpreted as a willing victim, or rather, as a knowing participant in a covenanted sacred act wherein the mystery of life, which lives on life, is comprehended in its celebration."[2] The mythology of the covenant, which includes a powerful taboo against the taking of life without ritual expression of reverence for it, was taught for a human season of some 20,000 years, and memories of the animal envoys of an Unseen Power still must sleep, somehow, within us. *The Man Who Killed the Deer,* a novel about an Indian who ignores the covenant and is subsequently haunted by the deer he has killed, is part of the evidence.

Although the narrative unfolded its pattern easily, the formal perfection of structure—beginning with a first chapter which is technically one of the most adroit in modern prose fiction—and the beauty of style signaled the appearance of a classic. After reading the manuscript for its first publishers, Farrar and Rinehart of New York, Stephen Vincent Benét was so enthusiastic that he insisted that not one word be changed.[3] Burton Rascoe, one of the most respected reviewers of the period, stated in his full-page review in the *Saturday Review of Literature,* "This is by far the finest novel of American Indian life I have ever read,"[4] and noted its superiority to Oliver La Farge's Pulitzer Prize-winning sentimental romance about Navajo Indians, *Laughing Boy* (1929). Yet the novel was a flop commercially. In the mobilization for World War II following the Japanese attack on Pearl Harbor on 7 December 1941, no one seemed to be interested in a book whose background was the life and religion of a remote Indian pueblo in Taos, New Mexico. Soon the publishers contributed the metal plates to the war effort and remaindered the stock for whatever price they could get. Still, some word about the classic novel had spread, and in 1950 Alan Swallow of Denver decided to bring out a new edition. In 1971 Pocket Books published a paperback edition. Numerous reprintings of these editions have followed, and foreign translations have appeared in German (1960), French (1964), and Dutch (1974). Although it is impossible to estimate with any accuracy the number of copies of *Deer* that have been sold in its first fifty years, the figure may possibly be more than three-quarters of a million. At any rate, sales continue steadily. The latest—and best designed—paperback reprint appeared under the Swallow Press and Ohio University Press imprint in 1989.

One reason for the novel's popularity is its subject matter, Pueblo Indian life. As a Southwestern "lifestyle" currently sweeps the country, anything "Indian" attracts attention, and tourists in New Mexico may well be including *Deer* along with their haul of squash-blossom necklaces and reproductions by R. C. Gorman. And here, although I am speculating, lies a critical problem: *Deer's* background materials may obscure its universality and the art that reveals it. Pueblo Indian life is the novel's background, the vehicle for another kind of story and not the story itself. Fascinated by materials with which we have little or no familiarity, we may confine our experience of *Deer* to expository data, to cultural anthropology, and ignore the novel's figurative meanings, its allegoricalness. If we recall that the greatness of *Moby-Dick* can be attributed to what Melville called "the part-&-parcel allegoricalness of the whole,"[5] rather than to the exposition of whaling on which that allegory expands, we may be prepared for an analogous attribution in our reading of *Deer*. The Indian data are controlled throughout the novel by an allegorical meaning which is not in any necessary sense "Indian" at all.

Because the allegoricalness of the novel depends on its total organization, an exposition of plot and background is necessary to show the foundation on which the fable builds. Background materials with which many readers may be unfamiliar I have highlighted in capital letters that they may be discussed later, and, once familiarity with these is increased, the hidden allegory may seem to rise naturally, like a photograph emerging from solution. An allegorical mode aims at both clarity and obscurity together, each effect depending on the other.[6] Although the numinous meaning of a symbolic or iconographic deer can be only enigmatically suggested by the words *mystery* and *wonder,* the deer assembles various accretions of figurative significance which form a clear patterning.

SYNOPSIS

The events of the novel take place in or near an Indian PUEBLO in northern New Mexico over a two-year period in the 1930s. Before the action unfolds, Martiniano[7] is already a pueblo outcast born of an Apache mother and a Pueblo father. When, about twelve years old, he comes of age for traditional religious education in the KIVA, he attracts the attention of the Indian Service, which is looking for "smart" boys, and sent for six years to a white man's school ("AWAY SCHOOL"), the council of elders having offered little resistance and forced the father, under threat of a public whipping, to agree to the removal. Martiniano is trained as a carpenter and acculturated to the ways of whites. When he returns to the pueblo, he has a young white man's outlook: rationalistic, individualistic, willful. His parents are dead, and his "uncles" have appropriated part of his inheritance, leaving him only two small farms outside pueblo walls. Resentful and rebellious, Martiniano refuses to conform to what seems a petty dress code (knocking the heels off his shoes, cutting the seat out of his trousers, and covering his middle with a blanket) and to join in the ceremonial dances, for the meaning of which he has never been prepared. These refusals earn him fines and a public whipping from the council of elders. He scorns them for their injustice and pridefully seeks outside the pueblo's ceremonial life a spiritual meaning to his existence. When he meets Flowers Playing, a "mountain" Indian (part Arapahoe, part White River and Uncompahgre Ute) as opposed to a "city-dwelling" Indian (or Pueblo), herself a product of "away school," he does not ask permission from her family for a marriage or request from the pueblo that she be adopted into the tribe. He woos and wins her in a white man's way, without regard for such relationships. Although his nascent intuitive powers have attracted him to Flowers Playing and prompt him to place his faith in the marriage ritual, he is bitterly aware that she must share in his poverty and disgrace. She does so willingly, even though, in addition to everything else, her exceptional gifts as a dancer are ignored by the pueblo. Only Palemon, who belongs to the old ways but believes in their substance, not their outer form, befriends the couple inside the pueblo; outside it, only Byers, the white trader for whom Martiniano does odd jobs, befriends him.

And now, on a mountain trail leading to the pueblo's sacred DAWN LAKE, Martiniano has killed a deer. He has assaulted a ranger who seeks to arrest him because the killing is out of season, and the ranger, retaliating, has left Martiniano for dead. Palemon, he who is gifted with extraordinary intuitive powers, "knows" something is wrong, finds and rescues his friend, and brings him and the slain deer back to the pueblo. Here Martiniano is censured by the council, not for the assault, but for having failed to perform rituals that amount to asking the deer's consent to the killing. Brought to the white man's court, he is sentenced to three months or $150, but Byers advances money for the fine. The case seems closed. The pueblo governor, however, wonders why rangers should be present on land historically the pueblo's. Reluctantly, an Indian Service attorney promises to get in touch with officials in Washington. And thus from the killing of the deer there unfolds a connected train of events: the pueblo has been moved to action over land seized by the federal government, and Martiniano is afflicted with a sense of guilt.

As conscience plagues him, Martiniano feels estranged from Flowers Playing. Seeking faith elsewhere, he tries the PEYOTE ROAD, the "church" that the federal government is pushing as a substitute for traditional religion. The council will have none of this. Martiniano, too, rejects use of peyote but must endure fifteen lashes for having participated in a ceremony requiring the outside stimulus of a drug. Moreover, the punishment is administered by Palemon, who has tried to shield his friend from discovery, and so Martiniano feels especially ashamed for having involved another person in his fate. Influenced by the power of a relationship, he accepts his responsibility and for the first time, instead of being haunted by the spirit-deer, senses its guardianship. Martiniano is reunited with Flowers Playing, she becomes pregnant, and there is contentment in their lives—but Martiniano's acculturation in the ways of the white man continues. Admirably enough, he refrains from killing deer who take shelter on his farm, and he works his land in order to pay off the debt to Byers, but he still thinks that *he* makes the land fruitful, that *he* truly possesses it. Accordingly, he violently ejects from the land a Mexican sheepherder. This act once again brings the pueblo's land claim to the attention of the authorities. Because the council begins to regard Martiniano with a measure of respect, he believes that he has bridged the gap between himself and the pueblo and become its legendary hero. Thus, on San Geronimo Day he attempts to "save" the pueblo from disgrace—the ceremony of the POLE CLIMB has been botched—but he, too, fails to climb the pole and bring triumph out of defeat. Humiliated at last, he begins to perceive the power of the deer as one of necessary relationships to life instead of as an adversary.

Meanwhile, Flowers Playing has been invited by the pueblo to enact the role of a Deer Mother in the DEER DANCE. As Martiniano observes her performance, there are illuminated for him the primal forces with which pueblo ceremonialism has always been concerned. In the sequence of events that end the novel, the slain deer ceases to haunt him, Flowers Playing gives birth to a son, and Martiniano repays the debt to Byers and takes part in the pueblo's ceremonial foot races. Above all, he is in touch with his own intuitive powers, and these lead him to rescue Palemon's son from a death in the mountains, in a scene somewhat parallel to that in which Palemon had rescued Martiniano in the novel's first chapter. Because the pueblo has brought the Dawn Lake controversy to a victorious conclusion, Martiniano can take legitimate satisfaction in watching the pilgrims depart for their annual Dawn Lake ceremony. Lacking the religious training to join in it, he nevertheless understands its necessity and vows that his own son will be educated in the traditional manner. He wraps himself in a traditional blanket and is content.

BACKGROUND

"[Waters] is concerned primarily with the inner drama that lies beneath the surface of ethnological documentation." So wrote Harvard anthropologist Clyde Kluckhohn in his foreword to *Masked Gods: Navaho and Pueblo Ceremonialism* (published in 1950). The inner drama of *The Man Who Killed the Deer* is also of primary concern, but the ethnological surface or background material plays its part. To describe it, I shall draw summaries almost verbatim from *Masked Gods*. Neither it nor *Deer* has, to the best of my knowledge, ever been seriously challenged on the grounds of authenticity. On the contrary, *Deer* has found acceptance in the Taos Pueblo itself. Fearful lest his Indian friends think his novel a violation of traditional secrecy and religion, Waters mailed the first advance copy to the interpreter for the Taos Pueblo council, but there were no repercussions. In fact, Waters has often been approached by a man or a woman in the pueblo who tells him how glad they are he wrote "that book," for from it their children can understand the "old ways." Moreover, when the Blue Lake (fictionalized as Dawn Lake) controversy came to a head, *Deer* was sent to members of Congress and supporting committees and organizations, as background material, and proved at least partially instrumental when, on 15 December 1970, President Nixon signed into law the bill providing that 48,000 acres of sacred land be kept in wilderness status under Taos Pueblo ownership with the national government acting as trustee.[8]

As mentioned earlier, the rituals whereby an animal consents to be sacrificed have their origin in the Paleolithic Age, an archaeological period which forms a general background for the North American Indians. Even as Waters was writing *Deer* in 1941, the University of New Mexico was excavating preglacial remains in a cave in the Sandía Mountains near Albuquerque, crediting Sandía Man with having existed 25,000 years ago. Moreover, if Campbell is right, the system of rites actually brought together two mythologies, that of animals and that of female humans, so that there are two contexts, moral and regenerative, to be associated with ritual and taboo.[9] This joint context helps to explain why the male deer killed by Martiniano is nevertheless viewed symbolically as a feminine power.

The story of the PUEBLO Indians begins about 2,000 years ago, according to the earliest dates of Southwestern Indians established by dendrochronology. About this time the Indians were dressing themselves in animal skins, weaving baskets, planting corn, and storing surplus grain. When many families at a time gathered in larger caves and expanded the storage pits into stone pit houses built in the shelter of overhanging cliffs, settlements began and, with them, society, as from caves the people climbed up the faces of cliffs to create cities wherever a horizontal ledge provided support. Great communal houses were built on top of the cliffs, and kivas—round, subterranean structures used for religious ceremonies—were built in open terraces in front of the house groups. Then about 1,000 years ago the people descended from cliffs to establish the great pueblos on the plain, city-states such as Pueblo Bonito in Chaco Canyon that may have rivaled those of ancient Greece. From what we presently know about this civilization of what *Deer* calls the "Old Ones" (called *Anasazi* by the Navajo, nomadic Indians who are late arrivals in the Southwest), its social structure was matrilineal, polarized to the intuitive and feminine in that "man, unguided by reason, maintained a direct intuitional relationship with the primal forces of a living universe" (*Masked Gods,* 30). Although this civilization vanished about A.D. 1300, some people remained and built up pueblos in the desert Southwest and along the Rio Grande. In fact, the oldest occupied towns in the United States are said to be Oraibi and Acoma, both dating from around A.D. 1200, and the Tiwa-speaking pueblo of Taos has probably been occupied for more than 700 years.

Taos Pueblo is located in the mountains about seventy miles north of Santa Fe. Three successive nations—Spain, Mexico, and the United States—legally confirmed the pueblo's ancient rights to its land, and President Lincoln presented the governor of the pueblo with a silver-mounted cane in token of the people's right to govern themselves by their own laws. Such confirmations notwithstanding, Spanish, Mexican, and Anglo settlers usurped pueblo lands and water rights. Much of the surrounding area, including Blue Lake near Mount Wheeler, was constituted as Carson National Forest. Not until 31 May 1933 did Congress pass an act giving Taos Pueblo a fifty-year tenure of their lands surrounding Blue Lake.

Pueblo ceremonialism "is concerned with the fact that the deeds of individuals are not confined to their own spheres of social action; they vitally affect the earth, the waters, the mountains—the whole web of life" (*Masked Gods,* 246). It is, therefore, essential to the maintenance of tribal culture that boys between the ages of twelve and fourteen be separated from their families and given religious instruction in the KIVA. A prolonged ritual initiation breaks the "cord" to a boy's mother and to the earth, and the child is born again into a consciousness of the greater life of the spirit, learning that "gods are the invisible cosmic forces of the universe" residing in man "who, if he wills, can evoke them for the common good . . . a prophecy and a promise of that time when man shall return to and be synonymous with the source power of all creation" (*Masked Gods,* 212). According to Waters, the Emergence myth is introduced to children at this time in the kiva, whose members develop a conscience with respect to all forms of life.

Beginning in the 1880s, the American government set about the task of educating Indian children in "AWAY SCHOOL." Nonreservation schools were established in Carlisle, Pa.; Lawrence, Kans.; Riverside, Calif.; Phoenix, Ariz.; and Albuquerque and Santa Fe, N. Mex. Once captured and sent to "away school," the Pueblo children suffered everything possible that could be done to erase all vestiges of their racial culture and identity. Their hair was cut; they were forbidden to speak their own language, to wear their own clothes, to keep their traditional customs, even their own names. Dismissed from school, they were untrained for anything but manual or menial labor. When finally they did straggle back to the pueblos, they did not know how to adapt themselves. And yet, in spite of their lack of kiva training, many returnees went "back to the blanket," the government schools having given them little more than a thin patina.

On their way back to the blanket, young men returning from government schools often found the PEYOTE ROAD attractive. Pharmacological experience of the ineffable (in various Indian languages *manitou, wakan, orenda,* and the like), has in some regions always been sought by young men in a "vision quest" and everywhere at least by shamans. Certain substances such as peyote, introduced to Native American tribes from Mexico about 1880, were and are alleged to inhibit metabolically the "restraint" of symbols, languages, and cognitive maps enculturated into people by society and thus to produce a "heightened" perception of ineffable truth. Although Aldous Huxley popularized the drug in *The Doors of Perception* (1954), an authority on the peyote cult, Weston La Barre, finds it hard to believe that an impaired brain functioning somehow becomes its physiological opposite: heightened perception may in fact be a lowered critical faculty, as in drunkenness and dreams.[10] Perhaps because the Taos Pueblo Council suspected that drugs were no substitute for their religion, the use of peyote had a stormy history there. In 1921 a peyote meeting was raided, and the blankets and shawls of all participants were confiscated. In 1923 two adherents of the cult were whipped and three men given large fines. Nevertheless, the cult has been accepted by various Indian tribes and officially recognized by the Bureau of Indian Affairs as the Native American Church.

The POLE CLIMB, DEER DANCE, and DAWN (i.e., Blue) LAKE episodes or references in *Deer* are obviously of religious significance. According to Waters in *Mexico Mystique,* the pole climb may have originated in ancient Mesoamerica when a great feast was celebrated in honor of Tlaloc, a god of rain and hence of regeneration. A tree was cut down, its consent having been asked, brought to the temple of Tlaloc with songs and dancing, and ceremonially planted. There are modern parallels to this ceremony in Mexico and the Southwest, and the climbing of a pole is a feature of the end-of-September, San Geronimo fiesta in Taos Pueblo. There, a tall, straight pine of considerable circumference (about 48 inches at the base, according to my rough measurement of the pine used in 1989) is planted in the Taos plaza, the fruits of harvest suspended from its top—a deer or sheep carcass, squash and corn, a bundle of groceries. An accomplished climber shinnies up the pole, lets down the treasure to the shouts of the crowd below, and then balances on top of the pole, singing his eagle song of triumph. Although athletic skill is required for successful climbing, a climber's triumph, as I understand it, is not a claim of excellence. It is, rather, a kind of sacred reciprocation between the people and nature, which made the harvest possible, and so it is believed that any break in this interaction, such as a failure to climb the pole, might result in disease or calamity.

As for the Deer Dance, which is prominent as a winter ceremony at Taos Pueblo, its religious significance is translated by Waters into a psychological allegory, as we shall see presently. But the Indian concept of harmony among all things may seem so alien to non-Indian readers that we don't conceive of a spiritual conviction that is communicated through dance, a unique expressive act in which there is immediacy and a perfect unity of thought and feeling. As Jamake Highwater argues in *The Primal Mind,* "The idea that spirituality can be associated with the body is extremely remote from the white man's belief in the dichotomy of mind and body, spirit and flesh."[11] Be that as it may, primal people regard movement as the embodiment of a mysterious force, so that they may imitate an animal in movements (but also in costume) in order to influence the circumstances of nature.

Just exactly why a mountain lake is considered as a sacred place of tribal origin seems to be a question related to Emergence, or the process of evolution considered in mythological terms. One interesting theory, presented by Waters in *Mountain Dialogues* (61–62) is that in the Mesoamerican number system the founding concept of zero represented the ocean, or endless space and time; hence the "foundation" of pyramids in Teotihuacán was water, the first "lifting up" or step or world (the second being fire, the third earth, the fourth air, and so forth). Perhaps an analogous idea is expressed by the sacrality of Dawn Lake, water being the first in the progression of life forms. In the psychology of symbols, water represents the unconscious, and it is this meaning which seems best suited to the allegory of Emergence in *The Man Who Killed the Deer.*

Allegory traditionally presents a gradual evolvement of correspondences between a narrative and a cluster of pieties or religious formulae familiar to the reader. But there is the use of analogy which places most of the weight of a narrative's meaning on correspondences evolved within the story itself, depending hardly at all on borrowings familiar to the reader. Melville, Conrad, Franz Kafka, and D. H. Lawrence tend to effect allegoricalness in this manner, and the same is true of Frank Waters. In *Deer* the various analogies that can be drawn between Indian religion and modern psychology simply point to the oldest idea about allegory, defined by Angus Fletcher as "a reconstitution of divinely inspired messages, a revealed transcendental language which tries to preserve the remoteness of a properly veiled godhead."[12] No one, I think, can read *Deer* without sensing this remoteness, even though revelation may be imputed to Indian sources with which one is unfamiliar rather than to the creative mythology of Waters, a non-Indian with some Indian heritage. But the mythic tenor of *Deer* must be distinguished from the anthropological vehicle, and the distinction, often productive of a powerful dramatic irony, becomes the mark of the work's allegoricalness, the whole work becoming what Edwin Honig calls "the allegorical unit." The whole work partakes of the allegorical unit and also fulfills it, the allegorical unit then resounding with "inherent meanings . . . built up on all levels of connotation" until "the expository data serve the theme in a way parallel to the way Christian analogy served for the medieval writer." Honig develops his insights further:

> It must seem that the meanings grow naturally out of each action in the narrative. The more complex a writer's grasp of psychophysical relationships, the richer the work is likely to be. For the meanings of allegory depend, as in poetry, upon the accretion of certain tropes. These tropes make evident a consonance between objective facts and their moral or psychological counterparts, so that the reality—the hypothetical nature of the literal—is ultimately transcended by the total organization of meanings, which is the fiction itself. And so we may say that the language of allegory makes relationships significant by extending the original identities of which they are composed with as many clusters of meaning as the traffic of the dominant idea will bear.[13]

Honig's statements about "psychophysical relationships" explain why Moby-Dick is more than a whale, Pike's Peak more than a mountain, and the deer in *Deer* more than a deer. Expository data are transcended by the accretion of symbolic meanings driven by a "dominant idea."

As I interpret *The Man Who Killed the Deer,* its dominant idea is Emergence. In the Waters canon, Emergence represents a stage of human consciousness that reconciles the duality of reason and intuition and supersedes these on a numinous plane of increased awareness. This plane is, moreover, an effulgence of an immanent power which relates the inner world of man to the living universe, itself composed of expanding psychic as well as physical energies. From this perspective, which is above all evolutionary, the long journey of mankind has been through successive states of ever-expanding consciousness. From complete polarization to the instinctive or unconscious mentation, man has emerged to his present state of rational consciousness and must not surrender this advantage over the lower forms of life or sink back into the unconscious, a condition mythologically associated with the Cosmic Mother of Creation. Modern man, however—and "modern" here largely refers to Euro-American peoples since the advent of scientific and materialistic civilization in the seventeenth century, with its attendant cult of individualism—has become excessively rationalistic and consequently alienated from the source of life, suffering a loss of relationship to nature and reaching an ethical dead end. Consequently, there must be a redressing of the balance, human survival being at stake, and the reconciliation of reason and intuition will once more enable people to live in harmonious relationship with the emergent life forces of Creation.

Waters's idea of Emergence resembles the Jungian psychology of "individuation" but was developed, at least through 1941, without Jungian influence.[14] Undoubtedly, though, Emergence has been influenced both by oriental and by Amerindian mythologies inasmuch as these lay stress on a Way or Road of self-fulfillment. In particular, the Pueblo and Navajo myths of Emergence (as it is called) are a component part of Waters's idea or myth of Emergence; he has simply translated or interpreted them in the light of his own moral and religious philosophy. According to Waters himself, the "worlds" in Indian myths of Emergence are "allegories" (*Mountain Dialogues,* 159) of a process of evolution. There have been four successive "worlds," all embodied within the Cosmic Mother of creation, from which man has been born: the fire element of the first world gave him his life heat; the air element of the second world gave him breath of life; from the third world of water man derived his blood and other bodily constituents; and the earth element of this present world gave man his flesh. This Road of Life is thus participated in by every organ and faculty, and the process is cumulative, affirming another "world" or "worlds" to come, identified as a new world of consciousness, this being the lone human faculty left with room to expand. Given that man is intimately related to all forms of life, there is an ethical basis to evolutionary en-

largements, and man has, whether he recognizes it or not, an indebtedness to
those forms and a responsibility to them. It follows that human conscience,
though it may be local and tribal in orientation and enforcement, serves all
humanity in a world culture, because conscience pulls individuals back from
ego-centeredness into harmonic relationship at all levels—family, tribe, society, all peoples, all living things, the universe itself—and thus pulls individuals forward on the path of Emergence. In fact, conscience in all of Waters's
novels but especially in *Deer*—and the point needs emphasis because conscience in American literature (e.g., *Huckleberry Finn*) usually means moral
indoctrination—is regarded as the voice of Absolute Consciousness speaking
within us to our limited conscious selves.[15] Self-fulfillment is not an achievement of an individual; outstandingness has nothing to do with it. On the contrary, participation in the macrocosmic universe requires "complete obliteration
of self that merges at last into one flowing, living whole . . . that has been,
that will be, fused in the ever-living, indestructible now" (*Masked Gods,*
336). And that is why Emergence checks the ego-centered individual's wild
lunges for freedom and obligates him "to the dictates of the unconscious
which embodies all his primordial past," necessitating "those thaumaturgical
rites which acknowledge his arising from the one great origin of all life and
which keep him whole"—so that "there can be no Emergence to a higher consciousness without a Return to the fathomless deeps within us" (*Pumpkin,*
64, 153). A return to the Cosmic Mother is the prerequisite for emergence to
a new world of the mind.

Emergence is the dominant idea or creative myth that is allegorized in
The Man Who Killed the Deer. The allegorical hero's actions and thoughts
resemble those of a man possessed by a primary illusion that he is in control
of his fate. Specifically, he is "cursed" by the egocentric, Euro-American individualism in his outlook. Then the powers of conscience and intuition—the
two are envisioned as synonymous—appear in the form of a spirit-deer. The
hero loses his illusion by recognizing his obligation to the dictates of the unconscious and emerges to a state of increased awareness. There is a culminating
character to this allegory: the hero experiences final moments of illumination,
and love and creation triumph following the destructive battle with evil.

Yet it is characteristic of figurative images that their allegorical status is
not recognized. "Only a mind which can apprehend *both* a literal and a
'poetic' formulation of an idea," Susanne Langer claims in *Philosophy in a
New Key* (published the same year as *Deer*), "is in a position to distinguish
the figure from its meaning."[16] Transposed into Waters's terminology, this
statement asserts that the form or shell of spiritual endeavor is not to be confused with its substance. Although there are critics of *Deer* who either praise

it as a precursor of Native American novels or condemn it as a fictional impersonation of Native American consciousness, Waters not only never pretended to write an "Indian" novel but also took precautions in the novel itself to distinguish between the form and the substance of Indian life.[17]

While *Deer* was still in manuscript, Waters wrote Mabel Dodge Luhan on 14 February 1941, justifying his fictional approach to Indian life as a direct one without intervention of a non-Indian point of view yet nevertheless an outside viewpoint:

> I think a completely true all-Indian novel will never be written. Not by a white for it would stem, as you say, from his own white psyche. And not by an Indian for the very reason that his own psyche is given to an instinctive, intuitive, non-reasoning and non-evaluating approach, too deeply rooted to emerge into a foreign word-form. His own natural forms exist only as great myth and dance-dramas, ceremonials and sand painting, etc., whose meanings are intelligible to most whites only by translation of their values—and which are gradually becoming less intelligible and lost to the Indians themselves.
>
> So that I feel the truest writing possible of Indian substance is from an outside viewpoint, an honest and direct attempt at translation, rather than the fictional method of working out from within. . . .
>
> Now this, in your sense and mine, is not an Indian novel. To consider it such is to accuse me as a man of sentimentality, and as a writer of real hokum or self-illusions about what I am trying to do.
>
> To write at it in sketch form or essay—coldly; to look at it fictionally through a white participant, as THE WOMAN WHO RODE AWAY [novella by D. H. Lawrence]; or to project the Indian only as a shadow against a white background, as the SAD INDIAN;—these are the easiest methods. And they are all indirect and depend upon contrast. What this is, is an outside viewpoint with the looker merely eliminated from within the Indian envelope. [Tanner, 57]

Waters's decorum does seem justified. If we accept his premise that the Indian is polarized to intuition and to a nonverbal epistemology and the white is polarized to reason and to a verbal epistemology, "a completely true all-Indian novel" is unavailable to the psyche of either Indian or white; and even an Indian novelist writing from within Native American consciousness about the nonverbalized substance of spiritual power would be basing his or her attempt, as the white novelist's, on rational modes of expression. The Native American novel has not been ruled out—D'Arcy McNickle's *Surrounded* (1936) had already appeared, and the novels of N. Scott Momaday, James Welch, and Leslie Marmon Silko would appear in the period from 1968 to the present time—but it is Waters's contention that the substance of Indian life will remain ineluctably bound up in myth and ceremony, for which language can but produce translation. The category "Indian novel" makes no absolute sense, but an approach to Indian values through fiction can be attempted by means of translation of the "natural forms"—myth, dance, ceremony and the like. The approach in *Deer* is direct and honest, but the translation of substance into word form must be an approximation and an interpretation, never the substance itself.

The human substance of Indian life is another matter, for Waters presupposes a common humanity. The difficulty of interpreting, still more of intuiting, the thoughts and intentions of persons from an ancient culture is perhaps insuperable and would display itself awkwardly, as if Montezuma II were being interviewed on television. In a technical sense Waters meets this difficulty by translating what is essentially Indian silence into italicized passages. Philosophically he meets it by assuming the presence of constants among persons of different races. This is standard procedure for novelists and historians. As Martin D'Arcy declares in *The Sense of History,* "We are aware that individuals differ and that freedom makes human action unpredictable; nevertheless we presuppose without any hesitation that certain instincts remain constant, that there is a broad way and a narrow way, that the struggle between mind and heart, selfishness and generosity is unabating, that communities form naturally and exhibit common characteristics, and that these and other traits of men can be discerned."[18] Waters's letter to Luhan justifies his procedure in *Deer* on a similar humanistic basis:

> I believe, differently from you, that [Indians], like a Fiji Islander and an Eskimo, like people everywhere of all races and conditions, are yet human entities bound by the same simple human ties of human passion. From deep within us all well up old, dark, racial blood-forces. Around us, whether in jungle, mountain or city, exist the same problems of existence and environment. And above us, the same spiritual plane to which we all some day will converge. We are all middle-men, all human, Indian, negro and white. Whatever you say of tribal feeling, there does exist in an Indian the simple emotional ties between man and wife, mother and son, regardless of whether he acknowledges it under the name of love, and despite the fact that the individual feeling is quickly submerged in the tribal. In the Indian this is not the important part of life; it is how this is deepened, enhanced, by the wonderful, unspeakable essence flowing up into it from deep within.
>
> Now this exists, in some measure, in all men. And the problem has forever been how to admit it in a clearer stream, a more unimpeded flow. And so the great religious systems have arisen, age upon age, throughout the world. And as man has striven upward, he has spiritually, as temporally, gone through the same evolutionary changes. The core of Indian esotericism is the belief that he holds, unsullied because unspoken (i.e., not allowed to become dead through crystallization), the dark flower of primeval truth and power. The Lhasas of Thibet believe, likewise, that in their hands they hold alive against time the same spark of

the one timeless flame. Nor do they give it up to all to become a dead, crystallized concept. Only to initiates, to initiates who win to it through many reincarnations if necessary. But toward it grope, and have always groped, all men. The Taoist Way, the Buddhistic patterns, remain their shells of endeavor. Now I don't know the Lhasa secret doctrine, nor do I know the Indian belief. But within the Indian form of life, which is as valid as any other, I can suggest briefly the gropings of all men in the groping of Martiniano. For he, like all Indians, is human, fed by the dark irrational flow yet unilluminated for him, and by the need for resolving his faith consistent with the pattern which forms his outward life. . . . He may be Indian, but he is human. [Tanner, 57–59]

Regarded in this way, the substance of Indian life and religion partakes of universality, and "the gropings of all men," unlike esoteric "belief," are known to us. It is therefore justifiable to present an Indian protagonist who is in quest of the wordless ineffable: this is the allegorical aspect of the novel's figurative images. The fact that the protagonist resolves his faith "consistent with the pattern which forms his outward life" is no warrant for denying the universality of his quest. It is true that he has returned to the blanket (that is to say, departed from white culture and rejoined Indian culture), and readers with a preference for literal meanings alight here. In fact, it is quite easy to read *Deer* as if it were only the story of an "individual" who eventually submerges himself in the "collective," and in our noncollective society that is a negative outcome, because the protagonist seems to have given up his freedom (in our usual sense of the word as a lack of requirement), and capitulated to his persecutors, the Indian councillors. Of course, students of the culture of Pueblo Indians attest that the highest personal autonomy is often found in the most intricately developed social structure; that the individual who learns to walk safely through life by observing a large number of taboos and procedures is not being inhibited by the structure but guided by it in the acquisition of an essential skill, the freedom to act and to be, and hence is not being required to surrender spontaneity; and that, as the individual develops his inner potential by enhancing his participation in the ceremonies of the unit, which in the last case is no less than the entire universe, so does the entire universe become invigorated, and one's unique being is made significant in this way.[19]

Deer, however, is not a treatise in cultural anthropology, and so these nuances about the meaning of freedom in Indian life will do little to affect an impression of retrogression: the protagonist has returned to the blanket, and that is somehow a resolution foreclosed to the rest of us. On the other hand, once we recognize the allegorical status of *Deer,* the protagonist's return to the blanket is but figuratively a return to the Cosmic Mother, to the feminine power of the unconscious, and his groping for a faith eventuates in a vision which is not culture-specific but universal—in short, a myth. The protagonist, far from abandoning the modern world, has become the type of the truly free, nonalienated *modern* individual who has recovered the richness and wonder and mystery of life. Thus *Deer* remains faithful to the form of Indian life and religion while revealing to our noncollective society a substance that is at the forefront of contemporary ethics: in psychic integration only is there freedom, the ethic of fullness demanding an organic relationship whereby an individual is dependent on the existence of all other persons and of all living things, "*breathing mountains, the living stones, each blade of grass, the clouds, the rain, each star, the beasts, the birds and the invisible spirits of the air*" (18),[20] for all of which the metonymical figure is a deer.

Now, I live in an area of the country where the slaughter of *tame* deer is an event authorized by the United States government. Every year, hunters are invited into the forested premises of the United States Air Force Academy for the alleged purpose of thinning out the herds of these half-domesticated animals. So it wouldn't surprise me if there are readers of *Deer* who write off the symbolism of the deer as yet another "mystical" expression of Indian life, and certainly from the Euro-American perspective the idea of a deer as a "spirit" must seem at the very least extraordinary. And it is true that the Native American grasp of the solidarity of life is often expressed as a kinship with animals, who are not addressed as underlings in the world of nature but as representatives of the abiding power of the cosmos, a power with which to seek communion.[21] Yet I do not think that conscience and intuition are confined to the sensibilities of Native Americans, nor does Waters think so, as revealed in his letter to Luhan:

> We all break away. We look outward, and inward, and finally see in ourselves the macrocosmic universe, and the world outside as a microcosmic replica of ourselves. And what prompts us, and ever keeps us on the track of self-fulfillment, is that peculiar thing we call conscience which turns us back, or the intuition which illumines the forward step. It might just as well be called a deer. [Tanner, 58]

Even though the fundamental life force may appear to the Indian in the form of an animal, people everywhere depend on intuition for their life-affirming discoveries and imaginings and on conscience for the preservation of life. We all, so to speak, have our deer.

There is one character in *Deer* whose primary narrative function is to keep us alert to the distinction between the form and substance of Indian life: Rodolfo Byers, the white trader who lives on the boundary of the reservation.

Long experience has brought this old man, like the sage Dansker in Melville's *Billy Budd,* to a kind of bitter prudence and to representative authority, for he has "something of all men, and of the wilderness around him" (26). Having studied books about Indian history, ethnology, and anthropology, he finds them lacking in "the substance of life he loved" (29), which he identifies as the Indians' "living awareness" (31). He asserts that their "premises of life were based not on the rational, the reasoning, the evaluating approach, but wholly on the instinctive and intuitive," and it is this power of intuition which is "the very core of the life and the wonder and the mystery which had ever held him" (32). Intuitive himself, a man with "two natures, two lives" (28), he can approach understanding of Indians, but the living awareness itself is something that "could never be put into words, even by an Indian" (31). In these respects, Byers serves as Waters's spokesman, and Waters echoes his character's language at the critical moment when the protagonist himself is losing ego-identity and becoming receptive to substance: "So little by little the richness and the wonder and the mystery of life stole in upon him" (134). Byers puts us on guard against expectation of an inside viewpoint and in effect can do no more by way of interpreting Indian life than to isolate one factor, intuition, which he himself possesses even though he is polarized to the rational. At the same time, he effectually warns us against a too-literal reading of a novel with a psychological theme.

To liberate his allegorical hero into the substance of Indian life, Waters shows that a strong sense of tribal unity has been achieved and at the same time articulates feelings productive of a complex, permanent attitude which governs all individual lives once it is recognized. In the light of the mystery of life, we may perceive our own role in the cosmic plan and return to psychic balance and right attitudes. *The Man Who Killed the Deer* is not an "Indian novel" in the usual senses but an "Everyman novel," in which salvation is at stake.

The consonance between objective facts and their moral or psychological counterparts provides the basis for an allegory. As correspondences evolve within the story, the dominant idea begins to be revealed through accretion of meanings. Thus the deer that Martiniano kills is a figurative one and is increasingly amplified to "become" any deer, the constellation of the Pleiades, the Deer Mother in the Deer Dance, the Cosmic Mother, conscience, intuition, the unconscious, the ineffable, and so on. As Martiniano progresses through successive states of mind, so his capacity for relationship to the symbolic deer grows until he lives in harmony with it. When he is not in harmony with it, an ironic discrepancy between symbol and state of mind invalidates authenticity. Like as not, he will seek to accept substitutes for the reality as yet unilluminated for him. This is a pattern cherished by allegorists. For example, because Christendom in the Middle Ages was fond of listening to homilies on people's futile efforts to find a substitute for salvation, *Everyman* presents an allegory of a person who accepts all the substitutes society offers but finds himself suddenly confronted with the reality of death. Martiniano defies the pueblo, seeks legal redress for his grievances, looks for a faith in marriage and then in peyote, wants, like Captain Ahab, vengeance against an animal, and works up a savior complex, only to be haunted and "defeated" by the spirit-deer, with which he must finally learn to live, in order to be "saved," to be authentic, to emerge. I do not of course intend to imply that *Deer* is homiletic. Its moral sense is consistent with the familiar aesthetic enunciated by Henry James in *The Art of the Novel,* namely, "the perfect dependence of the 'moral' sense of a work of art on the amount of felt life concerned in producing it."[22] Martiniano's gropings are indeed *felt,* and if we were not engrossed in the fable, were not persuaded of its human truth, were not warmly allied with a proud social outcast who is, after all, behaving in a manner that few of us would question as irregular, let alone futile, we might wonder whether morality is even an issue. Only the total organization of meanings, in other words the allegory of Emergence, places events in a moral perspective from which we perceive a rightness in the outcome and a wrongness in the hero's lunges for freedom. This moral perception arrives, not as a comforting affirmation of received ideas and accepted norms but as a reconstitution of these in a new key of harmonic unity.

Actually, the "new" worldview is very old indeed and differs from modern styles of thinking chiefly in the extent to which it is analogical. To antiquity, as to the Middle Ages and the Renaissance, analogy was a natural method of perceiving truth. Because "this" happens in one sphere, so "that" happens in another sphere. There is a plague in Thebes because Oedipus is a patricide who has married his mother. There is madness, political disorder, and a raging storm because Lear has broken up his realm and renounced his daughter. It is not that Sophocles and Shakespeare imagined in any naive literal way that whenever a king violated a taboo or lost his mind the world of nature obliged with disease and thunder. In analogical thinking, these are symbols of disorder in that all life depends on observance of the natural order. If, for example, a farmer spreads a chemical pesticide over a given area, the disappearance of the insect disrupts the food chain, leads various species to prey on one another, pollutes the drinking water hundreds of miles away, and generally causes trouble in unforeseen ways. So the idea of order is by no means obsolete, even though we may describe this order in terms widely different from those of Sophocles and Shakespeare. A Frank Waters speaks of the reconciliation of reason and intuition, only going beyond this idea of order to postulate, on the basis of various philosophical and scientific systems, a new and higher world of consciousness to come. But always, what is being desiderated is an idea of order that makes for balance, health, and peace. And yet it is symptomatic of modern times that representation of an idea of order—by a Waters or, for that matter, by an Einstein—is brushed aside as "mystical," unless, of course, the idea is attributable to a religious system considered nonobsolete (such as Christianity) or to a materialistic Utopia (such as that put forward under the banner of Karl Marx).[23]

The point I am trying to make is that *Deer* has an inherent pattern based on analogical thinking. As soon as Martiniano kills the deer, a disruption in the natural order occurs, and Palemon, whose intuitive powers are fully alive to the world, picks up the vibrations and rescues a friend not even "known" to be missing. The cause of disorder is then traced to the breaking of a taboo: Martiniano has ignored the covenant between men and animals, itself in ever-widening circles of implication a sacred bond between microcosm and macrocosm. On further inspection, the moral and religious nature of the disorder is traced to its source in the mind, for the reasoning, analyzing, evaluating mind of Martiniano is but half a mind, the all-but-forgotten hemisphere of intuition, instinct, or the "feminine" unconscious not having been called into play. In analogical thinking, the natural order is symbolized by the deer, and so it is the "deer"-ness of life, which is everywhere manifested and which is but dormant in Martiniano himself, that is gradually recognized as the ego-fog clears. The restoration of order is then symbolized by fertility (Flowers Playing gives birth to a son, and Martiniano's fields yield enough produce to pay off his debt), by atonement (Martiniano participates in ceremonies), and by Emergence (he rescues Palemon's son because reason and intuition are reconciled, and he is aligned in the direction of Dawn Lake, to the origin of life forms).

In working out his idea of order, Waters uses the imagery provided by Indian culture, even though the order he envisions is largely independent of it. Thus at the turning point of the novel, after Martiniano has been humiliated by his failure to climb the pole and while he is watching Flowers Playing befriend two does on his farm, his own analogical perception of truth comes to him in a flash of intuition about his people:

> A snake wriggled up Martiniano's backbone; his knees trembled. A vision clutched him by the throat. He had cut his corn stalks and stacked them in little, upright conical piles to shed rain. In the dusk they looked like a far, vast village of tepees standing on the plain. Striding between them, distorted and fantastically enlarged by perspective, came the deer—giant, ghostly figures looming above the highest tips of protruding lodge poles. For an instant, as the

old myth-wonder and atavistic fear rose up and flooded him, he saw them as his people had long seen them, one of the greatest animalistic symbols of his race: the deer which had populated forest and plain in uncounted myriads on the earth, and gave their name to the Pleiades in the sky; whose hoofs as cere-monial rattles were necessary for every dance; who complemented at once the eagle above and the snake below; gave rise to Deer Clan and Antelope Priests; and lent the mystery of their wildness, swiftness and gentleness to all men. In a flash of intuition it all leapt out before him. And in its brief glimmer stood out a strange woman with the same wildness and gentleness which had first drawn his eyes to her as she danced—a woman no longer his wife, but as a deer clothed in human form and thus possessing the power to draw and control the great shapes that moved toward her. [162]

This mythological deer is a power to be accepted and lived with—quite literally, for Flowers Playing has the power—and Martiniano is properly filled with fear and trembling. Like Lee Marston in *Lizard Woman,* he has seen both the luminous and the fierce and terrible aspects of God.[24] Formulated as if through a Native American consciousness, the idea is a realization of profound religious import, well known to us in the Western tradition from the Book of Job to the Book of Revelation: *God can be loved but must be feared.*[25] And that this *is* a moment of illumination and self-fulfillment is conveyed by the imagery of a snake uncoiling from some instinctive realm and wriggling up the backbone into the visionary region of mind, for this is the serpent power of yogic wis-dom, as well as of Indian mythology, and its release signifies the beginning of the hero's emergence into higher consciousness.

The culminating point in Martiniano's quest is reached when he observes the Deer Dance, in which Flowers Playing plays the role of a Deer Mother, *the* Cosmic Mother of all Creation. Significantly, Waters translates the movements of the dance into a psychological allegory about the bipolar ten-sions of conscious and unconscious forces and about the dangers of allowing a dominating rationality, or the light, male principle, to break free from the dark, feminine principle with its emotions and instincts reaching back into the depths of time and rooting us to our past and to relationship with all the living universe. As the Deer Mothers dance softly before the male dancers, who represent deer in bondage, we are given this description:

They gave way before her as the male ever gives way to the female imperative. They tried to break free of the circle only to be irresistibly pulled back as man in his wild lunges for freedom is ever drawn back by the perpetual, feminine blood-power from which he can never quite break free. And all the time they uttered their strange, low cries, the deep, universal male horror at their submis-sion. Out of them it welled in shuddering sobs of disgust, of loathing and de-spair, as still they answered the call. On all fours, as the undomesticated, untamed, archaic, wild forces they represented, impelled to follow her in obedience to that spiritual cosmic principle which must exist to preserve and perpetuate even their resentment. [174]

Martiniano watches this performance with "a hypnotic horror" and recognizes his own fate:

> He felt himself cringing before that manifestation of the blind force which had pulled him back from his own strivings toward a new and resplendent faith— back into that warm flow of human life of which he was still a part. His own revolt, his anger and his fear; it all came out of him anew and was echoed by the sobbing, tortured cries of the deer before him. [175]

As the dance redefines the bondage that each person (not just the male) owes to the cosmic principle of origin and unity, Martiniano comes to grips with the meaning of his life, its misdirected attitude transformed by perception of its limitations:

> Now, for the first time, he sensed something both of the conscience which turns us back, and the intuition which illumines the forward step, and so holds us on the upward road of self-fulfillment. Sensed dimly, as one only can, the invisible, undefined and irrational force that has no meaning outside its living truth. It stood before him, silent, inscrutable, clothed in loose white buckskin— in the anonymous shape of a woman who had been his wife, and was now the commanding mother of all men. [175]

Thematically secured, much like Dante's Beatrice, as an earthly woman, incarnate creative force, and judicial principle, Flowers Playing has the most significant role in Martiniano's quest for redemption, albeit that the terminology for divine grace in the Christian allegory has been shifted into transpersonal psychology. Martiniano's consciousness still resents and fears the numinous power of the unconscious, but recognition of the reality of the natural order has still transformed his personality into a higher consciousness of his total goal on "the upward road of self-fulfillment." Irrespective of the wishes and fears of his conscious mind, the goal of life has been spontaneously produced by the unconscious, and his conscious realization of what he is living out and his acceptance of responsibility for what he has done or proposes to do make all the difference before the bar of nature and fate. He can no longer regard himself as a victim of the natural order because the meaning of the numina has manifested itself before his very eyes.

The ambivalence in attitude toward the irrational is typically suited to the method and purpose of allegory. Among modern critics Edwin Honig, for one, asserts that in allegory the irrational is "given an authentic, undiminished force which otherwise—according to law, custom, dogma—would be distorted or obscured."[26] The constant layering of meaning in allegory proves to be decisive in creating the whole effect a literary work can have upon us. The irrational becomes viable, and thereby marvelous and forbidding insights assume a form which, if taken literally, might be destructive of social codes. Certainly in a society such as our own, one that favors the patriarchal principle and harnesses the idea of freedom to rational consciousness and the idea of God to a one-sided power of goodness and love—even as the threat of world destruction hangs over us like the sword of Damocles—an archetypal vision on the order of *The Man Who Killed the Deer* looks to allegory's quality of elusiveness to conceal seriousness of intent. Perhaps that is why Martiniano's emergence is not expressed in the language of ecstasy but in that of resentment. Like Job or an Oedipus, he resents the limitations imposed on him by the horrible and irrational. Nevertheless, the allegory of Emergence, formulated in *Deer* as the redeeming necessity of a return to the unconscious, creates a new sense of wonder out of the mystery that lies buried, apparently, in us all.

ARCHETYPAL PROMISE FROM

APOCALYPTIC PREMISE:

THE WOMAN AT OTOWI CROSSING

It seems strange to me now that when I first arrived
I was not conscious of the myth beginning to take
form. Not only the myth of the Project on top of the
mesa, but the myth at its foot, at Otowi Crossing.
Only now can one realize they were two sides of the
same coin, neither of which could have existed
without the other. Both growing, as all myths must
grow, with agonizing slowness and in secrecy.
Forming one myth as we know it now—perhaps the
only true myth of these modern times.

(*Otowi*, 74][1]

This statement attributed to Dr. Edmund Gaylord, an atomic physicist
who has awakened from his sleep in conscious will and instinctive behavior
and who seeks a new world of the human spirit, is part of Waters's most original fictionalized attempt to resolve the apparent contradiction between
science and mysticism, matter and mind, reason and intuition. The myth of
the Project, which is based on the discovery of a New World of enormous
physical energy locked inside the atom, is evidently one polarized to consciousness, with its credo of rationalism, materialism, and the concept of linear time. The myth of the Woman at Otowi Crossing, which is based on the

discovery of a New World of enormous psychic energy locked inside the mind, is evidently one polarized to the unconscious, with its powers of perception of and being within the wholeness and timelessness of Creation.[2] These myths are said to be "one myth," complementary and united or reconciled, "perhaps" a single psychophysical energy—Absolute Consciousness, or Irreducible Reality—that may be realized once humanity has evolved to a new and higher stage of awareness. *The Woman at Otowi Crossing* presents Waters's mature novelistic vision of Emergence.

What might be surprising is Gaylord's earlier misconception of his own intellectual powers and of the methods of science that he has applied in helping to bring about atomic and thermonuclear explosions. But it is a historical misconception deeply engrained in our thinking, not easily remedied; and it is shared by many scientists still today who, while conducting experiments based on the matter-energy equation and on the relativity theory that events occur in a space-time continuum, are reluctant to discard the outmoded Newtonian view of a mechanistic universe. This situation, reported by such scientific philosophers as Arthur Koestler, Fritjof Capra, and F. David Peat, may well have its source in the Western idea of "mind."[3] When science is properly conceived, it is creative, its processes of thinking vividly intuitive, subjective, and irrational until after the experimental event. Science, like mysticism, depends on the unconscious mind. Scientific thought, properly conceived, is compatible with mysticism and a principal manifestation of individual, unenforced spiritual experience. But of course scientific thought is seldom so conceived: science is believed to be a branch of knowledge which operates predominantly with abstract symbols whose entire rationale is objectivity, logicality, and verifiability.

Whence arises this paradox, namely that the creative act emerging from unconscious mentation is regarded as depthlessly conscious? It arose with modern science itself under the influence of Descartes, who identified "mind" with consciousness alone, as if conscious and unconscious experiences belong to different, opposed, and irreconcilable compartments. Although the concept of the unconscious is an ancient one, it has for more than three centuries evoked a feeling of wary skepticism that in turn blocks the way to psychic integration with our individual selves and to comprehension of a worldview whereby everything in the universe is interrelated and interdependent. That has long been Eastern mysticism's worldview, and Einsteinian physics and Jungian psychology have only in the twentieth century begun to approximate it and to synthesize the insights of East and West. At the present time, late in the twentieth century, there are signs of change indicated in the titles of popular scientific books such as *The Tao of Physics, The Dancing Wu Li Masters,* and *Synchronicity: The Bridge Between Matter and Mind*—and in the characterization of an atomic physicist in *The Woman at Otowi Crossing*. For the most part, however, modern science has ignored and continues to ignore the grave and the constant in human affairs, the unconscious and its archetypes.

And now this same one-sided, materialistic, and hubristic science has bequeathed to the world since 16 July 1945, when the first atomic bomb was detonated in New Mexico, the apocalyptic premise to survival, the possibility of annihilation of all life as we know it.[4] Although Waters does not personally believe that such a dire catastrophe awaits us, the development of this power of destruction has occurred when, by all accounts, modern culture has reached a highly alarming stage of crisis of social, ecological, moral and spiritual dimensions.[5] Today there are no boundaries, and the old ethnically oriented mythologies which centered authority in gods "aloft" rather than in the individual human spirit are dying except in archaic cultures. So it seems that humanity faces man-made apocalypse at the very moment in history when the archetypal promise of myth, individually centered yet universal in meaning, has only begun to announce itself through creative minds as if urgently summoned to our aid, from the depths of the unconscious psyche, in the hour of dread.

Therein, I think, lies the prophetic greatness of *The Woman at Otowi Crossing*. Begun in 1953, though not published until 1966 and even then not brought out in a definitive edition until 1987, the novel carries forward and enlarges on a comparison-contrast developed in 1950 in *Masked Gods:* the atomic reactor at Los Alamos and the Sun Temple of Mesa Verde, considered as allegories about physical and psychic energies, reveal that "both the transformation of matter into energy, and the transfiguration of instinctual forces into creative energy depend upon the reconciliation of the primal dual forces of all life" (*Masked Gods,* 421–22). By preempting the fission-fusion language for nuclear energy as a metaphor for a psychological conflict resulting in release of new energy, Waters was prepared within a few short years after the Hiroshima bombing on 6 August 1945 to accept the Atomic Age as a revelation of reality (albeit an age tragically introduced in a destructive form) and to confront the apocalyptic premise—that one nuclear war forecloses the future—with the archetypal promise of the creative myth of Emergence. If we evaluate an author's achievement not only with respect to the ordinary recalcitrance of his materials but also with respect to the magnitude of conflict imaginatively confronted and artistically contained, *Otowi* will have to be considered as perhaps the supreme visionary novel in world literature at present. Although many modern novelists have confronted the facts of death in the self and in the heart of culture, it is Waters who convincingly invigorates the primal powers constituting hope.

While he was writing *Masked Gods,* Waters was influenced by aspects of Jungian psychology and was in particular drawn to Jung's idea of a "reconciling symbol" as explained in M. Esther Harding's *Psychic Energy* (1947). According to the theory, a solution to conflict will not appear in the form of an intellectual conclusion or in a change in conscious attitude, such as might be brought about by education or precept, but will develop spontaneously in the unconscious, arising as an image or symbol which has the effect of breaking the deadlock. The potency of the reconciling symbol "avails not only to bring the impasse to an end but also to effect a transformation or modification of the instinctive drives within the individual: this corresponds in the personal sphere to that modification of the instincts which, at least in some measure, has been brought about in the race through the ages of cultural effort."[6] Almost incredible as this proposition seems, the psychological imperative to bring about a radical change in the instincts and a promotion of human development has long been believed to be possible in the East, in the various forms of yoga, for instance. The reconciling symbol leads, Waters feels, "whole races, nations, and civilizations in great bursts of creative energy to another Emergence, a new stage of consciousness" (*Masked Gods,* 410). He speculates that such a symbol might be the circle: just as in relativity theory "a ray of light-energy travelling from the sun at 186,000 miles per second will describe a great cosmic circle," so the "evolutionary Road of Life completes its circuit by returning to its source" (*Masked Gods,* 434). He further speculates that a phenomenon such as telepathy points to the possibility of future emergence, through the unconscious, to a psychological fourth dimension in which past, present, and future are "coexistent" (*Masked Gods,* 431).

These speculations would help to shape the theme of *The Woman at Otowi Crossing.* Through an imperative of the unconscious, the protagonist breaks through to a mystical experience of timelessness, finds a solution to conflict, and emerges to an awareness which is, so to say, the paradigm for cultural transformation. Likened to a mandala-shaped kiva, the protagonist is herself a kind of personification of a reconciling symbol. By counterpointing the myth of the Project and the myth of the Woman at Otowi Crossing and unifying these in the myth of Emergence, Waters shapes for those who can respond to it a vision for the future, in which world crisis is resolved on a higher plane of at-one-ment with the cosmos.

The rediscovery of the unconscious mind and of its capacity for spontaneously releasing the energy of archetypes as solutions to crisis is of the highest interest in contemporary consideration of the "death of mankind."[7] The unconscious mind has power to effect alteration of our inner life and of the outer forms in which life finds expression and support. The promise of the unconscious mind lies in its creativity.

But if creativity may free us from a plunge into world catastrophe, is it not also a form of human motivation? Early twentieth-century psychology, influenced by Freud, reduced motivation to escape from anxiety and tended to leave out of account activities that might be self-rewarding and urges that might be independent of such biological drives as hunger, sex, and fear. Nowadays, nonreductionist theories have dramatically revealed the deleterious effects of protracted stimulus starvation as well as the organism's need for more or less constant stimulation, or at least a steady flow of information—a hunger for experience and thirst for excitation probably as basic as hunger and thirst themselves. In other words, living organisms exhibit an exploratory drive and demonstrate an essential creativity. It follows that what is self-rewarding can be at the same time self-transcending and other-rewarding, and here, at the psychological rather than at the consciously ethical level, we encounter our gift for empathy. In the manifestations of the unconscious, such as in dreams, the boundaries of the self are fluid, and one can be oneself and somebody else simultaneously. The gift for empathy then activates our participatory emotions, those which answer the human need for meaning whereby the self is experienced as part of a totality, which may be God, nature, and mankind. Therefore, the full human self is a power for human survival because in its most developed representatives—in mystics, for example—a whole new body of possibilities is brought into the field of experience, breaking the crust of closed societies and opening them to the perception of dimensions in which all life is timelessly incorporated as a unity.[8]

And so we come to see that a process or emergence to a higher consciousness, in which rational consciousness is reconciled with the unconscious, becomes the realization of a common humanity and an orientation in the direction of world culture.[9] Mankind's development is then not determined by catastrophe but by, in Waters's philosophy, "the periodic synchronization of human and cosmic rhythms" (*Mexico Mystique,* 274). As consciousness expands to relate the inner life of man to his material outer world, the cataclysmic changes that many people have predicted since the release of atomic energy may prove instead to be transformation into a new world of the mind, due to the release of psychic energy.

If we grant that transformation is validated by mystical experience, we may still think that visionaries are people close to the edge of neuroticism; and they are, in the sense that they have moved out of society into the area of original experience, where they must interpret life for themselves. The actual crux of the matter where mysticism is concerned is not that it seems antisocial and not that all symbolic expressions of it are faulty but that mystical experience is the *function* of life. Campbell makes this point in one of his television interviews with Bill Moyers:

> *MOYERS:* In classic Christian doctrine the material world is to be despised, and life is to be redeemed in the hereafter, in heaven, where our rewards come. But you say that if you affirm that which you deplore, you are affirming the very world which is our eternity at the moment.
> *CAMPBELL:* Yes, that is what I'm saying. Eternity isn't some later time. Eternity isn't even a long time. Eternity has nothing to do with time. Eternity is that dimension of here and now that all thinking in temporal terms cuts off. And if you don't get it here, you won't get it anywhere. The problem with heaven is that you'll be having such a good time there, you won't even think of eternity. You'll just have this unending delight in the beatific vision of God. But the experience of eternity right here and now, in all things, whether thought of as good or as evil, is the function of life.[10]

What Campbell is saying in *The Power of Myth* (the interviews published posthumously in 1988) is what Waters has been saying in his visionary novels all along, but pointedly in *Otowi:* its protagonist is a mystic. It is she who is normal, who is functioning within the vision of eternity. The other characters—with the exception of an old Indian and eventually with the exception of Gaylord, who has a mystical experience of his own—only think of themselves as "normal," when in fact their thinking in temporal terms cuts them off from reality. So we have a protagonist who has been nudged into the realm of the paranormal but who is nonetheless truly normal, a paradox for those who haven't broken through into the mystery dimensions or been pushed into the interface between what can be known and what is never to be discovered.

Yet modern science itself has been pushed precisely into such an interface, unable, for example, to decide whether an atom is a wave or a particle, when it is both and therefore the manifestation of a transcendent energy source. Again, it is the thinking in temporal terms which creates the problem, for we are accustomed to regard events in nature as a causality of pushes and pulls to connect them. Now that scientists are beginning to postulate that events arise out of the underlying patterns of the universe, the similarities between the views of physicists and mystics are being acknowledged, and the possibility of relating subatomic physics to Jungian psychology and to parapsychology is being seriously studied. With such studies, the classical notion of causation is being modified to make room for what Jung called an "acausal connecting principle," or synchronicity.[11]

Synchronicity is the term employed by Jung to explain the coincidence in time of two or more causally unrelated events which have the same or similar meaning. According to the theory, archetypal energy could be manifested both in internal imagery and in external events, and the meaningfulness of this coincidence of a psychic state and a physical event is emphasized by the connection with archetypal processes. Synchronicities act as mirrors to the inner processes of mind and are thus to be associated with a profound activation of energy deep within the psyche. As described by F. David Peat, the very intensity of synchronistic happenings suggests their profile:

> It is as if the formation of patterns within the unconscious mind is accompanied by physical patterns in the outer world. In particular, as psychic patterns are on the point of reaching consciousness then synchronicities reach their peak; moreover, they generally disappear as the individual becomes consciously aware of a new alignment of forces within his or her personality.[12]

It seems that one cannot describe the advent of this psychic energy without using the language of explosiveness, of something that reaches a peak, like the critical mass within an atomic reactor, and then bursts, like a bomb. Indeed, Peat believes that synchronicities tend to occur during periods of personal transformation, when there is a burst of psychic energy: births, deaths, intense creative work, falling in love, and the like. As we shall see, the synchronistic happenings that occur to the protagonist of *Otowi* fit into this profile exactly: as her old way of life is dying, as she herself is dying, she "explodes" into visions that are meaningfully precognitive of nuclear explosions, and then, as she becomes aware of a transformed personality, the synchronicities disappear and her Emergence—the myth made manifest—consolidates itself in the new world of consciousness.

Significantly, I think, Jung first contemplated synchronicity at the time when Einstein, a guest on several occasions for dinner in Jung's home, was developing his first (or special) theory of relativity.[13] In relativity theory we can never talk about space without talking about time and vice versa. When all things are seen as interdependent and inseparable parts or manifestations of an ultimate, indivisible reality, with opposite concepts unified in a higher dimension of space-time reality, there is no "before" and no "after" and thus no causation. Accordingly then, phenomena such as telepathy, clairvoyance, and precognition, all of which suggest an explanation beyond the merely coincidental, might also point to the unfolding of an order which is neither matter nor mind. Indeed, the theory of synchronicity leads to the proposal that "mind and matter are not separate and distinct substances but that like light and radio waves they are orders that lie within a common spectrum." What may be reflected in a synchronistic happening such as precognition are, according to Peat, "the dynamics of the macrocosm as it unfolds simultaneously into the mental and material aspects of a person's life."[14] Synchronicity, in short, proposes a bridge between mind and matter and admits a spiritual element into the philosophy of science. Hence Erich Neumann wrote in 1955 in a eulogy to Jung, "If the premise of synchronicity . . . can be validated, this would mean no more nor less than that phenomena which have hitherto been described in theological terms as 'miracles' are in principle contained in the structure of our world."[15] Jean Bolen, another Jungian psychologist, declares in *The Tao of Psychology:*

> With the idea of synchronicity, psychology joined hands with parapsychology and theoretical physics in seeing an underlying "something" akin to what the mystic has been seeing all along. The important element that synchronicity adds is a dimension of personal meaning that acknowledges what a person intuitively feels when a synchronistic event is directly experienced. Theories and laboratory experiences make thinkable the idea of an underlying invisible connection between everything in the universe. But when it is an intuitively felt experience, a *spiritual* element enters. The human psyche may be the one receiver in the universe that can correctly apprehend the meaning underlying everything, the meaning that has been called the Tao or God.[16]

When Jung studied Richard Wilhelm's translation of the Taoist *I Ching* or "Book of Changes," he recognized that an acausal synchronistic principle had long been known in Chinese mysticism, which is primarily concerned with nature's Way, or Tao. The Chinese, like the mystics of India, believed that there is an Ultimate Reality which underlies and unifies the multiple things and events we observe, and Tao, in its original cosmic sense as the undefinable, Ultimate Reality, is thus equivalent of the Hinduist *Brahman* and the Buddhist *Dharma-Kāya*. The Tao differs from the Indian concepts, however, by virtue of its intrinsically dynamic character. As explained by Capra, the Chinese "not only believed that flow and change were the essential features of nature, but also that there are constant patterns in these changes." The Taoists, specifically, "came to believe that any pair of opposites constitutes a polar relationship where each of the two poles is dynamically linked to the other."[17] From this belief, so difficult for the Western mind to grasp, that contraries are aspects of the same thing, there was derived a further belief that any extreme development becomes its opposite within the limits for the cycles of change. When, for example, a culture consistently favors yang, or masculine, values and attitudes—analysis over synthesis, rational knowledge over intuitive wisdom, science over religion, and so on—and has neglected the complementary yin, or feminine, counterparts, such a one-sided movement reaches a climax and then retreats in favor of the other polarity. Thus, where synchronicity is concerned, the coincidence of events in space and time not only points meaningfully to a ground of unity but also suggests a dynamic web of patterns according to which the synchronistic event may signal a change of polarities of transpersonal significance.

We have reached the juncture where Jung's theory of synchronicity and Waters's myth of Emergence mingle to form the dynamic worldview of *The Woman at Otowi Crossing*. Waters, in 1950, had read Wilhelm's translation of the *I Ching* and Jung's foreword to it explaining synchronicity and realized "the universal significance of this profound book" (*Mountain Dialogues*, 114). It helped to confirm his speculations about the Mesoamerican symbology of life as a continuous transformation of opposites through movement, a movement mythologized in Indian America as Emergence through successive "worlds" when a civilization reaches a verge of extreme development and is replaced by another one on the Road (Tao, "Way") of Life. To Waters, that ancient myth of Emergence was and is an allegory for man's ever-expanding consciousness, and here in Jung's theory of synchronicity, although it represents phenomena on a lower temporal plane than Emergence, was a link: parapsychological phenomena occur mainly in the surroundings of an individual whom the unconscious wants to take a step in the expansion of consciousness. And so a fictionalized individual represented as having authentic mystical experiences, including synchronistic events, might be projected into the vanguard of a new age that is coming to birth as an old age has reached its climax in an apocalyptic premise. Assuming that every event in the visible world is the noncausally related effect of an archetype in the unseen world, one would have a fiction revelatory of a dynamic process in history. And that fiction is *The Woman at Otowi Crossing*.

On an immediate level *Otowi* is the story of an "ordinary" middle-aged woman, Helen Chalmers.[18] As the story opens, she and her lover, Jack Turner, are waiting at a railroad whistle stop for the arrival of Emily, Helen's twenty-year-old daughter by a previous marriage. It is soon apparent that Helen, who abandoned Emily in infancy, has accumulated psychological dynamite—guilt, shame, and fear of financial failure—during almost twenty years of lonely isolation in a remote area of northern New Mexico called Otowi Crossing, where she manages a tearoom in a small adobe house. Emily does not arrive that day, but an army colonel does, to inquire about a school called Los Alamos on the mesa above Otowi Crossing. Soon after experiencing a faint premonition, Helen discovers that she has breast cancer. Realizing that she cannot marry Turner, she contemplates the seeming futility of her life. Just then she has the first of her mystical visions, a "fusion" (21) of self into the complete pattern of the universe. After many misgivings and resentments about this awakening, she courageously accepts the power of destiny that drives her, commits herself to its fulfillment, and painfully sacrifices intimacy with the two persons she most loves, Turner and Emily. Doomed and yet reborn, with only Facundo, an old Indian from the nearby pueblo, to understand her integrity and psychic power, she has terrifying precognitive dreams, the content of which appalls her—nothing less, as we know through dramatic irony, than A-bomb and H-bomb explosions, even planetary disappearance. She nevertheless grows in spiritual power and becomes a benevolent influence on many who know her, including physicists from the secret city of Los Alamos, who are experimenting with another, seemingly opposite kind of power. Helen influences one of these physicists, Gaylord, so much that, as he is observing the first H-bomb detonation over the Pacific, he has telepathic knowledge of the moment of her death and transfiguration, the triumph of spirit over matter.

That is the story on one immediate level. Waters never permits us to lose sight of Helen as a flesh-and-blood woman who suffers into wisdom; who swims in the nude and responds exuberantly to the natural world; who enjoys sex and friendship; who cooks and who nurses the afflicted. Waters, however, counterpoints the four parts of her myth—breakthrough to hidden reality, learning to live in a new world of freedom, exercise of released psychic energy, and its constructive influence on others—to the myth of science, whose hierophants successively break through to the new world of subatomic energy, release it, and victimize themselves and masses of humanity with radioactive fallout. So another immediate level of the story is a history of the Atomic Age from the Manhattan Project through the Trinity Site explosion, Hiroshima, experiments in the Nevada desert, and the H-bomb explosion in the Marshall Islands. The interaction of the immediate levels of the story leads to a distinction between Helen Chalmers, the vessel of worldly experiences, and the Woman at Otowi Crossing, the personification of the myth of Emergence. Lest the woman in her mythic role seem to impose on modern sensibilities, Waters allows various characters to raise our objections for us: a strategy of an ironist. Turner believes Helen is a neurotic recluse in danger of becoming a psychotic lost in a meaningless dream state. Emily, an anthropologist with intellectual pretensions, is upset by her mother's mythological interpretations of historical signs. Throckmorton, a rich but puerile politician, sees Helen as easy prey for his manipulation. All these characters get their comeuppance. Turner's pragmatism is a betrayal of trust that loses him any chance for a complete relationship with Helen. Emily's science is of no emotional help; after aborting her child by Gaylord, she comes to an academic dead end in a Mexican university. Throckmorton's goose is cooked when Turner tricks him into making public a proposal for bombing America's enemies. While the fates of these characters may not remove all objections to the myth of Emergence, they do indicate some validation of Helen's normalcy and moral wholeness.

The most convincing validation of Helen's mysticism comes from the story of Gaylord, to whom focus shifts in the last third of the novel. Repeating the pattern of Helen's emergence, but with a terraced crescendo, he inherits her archetype as a moving principle of life. Thenceforth his spiritual effort is to hold to the experience in loyalty, courage, and love beyond fear and desire. In mythological terms this "gay lord" is like the questing hero from Grail legends: an impotent Fisher King of the Atomic Waste-Land is cured of his wound and given reign over a regenerated world. When we first encounter him, he is dedicated to science at the expense of emotional development. He is little more than a dehumanized robot isolated from his Jewish family and the teeming life of New York City. In spite of his duty to science, though, he feels drawn to Emily shortly after his arrival at Los Alamos. Therein lies his dilemma, for security regulations strictly forbid courtship. When Emily becomes pregnant, Gaylord promises marriage but procrastinates, betraying the dictates of his heart at the very hour when a historical Klaus Fuchs is passing atom bomb secrets to Harry Gold—*that* big a betrayal. Gaylord gets his bomb at Trinity, *his* secret; Emily gets an abortion, *her* secret. Gaylord, unaware of the abortion and beginning to mature emotionally, no longer feels alienated from his family and neighbors in New York. When he is apparently sterilized by radioactivity during an accident at Los Alamos, the tragic irony of his apparently irreversible fate—as guilt-ridden as Helen's had been—is his belated feeling of compassion for humanity. The climax of Gaylord's story occurs in Nevada when a "shot" fails to explode after countdown, and it is his duty to climb the tower to defuse the bomb. At this moment he experiences disassociation from the instinctual pattern of fear and guilt which has constituted his emotional field. Having attained spiritual detachment, Gaylord disconnects the jinxed bomb and, later in Las Vegas, finds the courage to "connect" his presumably lost manhood with a willing "show-biz" goddess, allusively a lunar deity named Monday Willis. In a wonderfully comic scene, Monday breaks down the barriers of Gaylord's isolation and comments, "Jesus, but it's taken you a long time!" (278).

But it is Helen Chalmers who is at the center of the novel. It is Waters's narrative technique to convey the mystery of her character not only through her interactions with other characters but also through the compressed imagery of her mystical experiences, through the counterpointing of life and death forces, through her own words as expressed in a *Secret Journal,* through the symbolism of her death scene, and through the perceptions given by a Chorus, as I shall call it, of major and minor characters after her death. Out of this narrative complexity we finally perceive Helen's experience in the perspective of myth, the paradigm for humankind.

The novel highlights five mystical experiences of which three are incidents frozen in time and two are dreams. The first experience is one of totality:

> Then suddenly it happened.
> A cataclysmic explosion that burst asunder the shell of the world around her, revealing its inner reality with its brilliant flash. In its blinding brightness all mortal appearances dissolved into eternal meanings, great shimmering waves of pure feeling which had no other expression than this, and these were so closely entwined and harmonized they formed one indivisible unity. A self-hood that embraced her, the totality of the universe, and all space and all time in one immortal existence that had never had a beginning nor would ever have an end. [21]

This vision of the interpenetration of space and time in which an infinite, timeless, and yet dynamic present is experienced instead of a linear succession of instants is the basis of Helen's emergence, but it is also a basis of theoretical physics and of pueblo ceremonialism. Little wonder, then, that Helen comes to be admired by the Indians of San Ildefonso Pueblo. After telling Facundo about a strange dream, he takes her to a kiva, and the meaning of her dream is revealed by its symbolic architecture:

> In a flash she saw it all. The kiva, the whole multi-world universe, was at the same time the body of man. The whole of Creation already existed in him, and what he called an Emergence or a round of evolution was but his own expanded awareness of it. Once again with ecstatic intuition she glimpsed what she really was. Constellations ringed her head and waist; planets and stars gleamed on her fingers; the womb-worlds of all life pulsed within her. [62]

Since a kiva reconciles all opposites (see *Masked Gods,* 421), Helen's precognitive dream of it connotes her participation in the reconciliation to the point of a mutual embodiment of all parts of the universe. The dream reinforces her original experience of totality, and the bowl incident, the next of her psychic experiences to be dramatized, both consolidates her sense of a timeless reality and brings into focus the redemptive nature of Emergence.

In one of the most powerful passages in the novel, Helen moves through three-dimensional time of past, present, and future to atonement with eternity. She has unearthed a piece of pottery on which is the thumb print of a

Navawi'i woman (i.e., a woman from a local tribe of perhaps a thousand years ago) at the same time that wild geese in a V-formation fly overhead. A psychic experience results:

> At that instant it happened again: the strange sensation as of a cataclysmic faulting of her body, a fissioning of her spirit, and with it the instantaneous fusion of everything about her into one undivided, living whole. In unbroken continuity the microscopic life-patterns in the seeds of fallen cones unfolded into great pines. Her fingers closed over the splotch of clay on the bowl in her arms just as the Navawi'i woman released her own, without their separation of centuries. She could feel the enduring mist cooling and moistening a thousand dry summers. The mountain peaks stood firm against time. Eternity flowed in the river below. . . . And all this jelling of life and time into a composite *now* took place in that single instant when the wedge of wild geese hurtled past her—hurtled so swiftly that centuries of southward migrations, generations of flocks, were condensed into a single plumed serpent with its flat reptilian head outstretched, feet drawn back up, and a solitary body feather displaced by the wind, which seemed to be hanging immobile above her against the gray palimpsest of the sky. [124–25]

While the passage glances only figuratively at the fission-fusion experiments of nuclear technology, the allusion to the plumed serpent, Quetzalcoatl, underscores Helen's experience of timelessness as the principle of all Creation and the theme of all world religions: in Waters's interpretation, "the agonizing redemption of matter by spirituality" and "the transfiguration of man into god" (*Mexico Mystique,* 126). As the feather is arriving as a symbolic annunciation of the way of redemption for humankind, the mythic Woman at Otowi Crossing assumes the role of the Plumed Serpent, that of a Redeemer.[19] From this moment, the nature of Helen's visions is shifted out of its initiating and consolidating phase into an apocalyptic and synchronistic phase, and she herself is authorized, in the fullness of achieved identity, to suffer the anguish of the forces of death and destruction in order to light the way to rebirth.

The mushroom incident and the candle nightmare illustrate this trend. Once, while Helen and Jack are walking in the woods, they find a monstrous mushroom, and Jack boots it into the air as Helen screams:

> At that instant it happened. With all the minutely registered detail of a slow-motion camera, and in a preternatural silence, she saw the huge and ugly mushroom cap rise slowly in the air. Unfolding gently apart, its torn and crumpled blades opening like the gills of a fish, the fragmented pieces revolved as if in a slow boil revealing a glimpse of chlorine yellow, a splotch of brown and delicate pink. Deliberately it rose straight into the air above the walls of the canyon, its amorphous parts ballooning into a huge mass of porous gray. The stem below seemed to rise to rejoin it; then, shattered and splintered, it

settled slowly back to earth. . . . Now again she screamed. Crouching down
in terror, she vainly covered her head with her arms against the rain of its malignant spores. Countless millions, billions of spores invisibly small as bacteria
radiated down around her. They whitened the blades of grass, shrivelled the
pine needles, contaminated the clear stream, sank into the earth. Nor was this
the end of the destruction and death they spread. For this malignant downpour
of spores was also a rain of venomous sperm which rooted itself in still living
seed cells to distort and pervert their natural, inherent life forms. There was no
escape, now or ever, save by the miracle of a touch. [173]

Helen registers this experience while she is still ignorant of its synchronistic,
deadly equivalent as atomic mushroom cloud. Similarly, she is prescient but
untutored when her dream of a candle visits her just before the bombing of
Hiroshima:

Then one night she had awakened screaming. It was as if everything, house,
mountains, the world, the heavens, was enveloped in one brilliant apocalyptic
burst of fire. . . . How horrible it was! That long narrow candle with a wick
on top casting a tiny radiance. Then the wick suddenly erupted into flame,
touching off a monstrous explosion that enveloped earth and sky, the whole
world in a fiery flame. . . . Her dream had been more than a hellish illusion,
but not another breakthrough like the first she'd experienced so long ago. That
had opened to her the one creative wholeness with all its peace and plenitude.
This last ghastly dream-vision, for all its overpowering brilliance, had been
impacted with something negative, destructive, evil. [204]

Her visions of creative wholeness now countered by visions of apocalyptic
destruction, Helen becomes the scale in which the forces of life and death are
weighed in precarious balance.

The narrative art of *Otowi* tilts that balance in favor of life. It is of the
utmost interest to observe how Waters goes about the business of validating
the authenticity of Helen's emergence. For Waters knows exactly how large a
stone he is casting into the shallow pond of modern civilization. In raising
Helen to the Woman, to the level of transfiguring myth, he is also, as I have
previously noted, careful to raise the possible objections. Just as in *Romeo
and Juliet,* for example, we are convinced about love's beauty because we are
given the cynical Nurse and Mercutio to set our threshold doubts at rest, so
in *Otowi* our conviction of Helen's health and wisdom is heightened because
we are given a cast that includes "tough-minded" characters who measure her
for us but in the final analysis are themselves measured and usually found
wanting. Emily Chalmers is one of these. Always guided by the rational and
scientific assumptions of archaeology and anthropology, Emily disdainfully
recalls her mother as having "come from a middle-class family distinctly

commonplace compared to the Chalmers" and as having "had no advantages and little education" (36). But this certified expert on the Indians is frightened by the primitivism of naked Navajos during a fire ceremony, is disturbed by the hoofbeats of a wild stallion, and considers the Indian myth of Emergence not as a parable of the evolutionary journey of mankind but as the literal record of ancient migratory routes. In a fit of narcissistic rage, Emily aborts her child, and the sterility of her life thus subverts her opinions about Helen.

Another and tougher character is Jack Turner. This honest newspaper editor and reporter loves Helen and is himself lovable, so when he scouts her mystical experiences as the result of a mental breakdown, he clearly represents a majority opinion in American culture and is doing the "right" thing by trying to lure Helen to the couch of a Freudian analyst. But Turner's limitations are revealed in a number of ways: his love of Western Americana is tainted with nostalgia, symptomatic of his addiction to thinking in terms of linear time (the Chile Line railroad a symbol here); he has a habit of doing harm through good intentions, such as when he helps Emily to find an abortionist; and he lugs around his own repressed guilt for having fathered an illegitimate daughter with an Indian woman. At the end of the novel he confesses to Meru, an investigator of psychic phenomena, that he has considered destroying Helen's *Secret Journal* because he feared it was the "product of an unbalanced mind" (312). Even though he has made some amends in life by setting up his daughter in a New York apartment, Turner's interest in promoting Helen's legend makes it doubtful that he ever understood her at all, for she has no wish for celebrity status or to impose her will on others. Of those closest to her, then, only Facundo initially and Gaylord finally comprehend her and feel compassion for a person visited by all the joys and terrors of the unseen life. One might think that an old Indian cacique and an atomic physicist would present the most formidable obstacles to acceptance of a mystic who is a white woman. Accept her they do, however, because each in his own way considers as valid Helen's emergence.

Further validation is accomplished through techniques of counterpointing and of witness bearing.

In American literature, structural, symbolic, and thematic counterpointing traditionally leads to simplistic juxtapositions of individual and society, nature and civilization, intuition and reason, timelessness and temporality, and the like. *Huckleberry Finn* and *Go Down, Moses,* for example, are developed by counterpointing, and the characters of Huck Finn and Ike McCaslin, once exposed to experience of absolutes, are isolated in the ideal. But Huck's idyll on the river and Ike's initiating encounters with wilderness and the bear represent nostalgic and negative reinforcements of American pastoralism; that is, the dream of a better way of life is seen by Twain and by Faulkner as doomed, as powerless to link past with present, individual with society. *The Woman at Otowi Crossing* breaks with this tradition by means of a reconciliation of opposites at "the still point of the turning world," as Eliot in his *Four Quartets* famously described this interplay.[20] Living at the "crossing" between counterpointed territories (Los Alamos versus San Ildefonso Pueblo), cultures (modern-scientific versus primal-mythopoetic), psychic polarities (rational consciousness versus unconscious), values (materialistic versus humanistic-ecological), and rituals (science with laboratory rituals enforced by a priesthood of intellectuals versus mysticism with tribal rituals enforced by a priesthood of hierophants), Helen dissolves differences by superseding them, in herself, in a higher state of awareness. She seems to be isolated, like the classic American boy-man protagonists; unlike them, however, as a Chorus figure remarks, she is at the hub of time:

> "She had it all right, a glimpse of the universal whole.
> "What a spot she was in to receive it! At the birth place of the oldest civilization in America and the newest. Probably in no other area in the world were juxtaposed so closely the Indian drum and the atom smasher, all the values of the prehistoric past and the atomic future. A lonely woman in a remote spot with few friends, she felt herself at the hub of time." [179]

Instead of being an outcast, exile, or rebel, Helen becomes an open individual, and her openness will, through its power, open society to transformation.

Counterpointing is a valid way of seeing opposites as two sides of the same coin, *if* contrasting images and symbols are meaningfully connected. They are in *Otowi* through the myth of Emergence. The reader of this novel not only has to question his or her habit of categorizing situations as either-or, but also has to participate in the myth of the Woman in order to perceive that it is *our* myth and that in judging her in her mythic role we are in effect evaluating life and death forces in our own spheres of being. We can understand well enough the contrast of a kiva and a nuclear reactor, though it's unlikely we've actually seen either one, but once we've synthesized these images as representing energies, we are no longer ignoring the esoteric and unconscious forces but *admitting* these to consciousness. And that is a pointer to Emergence. On the one hand, the sun is associated with creativity, fertility, Facundo (as sun-priest), the face of Gaylord's mother, the temple at Mesa Verde, the plumed serpent and rhythmic order; on the other hand, the sun is associated with atomic and thermonuclear destruction, the power of the sun having been usurped. Once we recognize that the sun has both constructive and destructive power, we have increased our moral awareness of the necessity of controlling excessive human intervention in the processes of a primal source. And that is a pointer to Emergence, too. Chronological time imagery links the Chile Line's whistle, Turner's guilty memories, and nuclear-test countdowns, whereas the imagery of eternity links stones, mountains, pools, circles, kachina forces, magnetic fields, a cooking pot, Earth, ancient America, and the Mother Goddess in her archetypal aspect as the Woman. When we perceive spiritual reality, it is then possible for us to be aware of living in a world of linear time, yet capable of experiencing the timelessness of an eternal reality of which we are a part. Our consciousness is then experienced as moving, rather than fixed.[21] And that is also a pointer to Emergence. In sum, life and death forces in *Otowi* both oppose each other and interact, and our "explanation" of the interaction turns out to be a mode of mythic consciousness.

Otowi has the power—and *power* is an oft-repeated word at the heart of this novel—to unsettle our sense of the self in its relationship to an "external" world and to recall us to a deeper mode of awareness beneath this self-consciousness which remains mythic in its overall patterns. The dualism of subjectivity and objectivity is not given with the human condition. What *is* given with the human condition, in the words of Falck, "may be an integrated mode of vision which comprises both the perceptual and the subjective or spiritual, and which we can recapture from the viewpoint of a later cultural stage only through a unifying and metaphorical effort of poetic imagination."[22] There is, so to speak, a mode of vision which accommodates as self-validating the emergence of Helen Chalmers.

Helen herself bears witness to her experience in the excerpts from her *Secret Journal* (1, 145–46, 250, 314) that frame the novel as prologue and epilogue and also appear at the novel's approximate midpoint, like a fulcrum by means of which vital powers are exercised. The myth she reveals is not dogmatically privileged, as would occur in the approach of traditional religion, and the questions of truth have not been prejudged. Like a piece of music, the novel gives us an immediate presence and presentation of ontological meaning, and the truth or satisfyingness of myth remains open to critical question. Helen questions it too: the fragments of her journal are not reiterations of her mystical experiences (though by implication these form part of an undisplayed journal) but philosophical reflections upon the meaning of the experiences; the reflections, moreover, are addressed to Turner in a spirit of love and bewilderment ("*I don't know, Jack. I don't know why this happened to me when it did,*" 1, italics in original). To her, Emergence is "*a normal, natural experience that eventually comes to every one of us,*" the import of which is that "*we're not separate and alone*" but "*part of one vast interconnected, living, conscious whole*" (146, italics in original). Moreover, psychic forces, "vast projections from the soul of humanity," have "the cosmic authority" (250) to deter nuclear war. The key passage of the journal, however, is not conveyed in the style of argumentation but in that of exaltation:

> *So all these scribbled pages, Jack, are to help you understand that an awakening or Emergence, as the Indians call it, is more than a single momentary experience. It requires a slow painful process of realization and orientation. Just like a newborn child, you get it all and instantaneously in the blinding flash of that first breakthrough—the shattering impact of light after darkness, of freedom after confinement. Then the rub comes. The learning how to live in this vast new world of awareness. The old rules of our cramped little world of appearances won't work. You have to learn new ones. The hard way, too, because everything you've known takes on new dimensions and meanings. This process of awakening with new awareness, a new perspective on everything about you, of perceiving the 'spherical geometry of the complete rounded moment' as Gaylord once called it—this is the wonderful experience I've been going through. . . . So when your turn comes, Jack, don't be afraid. Be glad! It's our greatest experience, our mysterious voyage of discovery into the last unknown, man's only true adventure. . . .* [314, italics in original]

The passage is a summation of the process already dramatized in the novel as a whole: realization and orientation of the inner self are the dynamics of characterization in a novel which must break with conventional form in order to be a disclosure or revelation of the true nature of the world in which we live, or at least of a meaningful world. It has been meaningful to Helen Chalmers, and her hard-won exultation is the song of life.

We are also given the testimony of ten individuals who have a wide range of responses to Helen. Most of these individuals are interviewed by an unidentified omniscient narrator. The interviews, interspersed throughout the present time of the novel, are "flashforwards"[23] (most take place in the future) effecting a sense that three-dimensional time (past, present, future) is an illusion from which few escape. Some of those interviewed are major characters in the novel—Emily (35–38; also author of a letter, 152–53), Turner (58–59), and Gaylord (73–74, 269–72; also author of reminiscences, 309–311)—while some are characters whose roles are minor or whose only appearance in the novel is through the interview—Dr. Gottman, Freudian psychologist in California, who rejects Jungian ideas as occult and considers Helen's "case" to be abnormal and morbid (132–34); Kaminsky or Kerenski, New York bookseller specializing in mysticism, who believes in the authenticity of Helen's experience (179–80); Alice Person, conventional Chicago matron once resident at Los Alamos, who is offended by Helen's lack of vanity as a "psychic" (207–9); Verna Taylor, shopkeeper in Cuernavaca, who discredits Emily's character and academic pretensions (241–43); Guy Alvord, big-time media reporter, who has popularized Helen's legend and who reveals Turner's self-interest in the same promotion (272–74); Milton P. Jasper, former political campaign manager now a Washington executive, who attests to Helen's power in transforming Throckmorton from a dangerous demagogue to a philanthropist (293–96); and M. Meru, New York authority on psychic phenomena, who accepts Helen's *Secret Journal* as the most complete record of a valid mystical experience in modern times (312–14).

Taken together, these ten characters form a Chorus with differing viewpoints. Emily, Turner, Gottman, and Alvord are dubious witnesses; Person, Taylor, and Jasper are a mixed lot; Kaminsky, Gaylord, and Meru are authoritative, Gaylord because he has mystical experiences of his own, including a telepathic "witnessing" of Helen's "death and transfiguration" (311), Meru because he has the privileged last word about her in the epilogue, understands the significance of myth, and is himself mythical. M. Meru, as his name implies, signifies Mt. Meru in Hindu and Buddhist cosmography, a metaphysical hub of the universe whose final judgment of Helen's spirituality is clearly to be heeded. Frances M. Malpezzi summarizes Meru's authority:

> Standing at his office window in his blue serge suit, enhaloed by fluttering white birds, bearing the name of a sacred mountain of Eastern mythology, Meru represents the amalgamation of reason, Christian mysticism, harmony with nature, Eastern mysticism. He is a synthesis of the sacred and the profane. As the *axis mundi* connecting the secular world with the divine, he authenticates the Emergence of Helen Chalmers.[24]

Malpezzi believes that Meru is central to *Otowi*. Although I believe that he should more properly be considered as a coda to the novel, introduced after the natural conclusion to its movement, I agree to the extent that Meru joins Gaylord in placing Helen's experience in the perspective of myth. For it is Gaylord, we recall, who, at the instant of a thermonuclear explosion over the Pacific, knows that Helen has become assimilated to indescribable light, her life energy suddenly liberated as a symbol of absolute inner unassailability and of life that survives death—a resurrection like a new sunrise.[25]

There is no actual death scene (though I have called it that); rather, there is a quiet vigil, a tableau, in which Emily, Turner, and Facundo wait for Helen's death. The focus is on Facundo, who is outside in the chill of night. Suddenly a band of seven deer becomes visible beyond the fence. To Facundo, the deer are her emblem, their celestial counterparts in the Pleiades, and this symbolic amalgamation of a living universe provides an eerie sensation of an Absolute Consciousness interpenetrating time and space. When Facundo taps a drum and sings a death song, the deer bound away, then slowly turn about, "and with quick delicate steps" (306) come back to wait at the fence. This tableau of the deer calls up various associations, all with the same meaning. As the Pleiades, they are glimpsed as the highest stage beyond the ascendent architecture of the kiva. Buddhism postulates seven stages for evolutionary development, the seventh stage ending the Road of Life, with man now divine and perfected. Whereas Western medical science recognizes seven physical centers ascending upward from the base of the spine to the brain, Eastern mysticism postulates seven centers (chakras) of psychic energy, with the seventh and most important chakra lying just below the crown of the head and regarded as the seat of universal consciousness. In Kundalini yoga the serpent power rises from the lowest physical center to the highest psychic center, pictured on Buddhist temples as the horned antelope. What all these representations of seven have in common is emergence to divinity.[26] But it is the superb feeling and decorum of the tableau with Facundo and the deer that may surpass its esoteric meaning and accomplish in one powerful image more than the reflective testimony of characters accomplishes. Waters approaches the mystery of death as John Donne does the mystery of love in "A Valediction: Forbidding Mourning":

> Our two souls therefore, which are one,
>   Though I must go, endure not yet
> A breach, but an expansion,
>   Like gold to airy thinness beat.[27]

The quick delicate steps of Helen's deer foretell a death which will not bring about a separation from life but a triumphant expansion of her essential spirit into the golden radiance of a larger sky.

8

CREATIVE MAN

FRANK WATERS IS A major American writer. That is the point of view of this study, the focus of which, however, has been a close critical examination of the texts of six novels in relation, first, to the concepts of unity, duality, and emergence and, second, to various contexts. Although some current critical theories hold in disfavor, if not in contempt, the idea that imagination is an essential power and quality of spirit and would like to regard as either willful or nostalgic the critic who speaks of "vision" in literature, it has seemed to me self-evident that imagination or vision is a force in which a writer feels implicated. It is the power, as Denis Donoghue asserts, "of making fictions and making sense of life by that means."[1] Colin Falck, who sees as our most urgent current need in literary theory the restoration of the concepts of truth or of vision to our discussions of literature, goes further: literature and literary criticism, he argues, "may need to be prepared to embrace, and to subsume, religion and theology if they are to discover or to rediscover their own spiritual meanings."[2] Through myths or "imaginative archetypes,"[3] Falck believes, art can reach beyond the appearances of ordinary life into reality itself and restore to its dignity the notion of ontological truth. In speaking, then, of the visionary novels of Frank Waters, and of their source in the archetypal imagination, I have not deemed it necessary to make an additional defense of imaginative literature; I am convinced that the claims of rationalist metaphysics and of doctrinaire religion to be our "real" access to truth lack a basis in intuitive life, and hence in art, and so I have never doubted great literary art's quintessential capacity of finding new ways of inscribing reality for us.

If there is a bias in my approach, it is one that can also be discovered in Jungian and Campbellian aesthetics. Jung, as we recall from *Modern Man in Search of a Soul*, warns us against reducing the visionary to personal characteristics or dismissing vision as illusion, on the basis that it defies rational understanding. That vision, he writes, "is not something derived or secondary, and it is not a symptom of something else. It is true symbolic expression— that is, the expression of something existent in its own right, but imperfectly known."[4] Campbell, especially in *Creative Mythology,* develops this point of view in relation to literary art in Europe since the twelfth century. He discerns four functions of a mythology: mystical, cosmological, sociological, and psychological. The first function is to reconcile waking consciousness to the mystery of the universe as it is. The second function is to render an interpretive total image of the same. The third is to shape the individual to the requirements of his social group. And the fourth is to foster the centering and unfolding of the individual in integrity, in accord with himself, his culture, the universe, and the "ultimate mystery which is both beyond and within himself and all things." According to Campbell, the failure in modern centuries of the third (sociological) function of a mythology has put the individual on his own, and consequently it is lived experience, not tribal or dogmatic authority, which leads to "creative symbolization." A creative mythology

> restores to existence the quality of adventure, at once shattering and reinterpreting the fixed, already known, in the sacrificial creative fire of the becoming thing that is no thing at all but life, not as it *will be* or as it *should be,* as it *was* or as it *never will be,* but as it *is,* in depth, in process, *here and now,* inside and out.

Creative myth, Campbell continues, "springs from the unpredictable, unprecedented experience-in-illumination of an object by a subject, and the labor, then, of achieving communication of the effect," by calling upon the "world's infinitely rich heritage of symbols, images, myth motives, and hero deeds." Ultimately, the art required is to make sounds, words, and forms

> open out in back, as it were, to eternity, and this requires of the artist that he should himself, in his individual experience, have touched anew that still point in this turning world of which the immemorial mythic forms are the symbols and guarantee.

The creative energy of the whole is in each of us, bare of egohood, and the individual is thereby mythologically considered as "Lord of the World Center," a *kosmogonos,* creator of all higher consciousness by means of "cosmogonic power."[5]

As I interpret them, Jung and, even more, Campbell, validate the high esteem in which Frank Waters may be regarded. Where American philosophy is concerned, he is clearly on a par with the Emerson who wrote in "The Over-Soul" (1841):

> We live in succession, in division, in parts, in particles. Meantime within man is the soul of the whole; the wise silence; the universal beauty, to which every part and particle is equally related; the eternal ONE.[6]

Where American poetry and imaginative literature are concerned, Waters, as creative mythologist, touches depths of experience that may remind us of moments in Walt Whitman, Emily Dickinson, Eliot, Robinson Jeffers, Theodore Roethke, and Faulkner but that are perhaps closer to Melville. But in that same respect—that is, creative mythology—there is no embarrassment in aligning Waters with a European tradition that begins with legends of Tristan and of the Grail Quest and emerges in the twentieth century with novels by Thomas Mann and James Joyce. An art that "opens out in back" to eternity, to the structuring laws and forces interior to the earthly being that is man, here and now, has the value of living myth. This is the value that I have placed on the visionary novels of Frank Waters. Therefore, I shall conclude this study, after summary of its findings, with a visualization of the novels as living myth and as a whole—namely, that they project in symbolic terms a composite, unifying, ontological, and cosmogonic character which I shall call Creative Man.

CONCEPTS

To celebrate Waters's eighty-third birthday, the Southwest Studies Program of the Colorado College in Colorado Springs invited him in July 1985 to discuss his work informally. Before an audience of over a thousand people, he spoke on a wide range of topics, including what he saw as the theme in his books of most relevance to contemporary civilization:

> I think I've been trying to illustrate the same theme in all of my books. The theme of the Colorado mining trilogy, the *Pike's Peak* trilogy, of course, was the search of this man Rogier for his self. It's a self-searching theme. Like most of us, he was a materialist and he thought the self was outside, and he finally

fixed it in the heart of the Peak. That was the self that he was searching for, that great heart of gold in the living mountain, instead of searching for that inner self, that identity within himself, an inner search. Now, this Woman of Otowi Crossing, in another sense, was a woman who for a long time had been pretty desperately searching for her self. A self-searching process. And about the time that I picked her up in the novel she had reached a dead end. She just couldn't go any further. . . . And that was when she got to bounce back. I think in a way that is what we are undergoing on a civilization basis today. We have become very materialistic, and we have projected happiness and fulfillment and completeness outside, and we are now just about reaching a dead end. . . . But as long as we have almost ruined the planet or almost ruined civilization as a whole, I think we've come right down to the point where we can't go much further, and that's when we are going to bounce back.[7]

This is Waters's main theme as he sees it: the search for the inner or spiritual self at a time when materialistic civilization is on the verge of collapse.

The theme is present in all his novels. The allegorical journey of Lee Marston in *The Lizard Woman* takes him from civilization to the burning center of a desert—his own center, so to speak—and back to civilization with a dawning inner selfhood. Surrounded by the crudely materialistic world of Cockroach Court, Tai Ling, the yogi, seeks for his self, belatedly discovers that his own ego is the barrier to fulfillment, and at the moment of death realizes his inner truth. Rogier fails in the quest for identity, but March Cable, Martiniano, and Helen Chalmers emerge, in varying degrees, into completeness. Maria del Valle is born with it.

The three interlocking concepts of unity, duality, and emergence can now be seen as the dynamics of the theme of self-searching. Unity is the completeness of identity, symbolized by a uroboric mountain range, by a heart of gold, by an inner light, by a deer, or by a character in her role as an androgynous, eternal female. Duality displays the crisis of identity: polarized pairs of opposites (such as a materialistic versus a spiritual view of nature) may reflect "a dead end" for a person or for a civilization but may also hold out the promise of new equilibrium, a reconciliation, a bouncing back. Emergence shows the way: it is self-fulfillment in creative process and joins the inner self to all Creation. The character who has emerged—and Rogier is the exception that proves the rule—arrives in a new world of consciousness or at an expanded awareness of the creative energy of the whole that is in each of us. The concepts which carry out the theme of self-searching produce narratives which, holistically, bring the timeless dimension of experience, the perpetual reality of the here and now, back to the materiality of the secular kind of temporal experience. The truth of the narratives, therefore, does not lie in everything that makes up a chronological succession of events but, rather, in characters who realize and embody essence. In the long view these are mythic characters. We know them by their actions and by their internal states of mind, but we also know them as symbols or manifestations of immemorial forms.

CONTEXTS

In the course of this study I have attempted to view Waters's novels in numerous contexts: geographical, historical, and cultural; literary, mythological, and philosophical. The question of "influence" arises from these contexts, and the answer to it, insofar as I have been able to determine, is that Waters has simply absorbed influences and cannot be categorized by any single one of them (such as "Jungian," "Buddhist," "Indian"). I have paid relatively little attention to mysticism as a context, partly because the subject is of a biographical rather than a critical nature, partly because Waters's motif of psychic landscape (i.e., mystical experience of earth) is a "given" that explains little, like the divine frenzy of the poet. But I shall look at mysticism presently.

The geographical, historical, and cultural contexts of the novels are, in two words, the American West. The vast space of the West—the horizontal broadness of plains and deserts, the vertical height of mountains—confronts the artist quite literally: the land threatens to overwhelm fictive character and to lead us away from the social sphere of the novel toward something inferior, such as the moral fable. Waters, in a symbolic approach, sees the West as the center of space experience, a heartland, and establishes centers within this space: Mexicali, Pike's Peak, Mora Valley, Taos Pueblo with its Blue Lake, the crossing between Los Alamos and San Ildefonso Pueblo, and a magic mountain in the Sonoran Desert. Thus he creates environments for his characters which are usually favorable (the exception being Mexicali) for the experiencing of intimacy between them and nature or of mystical insights. "Once established," as John R. Milton observes, "these centers then radiate the spirit of place outward in circles of influence, just as older civilizations spread outward from a central core."[8] Waters's West consists of symbolic spaces, as lake, valley, mountain, or bridge become representative of the cosmic reality or of psychic integration. By a similar token the West's history and cultural diversity lend themselves to mythic density. The land's antiquity, represented by the Indians and, to a somewhat lesser extent, by the Mexican-American settlers, serves to remind us that Euro-Americans are recent arrivals in the region, out of touch with the spirit of the land and often suffering from racial psychosis. The geographical, historical, and cultural contexts provide, as it were, a stage upon which a universal drama of contemporary concern can be enacted, a drama relating the individual not merely to society but ultimately to the cosmos.

The study of Waters's novels in the context of literature has, I think, opened a number of critical perspectives. First, his indebtedness to other authors seems to be relatively slight. Conrad is an early influence (as he was for Faulkner) but seems to have left few traces in the major novels after *The Lizard Woman,* apart from Waters's rhetorical use of negative universals such as *timeless, motionless, immemorial,* and the like. *Moby-Dick* is obviously a model for *Pike's Peak.* Perhaps Arthurian legends and the legend of the Grail Quest, with which Waters became familiar in childhood, lie in back (considerably far back, I think) of his theme of self-searching, especially when it takes an allegorical turn. Thomas Wolfe, whose *Look Homeward, Angel* appeared in 1929, may be felt as a presence in the trilogy of the 1930s, but Wolfe-like rhapsodic passages have been mostly expunged from *Pike's Peak.* Second, by relating a novel to genre, I have been able to discriminate among all the novels. The idea of a universal moral order, so important for a reading of Greek and Shakespearean tragedy, is an integral part of Waters's vision and helps to explain the destinies of his characters before the bar of justice and fate. In *Yogi* the idea is translated as karma and in *Deer* as conscience; in *Pike's Peak,* which is indeed a tragedy, the idea of order is represented as Self, or Absolute Consciousness, and those terms also can be used to describe the protagonist's experience of totality in *Otowi.* The study of *People* shows that it is not "just" a pastoral novel: it may be one of the greatest pastoral novels in literature, because it resolves, as few if any other pastoral novels do, the contradiction between technological civilization and the values of a rural microcosm. *People,* accordingly, is not plagued with the nostalgia and sentimentality that one associates with the pastoral genre in much of modern fiction. If there is no nostalgia or sentimentality in Waters's pastoral novel—I extend the implications of this fact—there is certainly none in his general outlook, regret at the encroachment of materialism notwithstanding. From the point of view of eternity, so to say, changes of any kind, whether it be the uprooting of people from their native soil or the development of thermonuclear weapons, are finally expressions, for good or ill, of human duality. The study of genre throws light, too, on the art of *The Man Who Killed the Deer.* By taking the approach that it is an allegory, I believe that I have shown why *Deer* is a universal story, not an "Indian" novel in an ethnic or regional sense, and why, therefore, *Deer*'s inherent form evokes the richness, wonder, and mystery of life: this is the beauty and economy of *Deer*'s effect. The one, perhaps slight drawback to this allegorical formation of *Deer* is that the hero, Martiniano, tends to be a function of a predetermined unfolding of psychophysical events; that is to say, his "character," though memorably caught between two cultures, two worlds, lacks the full social dimension that one is accustomed to find in many traditional novels. For that reason, although *Deer* is a masterpiece, *The Woman at Otowi Crossing* may be a greater one, or at least a more satisfying one: the character of Helen Chalmers moves to a visible world of large social dimensions.

Other contexts for a study of Waters's novels are the mythologies and philosophies that have influenced his thought and reflect its range and depth. He was introduced to Navajo myths while he was still in grade school, and his fascination with the Emergence myth may have originated at that time. Waters's developed myth of Emergence, however, illustrates his syncretism: he combines Native American and ancient Mesoamerican myths with oriental philosophy, particularly Buddhism and Taoism, and brings to the combination a scientifically informed knowledge of geological and human evolution. He also finds Jungian psychology congenial—to a point. Whereas the theories of the collective unconscious and of synchronicity may have helped him to clarify his position in *Otowi* and in the final revisions of *Yogi* and *Pike's Peak*, Waters rejects Jung's belief that the expansion of consciousness and achievement of the wholeness of personality is brought about by the ego "reflecting upon itself, acting as a symbol uniting the conscious and unconscious" (*Mountain Dialogues*, 176). There is, for Waters, a profound difference between the personal ego's experiencing itself as the Self and the absorption of the ego by the Universal Self, as postulated by oriental philosophy. Thus, his novels offer agreement with the Jungian concept of a duality between conscious and unconscious forces but disagree about the nature of their reconciliation. Ego-identity blocks Tai Ling's progress toward illumination, Rogier's search for self, and Martiniano's understanding of the spirit-deer; absorption of the ego by the Universal Self explains or leads to the wholeness of personality as manifested in Maria del Valle and Helen Chalmers almost from the beginning of their stories and in Martiniano and Tai Ling at the end of theirs. Since Waters was not acquainted with Jungian psychology until after the completion of *Deer* in 1941, I think it is fair to conclude that the informing ideas in the novels were largely developed by Waters without a decidedly Jungian influence. The influence of Evans-Wentz, on the other hand, is quite strong: the philosophy of Mahayana Buddhism, as explained by Evans-Wentz in his series of Tibetan books, guided Waters in the development of *Yogi* and may have contributed to creative symbolization in *People, Deer, Pike's Peak,* and *Otowi*. The point, nevertheless, need not be pressed, for the inclination of Waters's imagination is so powerfully archetypal that he has tended to greet the ideas of other philosophers as if on grounds of "prior" familiarity.

Two other contexts deserve a glance here: contemporary science and feminist criticism. The esoteric notion of the interrelationship of mind and matter is particularly evident in *Pike's Peak* and of course in the trilogy that preceded it. Therefore, in concluding my study of that novel, I gave a summary of certain theories in contemporary science that also seek to bridge mind and matter. Today, mysticism and science are revealing remarkable similarities, and what Waters began to envision more than sixty years ago assumes a prophetic quality. Similarly, as I pointed out in my study of *People,* Waters meets the most rigorous criteria of feminist criticism for the creation of fully human female characters in fiction. He may not be unique in this respect, but his achievement, as a white male author, keeps rare company with that of Hawthorne and Henry James. In a sense, then, Waters has created the kind of female protagonists that feminist criticism claims to be almost totally lacking in American literature, especially in Faulkner, Hemingway, and Steinbeck. His balanced sensibility is something to be reckoned with in future assessments of the literary canon.

A word, finally, about mysticism. The usual Western stereotype of the mystic is of a dreamy, unworldly individual with his eyes firmly fixed on a God-inhabited, subjective, faith-oriented view of reality. We seem to have a wrong idea about mystics and to overlook their demonstrated abilities: St. Teresa of Avila and St. John of the Cross, for example, were superb administrators. We also overlook their objectivity. The British philosopher C. D. Broad believes that the objectivity of mystics ought to be accepted at face value:

> To me the occurrence of mystical experience at all times and places, and the similarities between the statements of so many mystics all the world over, seems to be a really significant fact. *Prima facie* it suggests that there is an aspect of reality with which these persons came in contact in their mystical experience, and which they afterwards strive and largely fail to describe in the language of daily life. I should say that this *prima facie* appearance of objectivity ought to be accepted at its face value unless or until some reasonably satisfactory explanation of the agreement can be found.[9]

This opinion is strengthened by the fact that the language used by physicists and mystics to describe reality is almost indistinguishable when it comes to guessing who says what.[10] More to the point, where Waters as mystic is concerned, is the apparent correlation between mysticism and the mythic mode of consciousness with its apriori, instinctive impulse toward a different, sacred cognition.[11] The truth sought by mystic and mythmaker alike is that the universe is interrelated. The language for their experiences may fail the test of empiricism, but these experiences touch the realm of inner, primary meaning that transcends empirical testing. We are dealing, then, with an alternative mode of consciousness whereby the meaning sought is not one of social fulfillment but of a place in a larger, eternal order beyond the local boundaries of time and space.

Waters creates art out of mysticism: his experience of the still point of turning time, of eternity in the grain of sand, is manifested in true symbolic expression. Language, for him, derives from an original source before being reflected through mind and thought. Words, as he describes them, have a kind of annunciatory power:

> Words, words, words! Each has shape and color, sound and fragrance, a music and a meaning, all its own. How sharp and curt they are, how long and alliterative, how melodious and mysterious! They roll like the drum-thunder of hoofs from off the horizon, they swoop down like hawks to rend with bare talons; they purr from firelit pages, smooth the wrinkles from sleepless nights. But ever they speak as foci of unmeasured power with the mystery of divine origin.[12]

Words come to the creative artist from without. This is clearly a mystical conception, but the concept of the Word behind words surely requires no introduction (for example, "In the beginning was the Word, and the Word was with God, and the Word was God" John 1:1). Moreover, when the Word enters history, the archetypal imagery is often the same, the dove (for the Christian paraclete), the swan (in the myth of Leda and Zeus as interpreted by William Butler Yeats in his poem "Leda and the Swan"), and the hawk (for Waters). Symbolic birds bear mystical meaning as the Word they represent is conjured as vital expression of universal human experience.

CREATIVE MAN

Many years ago, G. Wilson Knight, the British critic and novelist, proposed that the way to read Shakespeare is to regard each play as a visionary whole and then to work into the heart of each play:

> Each incident, each turn of thought, each suggestive symbol throughout *Macbeth* or *King Lear* radiates inwards from the play's circumference to the burning central core without knowledge of which we shall miss their relevance and necessity: they relate primarily, not directly to each other, nor to the normal appearances of human life, but to this central reality alone.[13]

This, it seems to me, is a sound critical procedure for the reading of any creative artist whose vision of reality has carried him or her beyond the confines of superficial appearances. The remarkable aspect of Knight's approach, however, is not the distinction between appearances and reality but the assumption that certain literary forms are geometrical, having a central core, like the hub of a wheel, enveloped by a circumference. For, in mythological symbolization, the spoked wheel is the turning world, and the hub is like Self, Emerson's eternal ONE, holding all fast. Such a geometry of the spirit helps us to visualize not only the form of a particular play or novel but also the form of an entire oeuvre. But the focus of such visualization is on the hub ("the burning central core"), on a Power which is the apriority of space and time in the here and now that, radiating outward, becomes everywhere and always.

Campbell identifies this Power in world mythologies as the Goddess Mother of the universe. "It is into and through her," he writes, "that the god-substance pours into this field of space and time in a continuous act of world-creative self-giving."[14] The power is ontological, that is, having to do with the essence of things, and cosmogonic, that is, having to do with creative evolution. It is not, this Power, "out there," to be sought and found in transcendence, but is to be recognized in oneself, in every individual, and in all things.

Although my many readings of Frank Waters's books have perhaps only touched on the core of their meaning, I do believe that there *is* such a core and that it can be identified in the affairs of humankind as Creative Man. The human individual is constantly and truly visualized as seated at the hub of life, at the *axis mundi,* at the intersection of time and space. The seat of true religiosity, Waters writes in "Mysticism and Witchcraft,"

> is not the great formalized church but the human heart. Only here is lit that spark of mystical apperception which illuminates, if only for an instant, the darkness of our inner selves and the totality of the universe about us. By it we will realize that in the human atom resides all the creative power and all the time we need to transform this catastrophic era into an age more fruitful than any we have known.[15]

The human heart (meaning, of course, the mind) is the center. Around it are ever-widening circles of relationship and finally the cosmic circle itself. This is the geometrical figure with which, for example, *The Man Who Killed the Deer* begins and ends. When Palemon is seeking Martiniano on the mountain, he sees a boulder "marked with the strange signs of the Old Ones—a circle enclosing a dot. . . ." (3). Then at the end of the novel, as Martiniano is watching the Indian pilgrims dance in a circle, he reflects, "A man drops but a pebble into the one great lake of life, and the ripples spread to unguessed shores, to congeal into a pattern even in the timeless skies of night" (217). The large space and the small space have been brought into juxtaposition, and then, after Martiniano has at last grasped the meaning of the Deer, those spaces are congealed into one pattern. And we see Martiniano *in* the center of the larger spaces of earth and stars. As Creative Man he unifies everything in the picture—and in the novel.

But this unifying function of Creative Man is more than a spatial form horizontally or one-dimensionally perceived as in the image of the dot within the circle or of the individual as centered within the cosmos. Creative Man is perceived in depth, the third dimension of space, which translates into time, the fourth. As Quay Grigg observes about Waters's space-time, here-and-now, "Einsteinian" geometry of spirit, there is at its core a vertical image akin to a mountain peak. Waters's oeuvre is modeled, Grigg finds, "not on our rational, separate perception of time and space, but upon those denizens of the unconscious who point both backward and forward in time, and who float like mountain peaks above the dimension of space."[16] In other words, our usual perception of dimensions—past, present, future, length, breadth, depth— is configured as, instead, a mythic timelessness which, far from being static, is in paradoxical process of standing still and of being vertically heightened. It follows, I think, that at the visionary core of a novel by Waters the creative powers of the universe are centered in an individual and are therein emergent.

Creative Man, who is creator of all higher consciousness, is a composite of these individuals. In *Yogi* the horizontal plane of mundane consciousness is crossed by the vertical plane of supramundane consciousness, the plane of Tai Ling's search and eventual illumination. In *People,* Maria del Valle's hawklike eyes survey the world from a mountain top, and her life integrates the vertical plane from it to the womb-valley below. The tragedy of Rogier is that, in the psychological sense, he seeks selfhood *in* the mountain when his own inner self *is* the peak, the world's center. The experience of Helen Chalmers in *Otowi* is her breakthrough into the fourth dimension and her realization, in the words that begin the novel, that "*There is no such thing as time as we know it. The entire contents of all space and time co-exist in every infinite and eternal moment*" (1, italics in original). Helen exists for us in a space-time continuum, a centering and a towering of the human spirit. All these characters, including Martiniano but with Rogier excepted, represent Creative Man, Helen above all. She is the most fully realized and warmly beautiful manifestation of Creative Man, and the mystical, cosmological, and psychological functions of creative mythology have in her been brought into masterful focus in depth, in process, here and now. Creative Man reconciles waking consciousness to the mystery of the universe as it is, renders a total image of the same, and fosters the centering and unfolding of the individual in accord with self, culture, the universe, and that ultimate mystery which is both transcendent and immanent. Hence there is in most of Waters's visionary novels but especially in *Otowi* an immediacy and emotional power of mythical happenings, a power that can only be conveyed as a sense of Creative Man's ever becoming within a duration of time which has no beginning or end and within a continuum of space which is boundless.

Creative Man—this composite of Lee Marston, Tai Ling, March Cable, Maria del Valle, Martiniano, Palemon, Edmund Gaylord, and Helen Chalmers—has required of Waters an original conception of character in fiction. The possibility, for the poet and novelist, is always there, this conjuration from the depths of the imagination of the eternal mystery of human character. Melville, who had an extraordinary itch to tear off the masks of God, contemplated that possibility in *The Confidence-Man* (1857):

> original character, essentially such, is like a revolving Drummond light, raying away from itself all round it—everything is lit by it, everything starts up to it . . . so that, in certain minds, there follows upon the adequate conception of such a character, an effect, in its way, akin to that which in Genesis attends upon the beginnings of things.[17]

And, it is commonly agreed, the great interest of American literature arises from the sense of American feeling as making a new start, as seeking to express what William Carlos Williams calls "a new spirit in the New World."[18] But, for Frank Waters, more, I think, than for most American writers, the possibility of envisioning a new world has taken the form of projecting through original flesh-and-blood characters a *new mind*. The emergence of his Creative Man brings a vision of new, higher consciousness to American and modern world literature. For that reason, if not for that reason alone, his has been a classic achievement. Either *The Woman at Otowi Crossing* or *The Man Who Killed the Deer* belongs in the hierarchy of American fictions, along with Hawthorne's *Scarlet Letter,* Melville's *Moby-Dick,* Twain's *Huckleberry Finn,* F. Scott Fitzgerald's *Great Gatsby* and Faulkner's *Sound and the Fury*. Waters has brought the beauty of great art to the truth of creative mythology and has perceived the possibilities of which our minds, operating in society, are capable. His vision of our common humanity in process of creative enlargement engenders a feeling of hope for modern mankind, a sense of new and authentic beginnings, and a faith that life is not chaos but cosmos.

NOTES

FOREWORD

1. Terence A. Tanner, *Frank Waters: A Bibliography with Relevant Selections from His Correspondence* (Glenwood, Ill.: Meyerbooks, 1983), x.

2. The letter was reprinted with permission in *The Frank Waters Society Newsletter* 3, no. 1 (15 April 1985).

3. Quay Grigg, "Frank Waters and the Mountain Spirit," *South Dakota Review* 15, no. 3 (Autumn 1977): 46.

4. See, for example, Michael Loudon, "Mountain Talk: Frank Waters as Shaman-Writer," *Studies in Frank Waters* 5 (1982): 1; Thomas J. Lyon, "Frank Waters," in *Fifty Western Writers* (Westport, Conn.: Greenwood Press, 1982): 511; and Charles L. Adams, "Frank Waters' Changing Mountain Dialogues," *West Virginia Philological Papers* 36 (1990).

5. Thomas J. Lyon, *Frank Waters* (New York: Twayne Publishers, 1973), 18.

6. Reprinted in *Frank Waters: A Retrospective Anthology,* ed. Charles L. Adams (Athens: Ohio University Press/Swallow Press, 1985), 10–20.

7. Celeste Lowe, "Echoes from the Archives," *The Nevadan* in the *Las Vegas Review Journal,* 23 March 1975, p. 28.

8. Lyon, *Frank Waters,* 136.

9. Terence A. Tanner, *Frank Waters,* 37.

10. Ibid, 76.

11. Adams, ed., *Retrospective,* 66.

12. See *Mountain Dialogues* (Athens: Ohio University Press/Swallow Press,

1981) and *Sundays in Tutt Library with Frank Waters* (Colorado Springs: The Colorado College, 1988).

PREFACE

1. Teilhard de Chardin, *The Phenomenon of Man*, 218.
2. See Ferguson, *The Aquarian Conspiracy*.
3. The cries of despair in modern literature are regarded as a single motif in Engelberg, *Elegiac Fictions*.

CHAPTER 1

1. Falck, *Myth, Truth and Literature*, 167–68.
2. Ibid., 168.
3. On the pattern of mythic quest, see Campbell, *The Hero with a Thousand Faces*.
4. Waters refers to the Four Corners area of the Southwest as "indeed the heartland of America" (*Masked Gods*, 18) and as the "ancient, wilderness heartland" (*Pumpkin*, 3). He also envisions the heartland as a crucible for the creation of "the new American—a continent-soul reborn" (*Dust*, 482–83).
5. In any edition, this is line 341. See, for example, *The Complete Poems and Plays*, 47.
6. Melville's first novel, *Typee* (1846), was a popular success. With *Mardi* (1849) he lost his audience, and *Moby-Dick* (1851), although a few reviewers recognized its greatness, sold a paltry number of copies in his lifetime (he died in 1891). The flood tide of interest in Melville began rolling in after 1919, the centennial of his birth. See Luther S. Mansfield and Howard P. Vincent, Introduction to *Moby-Dick*, ix–xxxiii.
7. The neglect of writers of the American West is discussed by Milton, "Thoughts on Western Writers."
8. Eliot, *Selected Essays*, 14, 15.
9. Joseph Dozier (1842–1925), Waters's maternal grandfather, in whose home Waters lived in his youth, was one of the earliest residents of Colorado Springs and a distinguished contractor and builder in the Pike's Peak region for years. He was born in the Tulls Creek District, adjacent to the Moyock District, of Currituck County, North Carolina. The Doziers were of French extraction and had established connections with the Currituck County area by the end of the seventeenth century (see Maling, *The Dozier Family of Lower Norfolk County*). After Dozier's death, Waters came to reflect on his grandfather's extraordinary character, on which is based the character of Joseph Rogier in a trilogy of novels published in the 1930s and early 1940s, later revised as *Pike's Peak*.
10. On Faulkner as verse dramatist, see Donoghue, *The Third Voice*, 258–60.
11. Bucco, *Frank Waters*, 40.
12. The symbolic nature of the confidence man in American literature is discussed in my *Myth of the Picaro*, 145–200. Faulkner's Snopeses would seem to belong to the tradition of roguery in Old Southwestern humor.
13. Spencer, "Emerging as a Writer in Faulkner's Mississippi," 134.
14. Brooks, *The Hidden God*, 130.
15. Brooks, *William Faulkner*, 45.

16. Brooks, *The Hidden God*, 35.

17. On vision in literature, I have consulted Falck, *Myth, Truth and Literature;* Arieti, *Creativity;* and Stegner, *One Way to Spell Man.*

18. The nine visionary novels include *Nobility, Roots,* and *Dust,* a 1500-page trilogy reduced by half in the revision called *Pike's Peak.* The other visionary novels are *Lizard Woman, Yogi, People, Deer,* and *Otowi.* Because *Diamond Head* and *River Lady* were coauthored and intended for cinematic treatment, I have not included them as visionary. *Flight from Fiesta* might be included among Waters's visionary novels, but, because it originated in an idea for film, I have omitted critical consideration of it.

19. On recent scientific approaches to unity, see Peat, *Synchronicity.*

20. Capra, *The Tao of Physics,* 146. Capra's summary of duality in oriental philosophy is the basis of my own summary in this paragraph.

21. Cited ibid., 148.

22. Waters in *Mountain Dialogues* presents polarized views of the nature and meaning of man, as represented by Carl Jung of Switzerland and Bhagavan Sri Maharshi of India, but envisions eventual reconciliation between Western psychology and Eastern metaphysics.

23. Hoffman, *Freudianism and the Literary Mind,* 94.

24. *Collected Poems of Herman Melville,* 45, italics in original.

25. In any edition of "Burnt Norton," these are lines 64–65. See, for example, Eliot, *The Complete Poems and Plays,* 119.

CHAPTER 2

1. See Levin, *The Power of Blackness,* xi–xii, 7–8, 28–30, 100. Levin quotes Frost's "Desert Places" in this context.

2. *Fever Pitch* was published by Horace Liveright in 1930 and republished as *The Lizard Woman* (Austin, Tex.: Thorp Springs Press, 1984). All references are to this 1984 edition but have been checked against the first edition.

3. See Terence A. Tanner, *Frank Waters,* 7.

4. The coherence of the narrative is not seriously challenged by transformation of Arvilla's gold bracelet to "a cheap brass bracelet, such as may be bought as any souvenir" (136). While puzzled by this discrepancy, Waters has denied any intention to make Dane an unreliable narrator. "I didn't intend to intimate that Marston's story wasn't absolutely true, and the effect on Dane shows that to be true" (conversation, 21 July 1988). *Gold* may refer to color, not the metal.

5. Hoffman, *Freudianism and the Literary Mind,* 328–29. First published in 1945, Hoffman's book reduces archetypes to static symbols and is generally hostile to the psychology of Jung. Perhaps it is well to point out that Frank Waters himself did not begin to read Jung until he moved to Taos. From 1938 on, Mabel Dodge Luhan permitted Waters to borrow any books he wanted from her extensive library. In this way Waters became acquainted with Jung's books, but actually not until he had completed *Deer* in 1941.

6. The influence of naturalism on both *Lizard Woman* and *Yogi* (largely written in 1927) occasionally seems strong but not doctrinaire. Because men and women are part of nature, they are subject to its laws, such as those of heredity, and this deterministic outlook plays a part in Waters's characterization of racial types, especially those of mixed heritage (e.g., Arvilla in *Lizard Woman,* Barby and Guadalupe in

Yogi). Another favorite theme in naturalistic fiction is that of "the beast within," recognized when a character yields to lower instincts (e.g., both Horne and Marston in *Lizard Woman* temporarily degenerate when the veneer of civilization is stripped away). When he wrote *Lizard Woman*, Waters was familiar with naturalistic novels and stories by Frank Norris and Jack London. His view of life was and is, however, nondeterministic. "We're all animals to start with, then we develop mentality, then spirituality" (conversation, 21 July 1988). An excellent guideline remains Cowley, "A Natural History of American Naturalism."

7. Although Conrad's narrator in *Heart of Darkness* is likened to a Buddha, the narrative strategies are Jamesian (i.e., to make us see reality in a social sense). Waters's emphasis on the ephemerality of existence is more truly oriental than Conrad's, and none of the novels has a recognition scene that is merely social in its implications.

8. Waters's characters sometimes suffer a loss of feeling (Marston in *Lizard Woman*), a failure of compassion (Tai Ling in *Yogi*), or of the sense of community (Martiniano in *Deer*), or they are estranged from society because of a real fixation (Rogier in *Pike's Peak*) or imagined insanity (Helen in *Otowi*). The usual source for these losses and failures is attributed by Waters to a psychic imbalance caused by rationality and materialism. Attainment to "mystical" detachment presents a special case that necessitates estrangement from society as it is presently constituted; enhancement of personality, however, is not a perversion of humanity but a way toward its orientation in terms of all relationships, social and cosmic.

9. Waters makes frequent reference in his nonfiction to the Aztec Earth Mother called Tonantzin, who was recognized by the Catholic Church, ten years after the Conquest, under her name the Virgin of Guadalupe as the Christian patroness of all Indian America. This identification is particularly evident in the character of Guadalupe in *Yogi* and is relevant to the character of Maria del Valle in *People*.

10. See Campbell, *Occidental Mythology*, 7.

11. I am grateful to Robert Kostka for pointing out the similarity of this idea in *Lizard Woman* to one of the doctrines of Taoism.

12. Empson, *Seven Types of Ambiguity*, 44.

13. Tony Tanner, *The Reign of Wonder*, 36–37.

14. Ibid., 61, 166, 353.

15. Campbell, *Occidental Mythology*, 3.

16. Neumann, *Creative Man*, 250.

17. Neumann, *The Psychological Stages in the Development of Personality*, 342.

18. Ibid., 278.

19. Ibid., 299.

20. Ibid., 316.

21. Ibid., 358.

22. Ibid., 323.

CHAPTER 3

1. Romantic landscapes are defined as those upon which the artist has projected his emotions and mood, whereas psychic landscape involves the reverse—the projection of the land's spirit into the mind. See Fleck, "Psychic Landscape."

2. Adams, "Las Vegas as a Border Town."

3. An "instant city" of the interior West has little sense of its own history and is

characterized by phenomenal growth not "naturally" related to geography. Even though an instant city may not lie on the original east-west thoroughfare of the Union Pacific, it may still become a boomtown or a series of boomtowns and eventually an important crossroads. See Wiley and Gottlieb, *Empires in the Sun,* 121.

4. Grider, "Rightness with the Land," 50–51.

5. Ibid., 51.

6. All references are to the Sage Paperback edition of 1972 published by The Swallow Press.

7. The idea of death as a struggle at a decisive moment seems to be of archetypal origin, according to von Franz, *On Dreams & Death,* 22.

8. Govinda, *Foundations of Tibetan Mysticism,* 90–93, 107, 117, italics in original.

9. Ibid., 122–23.

10. *The Tibetan Book of the Dead,* 95.

11. Jung, "Psychological Commentary on 'The Tibetan Book of the Dead,' " xliii.

12. Evans-Wentz, Introduction, 2.

13. I have discussed the Spanish *pícaro* as an archetypal figure not limited by literary and geographical frontiers, in *The Myth of the Picaro,* esp. 19–20. The psychology of the *pícaro* (e.g., in *Lazarillo de Tormes*), reveals failed identity, alienation, and religious despair. Waters's characterization of Barby and his "picaresque" environment falls into the pattern.

14. One deconstructionist critic argues that the self-expression of female characters in literature filters through the discourse controlled by a male author. See Friedman, *The Antiheroine's Voice.*

15. Waters has commented in *Masked Gods* on the psychological significance of the sun in Mesoamerican myth: "Opposed to the dark, feminine, earth-born, unconscious principle, he embodies the light, masculine, conscious, spiritual principle of man's dual nature" (198).

16. The text has "vanished" where "banished" (as in the quotation from p. 206) fits the sense of the passage.

17. Although Conrad's influence on Waters diminishes after *Lizard Woman,* the protagonist of *Victory* bears a certain resemblance to Tai Ling. Life convicts Axel Heyst of a lack of self-knowledge, even though habit precludes realization of the significance of compassion. Heyst's victory over his conditioning in skepticism comes too late to save him.

18. "The longing for light is the longing for consciousness" (Jung, *Memories, Dreams,* and *Reflections,* 269). Bear in mind that Tai Ling has an irrepressible urge to rise out of primal darkness but is never fully liberated from instinct.

19. See Lyon, *Frank Waters,* 120.

20. Evans-Wentz, *Tibetan Yoga and Secret Doctrines,* 23.

21. Ibid., 46–47.

22. Cf. "We carry not only an individual karma, but a karma of the race and of the land mass to which we are attuned" (*Pumpkin,* 40).

23. The Spanish poem which serves as epigraph for *Yogi* is allegedly by "Hexotziquense" and appears on a convent wall painted by Diego Rivera, who had a reputation for inventing "ancient" myths and sayings. Waters was aware of the hoax. The words of the poem, however, reveal a message which Tai Ling must grow to understand. Roughly translated, they are: "They discredit us and diminish our worth because we are the common people. Only we who have felt it know what is grief, what is anguish, how well it is known."

24. Bradbury, "Style of Life, Style of Art and the American Novelist in the Nine-

teen Twenties," 18. On complex pastoralism as an alternative metaphor, see Marx, *The Machine in the Garden,* esp. 362–65. Waters completed the first draft of *Yogi* in 1927 and returned to it for revisions in 1937 and in 1945.

25. "Visions of the Good: What Literature Affirms and How" is an unpublished, 12-page typescript dated 16 July 1986, quoted by permission of the author but with page references omitted for quotations. The title was not chosen by Waters.

26. These distinctions are drawn from Campbell, *Oriental Mythology,* 13–20.

27. The real author exists outside the text, while the implied author leaves traces in the narrative. See Booth, *The Rhetoric of Fiction,* esp. 67–86, 211–40.

28. Evans-Wentz, Introduction, 89 n. 3, italics in original.

29. Ibid., 97 n. 1, italics in original.

30. Jung, "Psychological Commentary on 'The Tibetan Book of the Dead,' " xlii, italics in original.

31. Following the authorized Tibetan edition of the "Root-Verses of the Bardo," Govinda translates the opening words as "when the Bardo of Life is dawning upon me" and argues that the *Bardo Thödol* has to do "with life itself and not merely a mass for the dead" (*Foundations of Tibetan Mysticism,* 124).

CHAPTER 4

1. Differences between *Pike's Peak* and the trilogy are discussed by Adams, "*Pike's Peak*," and "Tailings from the Pike's Peak Load," and by Waters himself (Tanner, 206–11). After comparing the texts, I agree with Adams and Waters that *Pike's Peak* is a new novel but conclude that the essence of the story and of its meaning can be distilled from the trilogy. Textual criticism is here relevant to the history of ideas: the trilogy of the 1930s was not influenced by Jungian psychology (as *Pike's Peak* is) and anticipates by fifty years some postulates of theoretical physics today.

2. For this brief summary of tragedy, I am indebted to Wain, *The Living World of Shakespeare,* 163–64, 167.

3. Unless otherwise noted, all references are to the 1987 paperback edition of *Pike's Peak.* Hinduism conceives of the ultimate or Irreducible Reality as Spirit or Atman, which manifests as the Self: see, for example, Woodroffe, *The Serpent Power,* 26–27. In order to avoid using a culture-specific word for what is timeless, formless, and ineffable, I have used the uncapitalized words supreme universe, which is virtually synonymous with the idea of a sacred universe.

4. Waters's biography of Winfield Scott Stratton, *Midas of the Rockies,* was published in 1937 and was initially titled *Bowl of Gold* (Tanner, 16). Stratton's theory that the volcanic cone of Pike's Peak was a bowl of gold seemed to be verified when he discovered gold near Cripple Creek, Colorado, on 4 July 1891. In the novel, Rogier stubbornly ignores the theory and seeks gold outside and beneath the "bowl."

5. On the archetype of a lotuslike, golden heart, see Jung, "Commentary on 'The Secret of the Golden Flower.' " Rogier's "heart" symbolism as "golden flower" is evident in "faintly colored, fish-shaped petals slowly revolving around a yellow-bright center as if trying to arrange themselves into the pattern of a great golden flower" (*Pike's Peak,* 658). Rogier has projected upon the Peak an archetypal symbol of immanent divinity; hence the Peak itself is but a transient symbol. Although his search for the heart of the Peak is expressed in the imagery of Taoism, one is reminded of tales by Melville and Conrad in which an individual confronts an enigma at the heart of the natural world.

6. The pessimistic conclusion that nature is meaningless and designified influenced many Victorian and early modern writers, according to Lorsch, *Where Nature Ends.*

7. See Robinson, *Mexico and the Hispanic Southwest in American Literature,* 210.

8. Waters's admiration for D. H. Lawrence's *Plumed Serpent* is heavily qualified by Waters's belief that no people can return to the old magic of their ancient past. See *Masked Gods,* 405–8.

9. The essence of "Two Views of Nature" was first delivered as a talk at the fourth annual Arizona Historical Convention in Tucson in March 1963 and was published in *South Dakota Review* (May 1964).

10. See Henry Nash Smith, *Virgin Land,* 77–80.

11. Melville, *Moby-Dick,* 188.

12. On scapegoat psychology, see Neumann, *Depth Psychology and a New Ethic,* 50–55.

13. For a recent summary of the basic outlook of mystics, I have drawn on Weber, *Dialogues with Scientists and Sages,* 1–19.

14. Colorado Springs was affectionately called Little London after the first stake was driven in 1871. When the first census was taken in 1885, Colorado Springs had quickly passed through a frontier stage to become a cosmopolitan town with a population of 4,563; the greatest proportion of the foreign-born population that year was British, and a large sum of British capital helped to develop the town. (Adridge, "Little London"). For the fictional Rogier family in *Pike's Peak,* the title Little London suggests social, financial, and cultural frustration and deprivation. The nature and orientation of Rogier's religious feelings, which he keeps a secret even from his family, further isolate him from a Christianized society. In 1905, the city had a population of 30,000, a combined church membership of 10,000, 46 churches, 35 millionaires, and dozens of other people whose wealth reached into six figures. (Mobley, "Colorado Springs, 1905").

15. Of use in discriminating between the madness and sanity of a literary character is a chapter on *Don Quixote* in Auerbach, *Mimesis,* 293–315.

16. See Waters, *Cuchama and Sacred Mountains,* 162. Waters discusses Pike's Peak, as a sacred mountain, in a note on p. 60.

17. Sagan, *The Dragons of Eden,* 183.

18. Ornstein, *The Psychology of Consciousness,* 82.

19. See ibid., 137–40.

20. The revolution in neuroscience is discussed by Gilinsky, *Mind and Brain,* esp. 460–78.

21. For a summary of this movement, I have drawn on two sources: Weber, *Dialogues,* and Peat, *Synchronicity.*

22. Weber, *Dialogues,* 182. Prigogine's work challenges the validity of the second law of thermodynamics, long regarded as meaning that the universe is disintegrating.

CHAPTER 5

1. All quotations are from Frank Waters, *People of the Valley,* Chicago: Swallow Press, 1969.

2. Hick, *Faith and Knowledge,* 115.

3. Often hesitant to use the word *spirituality* in public, Waters writes, "So for the ultimate and divine observer within us, I prefer the term 'Being Within,' used by the great Shawnee chief Tecumseh during his impassioned address in 1810 . . . protest-

ing the United States usurpation of his tribe's homeland." ("A New Look at an Old Worldview," 124).

4. I have incorporated in this paragraph a number of insights about Waters's art in Lyon, "Does the Land Speak?" and "Frank Waters and the Concept of 'Nothing Special.' "

5. In conversation, 21 July 1988.

6. On the pastoral in literature, I have consulted Greg, *Pastoral Poetry & Pastoral Drama;* Empson, *Some Versions of Pastoral;* Lynen, *The Pastoral Art of Robert Frost;* Brooks, *William Faulkner;* Kermode, Introduction to *The Tempest;* Marx, *The Machine in the Garden;* Marinelli, *Pastoral;* Squires, *The Pastoral Novel;* and Ettin, *Literature and the Pastoral.* Because pastoralism sometimes shares with regionalism a vague yearning to look back toward a simpler life, the two are apt to be confused. Regional art becomes pastoral only when the contrast between past and present, simplicity and complexity, is taken seriously. The bulk of regional writing is second or third rate, because it consists only in a sentimental picturing of local color, making local differences seem charming, comic, and peculiar. For this distinction, see Spenser, "Regionalism in American Literature."

7. See Brooks, *William Faulkner,* 47–74.

8. Cited in Squires, *The Pastoral Novel,* 55, from Robert Speaight, *George Eliot* (London: Arthur Barker, 1954): 49.

9. Marx, *The Machine in the Garden,* 364.

10. Ibid.

11. Ibid., 7.

12. Lynen, *The Pastoral Art of Robert Frost,* 72.

13. Ibid., 189.

14. The archetypal motif of journey and return is studied at length in Campbell, *The Hero with a Thousand Faces.*

15. In conversation, 21 July 1988.

16. On the Hispanic people of northern New Mexico, I have consulted Mills, *The People of the Saints.* According to a member of the Chilean Society of History and Geography, Inés Dölz-Blackburn, in her article "Imagery and Motifs in Frank Waters' *People of the Valley,*" the Spanish soul is the same from America to Chile, and country women are often leaders who assume a macho role.

17. The use of an implied author to preserve a character's mythical dimensions is discussed by Friedman, *The Antiheroine's Voice,* esp. ch. 7, "The Mythic Narrator: *Tereza Batista* and the Utopian Alternative."

18. See Potter, "Coin of the Dead."

19. Peat, *Synchronicity,* 131.

20. Waters's acknowledged source on skull divination in the Southwest is a sketch by J. Frank Dobie. I have not been able to locate that sketch.

21. Kerényi, "The Primordial Child in Primordial Times," 43.

22. Jung, "The Psychology of the Child Archetype," 89.

23. Inés Dölz-Blackburn, "Imagery and Motifs in Frank Waters' *People of the Valley,*" notes that Hispanic women may demonstrate authority by smoking "male" cigarettes.

24. Campbell, *The Hero with a Thousand Faces,* 40–41.

25. The axial Rock of the Navajos is discussed in *Masked Gods,* 167–70.

26. On the symbolism of the crescent, see Campbell, *Primitive Mythology,* 446, and *Oriental Mythology,* 37, 41, 91, 94, 206.

27. Androgyny as an ideal is proposed by Heilbrun, *Toward a Recognition of Androgyny.* "The ideal toward which I believe we should move," she states, "is best

described by the term 'androgyny.' This ancient Greek word—from *andro* (male) and *gyn* (female)—defines a condition under which the characteristics of the sexes, and the human impulses expressed by men and women, are not rigidly assigned" (x). Drawing on Heilbrun's proposal, Malpezzi notes that Maria del Valle is in fact a depiction of the androgynous ideal ("A Study of the Female Protagonist in Frank Waters' *People of the Valley* and Rudolfo Anaya's *Bless Me, Ultima*"). For a further study of Waters's creation of nonstereotypical female characters, see Grigg, "*Man, Woman, People.*"

28. See Gladstein, *The Indestructible Woman in Faulkner, Hemingway, and Steinbeck.*

29. Cited in ibid., 1, from Carolyn Heilbrun, "The Masculine Wilderness of the American Novel," *Saturday Review* (29 January 1972): 41.

30. Heilbrun sees Hawthorne's Hester Prynne as one of a kind (*Toward a Recognition of Androgyny,* 66). Hester and, to a lesser extent, Isabel Archer in Henry James's *Portrait of a Lady* are certainly fine exceptions to the general rule, but Maria del Valle is possibly a finer one.

31. William Faulkner, *The Hamlet* (New York: Vintage Books, 1964), 95.

32. John Steinbeck, *The Grapes of Wrath* (New York: Viking Press, Compass Edition, 1958), 100.

33. Ibid., 286.

CHAPTER 6

1. Waters, "*The Man Who Killed the Deer:* 30 Years Later," 18–20.

2. Campbell, *The Way of the Animal Powers,* 76.

3. See Waters, "*The Man Who Killed the Deer:* 30 Years Later," 17.

4. Rascoe, "Two Worlds in Conflict."

5. "I had some vague idea while writing it [*Moby-Dick*], that the book was susceptible of an allegoric construction, & also that *parts* of it were—but the specialty of many of the particular subordinate allegories, were first revealed to me, after reading Mr. Hawthorne's letter, which, without citing any particular examples, yet intimated the part-&-parcel allegoricalness of the whole." The quote is from Herman Melville's letter of 8 January 1852 to Sophia Hawthorne, cited in Honig, *Dark Conceit,* 193–94, italics in original.

6. A point made by Fletcher, *Allegory,* 73.

7. Martiniano may seem to some readers an unusual name for an Indian, as is the name Palemon. In the fifth century A.D., a neoplatonic writer, Martianus Capella, announced an awakening to a vision that popularized the motif of an allegorical ascent to heaven. Possibly of Hindu origin, the name Palemon appears as Palamon in Geoffrey Chaucer's "Knight's Tale." Whatever the source, if there is one, Water's choice of names sometimes heightens the effect of universality. This is especially true when a character named M. Meru in *Otowi* brings in associations with Mt. Meru, a metaphysical mountain in Hindu cosmography.

8. See Waters, "*The Man Who Killed the Deer:* 30 Years Later."

9. See Campbell, *The Way of the Animal Powers,* 129.

10. See La Barre, *The Peyote Cult,* xv–xvi, 228. The 1938 edition of this book might have been used as a source for *Deer.*

11. Highwater, *The Primal Mind,* 135.

12. Fletcher, *Allegory,* 21.

13. Honig, *Dark Conceit,* 114.

14. The similarity between Waters's idea of Emergence and Jung's "individuation" is discussed by Hoy, "The Archetypal Transformation of Martiniano in *The Man Who Killed the Deer*."

15. Waters was reading works by the mystic Georges Gurdjieff (1872?–1949), in the late 1930s. Although Waters developed his idea of conscience prior to that time, he would have found a similar view of it in Gurdjieff's teaching, at the forefront of which is the contrast between morality, which is relative to time and place, and conscience, which is universal. In both Waters and Gurdjieff one finds the profound conception of conscience as a power in us that makes us sensitive to the workings of cosmic laws of interrelationship. See Bennett, *Gurdjieff,* 83–84, 257, 293, on Gurdjieff's conception of conscience.

16. Langer, *Philosophy in a New Key,* 149. Langer's seminal work, first published in 1942, indicates the widespread interest in literary symbolism at that time.

17. Davis views *Deer* as "an impressive forerunner of fiction ostensibly written from within the native consciousness" ("The Whorf Hypothesis and Native American Literature"). Fiedler lumps *Deer* together with Oliver La Farge's *Laughing Boy,* a novel with which it has almost nothing in common except superficial appearance, and condemns both for a "pretense of writing within the consciousness of Indians" (*The Return of the Vanishing American,* 170). The impersonation of native consciousness in Ken Kesey's novel *One Flew Over the Cuckoo's Nest* is spared Fiedler's scorn. Fiedler is neither consistent nor fair in his remarks about *Deer*.

18. D'Arcy, *The Sense of History,* 33.

19. See Lee, *Freedom and Culture,* 9–11, 20–24.

20. Page references to *The Man Who Killed the Deer* are to the readily available Pocket Books edition. Italics in original.

21. See Highwater, *The Primal Mind,* 69–74.

22. James, *The Art of the Novel,* 45.

23. For some of the ideas and phrasings in this paragraph, I am indebted to Wain, *The Living World of Shakespeare,* 163–68.

24. That *Deer* reflects some of the thinking in *Lizard Woman,* composed in 1925, strengthens the contention that Waters arrived early and independently at views parallel to Jung's.

25. See Jung, "Answer to Job," esp. 626–27.

26. Honig, Dark Conceit, 53.

CHAPTER 7

1. Page references are to the revised edition of *The Woman at Otowi Crossing,* Athens: Swallow Press/Ohio University Press, 1987.

2. The "discovery" of psychic energy has only recently been accredited. For instance, Dr. Joseph Banks Rhine and his wife Dr. Louisa E. Rhine spent some fifty years at Duke University trailblazing and then doing the work of establishing the scientific foundation for parapsychology, but final respectability was not granted to parapsychology by the scientific establishment until 1969, when the prestigious American Association for the Advancement of Science accepted, after rejecting two previous applications, the Parapsychological Association as a member organization.

3. See Koestler, *The Act of Creation;* Capra, *The Tao of Physics;* and Peat, *Synchronicity.*

4. The concept is surveyed in Lefever and Hunt, *The Apocalyptic Premise.*

5. In "Prelude to Change," Waters's commencement address at the University of

Nevada, Las Vegas, on 23 May 1981, he reviews the Hopi prophecy about world destruction and then rejects the view that cataclysmic changes will overtake the planet.

6. Harding, *Psychic Energy*, 8.

7. See Schell, *The Fate of the Earth*, 115. Scientific knowledge, Schell writes, has brought us face to face with the "death of mankind" and in doing so has "caused a basic change in the circumstances in which life was given to us, which is to say that we have altered the human condition."

8. In summarizing some conclusions about motivation, I have consulted Koestler, *The Act of Creation*, 495–508.

9. Waters's novel *Flight from Fiesta* emphasizes the theme of "common humanness" (102).

10. Campbell, *The Power of Myth*, 67.

11. Synchronicity was a concept long incubated. In 1930 Jung introduced the "synchronistic principle" in a memorial address to his friend Richard Wilhelm. The best-known references are Jung's Foreword to the *I Ching* (1950), "On Synchronicity" (1951), and "Synchronicity: An Acausal Connecting Principle" (1952).

12. Peat, *Synchronicity*, 27.

13. In a letter to Dr. Selig dated 25 February 1953, Jung wrote, "It was Einstein who first started me off thinking about a possible relativity of time as well as space, and their psychic synchronicity." See Singer, *Boundaries of the Soul*, 398.

14. Peat, *Synchronicity*, 186–87.

15. Neumann, *Creative Man*, 254.

16. Bolen, *The Tao of Psychology*, 84, italics in original.

17. Capra, *The Tao of Physics*, 104–5.

18. An incidental source for the characterization of Helen Chalmers is the life of Edith Warner, who befriended J. Robert Oppenheimer and other physicists from Los Alamos. Waters himself was acquainted with Warner, and he began composition of *Otowi* in 1953 (Tanner, 190). Therefore, he is not directly indebted to a book by Church, *The House at Otowi Bridge* (1959). On Waters's use of details from Warner's life, see Malpezzi, "The Emergence of Helen Chalmers."

19. Waters consistently views Quetzalcoatl as a Redeemer in *Pumpkin* (101, 161–63, 167), *Mexico Mystique* (57–59, 124–26, 133, 139, 193), and *Mountain Dialogues* (143) and believes that the original transcendental myth was distorted by the Aztecs into a secular, materialistic ideology. It was this Aztec vulgarization of Quetzalcoatl that D. H. Lawrence fictionally restored to Mexico in his novel *The Plumed Serpent*, according to Waters in "Quetzalcoatl versus D. H. Lawrence's *Plumed Serpent*."

20. In any edition of "Burnt Norton" this is part of line 64. See, for example, Eliot, *The Complete Poems and Plays, 1909–1950*, 119.

21. This point is made by Bolen, *The Tao of Psychology*, 9.

22. Falck, *Myth, Truth and Literature*, 121.

23. The term *flashforwards* for the interviews in *Otowi* is used by Lyon, *Frank Waters*, 128.

24. Malpezzi, "Meru, the Voice of the Mountain," 33.

25. The archetypal image of light as life energy suddenly liberated by the "explosion" of death is discussed in von Franz, *On Dreams and Death*, 84. Waters uses light imagery in this sense not only for the death of Helen Chalmers in *Otowi* but also for that of Tai Ling in *Yogi*.

26. Waters discusses some representations of the number seven in *Masked Gods* (222–23), *Pumpkin* (137–38), and *Mexico Mystique* (175, 191). There are allusions in *Otowi* to Amerindian myths of seven womb-caves (51, 95, 151), which Emily believes

are references to the seven traditional kivas within a pueblo, but which Helen considers a parable of Emergence. The tableau with seven deer obviously supports Helen's interpretation.

27. In any edition of "A Valediction: Forbidding Mourning," these are lines 21–24. See, for example, Donne, *Songs and Sonets,* 82.

CHAPTER 8

1. Donoghue, *The Sovereign Ghost,* 175.
2. Falck, *Myth, Truth and Literature,* xii.
3. Ibid., 37.
4. Jung, *Modern Man in Search of a Soul,* 162.
5. Campbell, *Creative Mythology,* 3, 6–8, 40, 94, 646, italics in original.
6. *The Complete Essays and Other Writings of Ralph Waldo Emerson,* 262.
7. Waters, "A Saturday with Frank Waters," 212.
8. Milton, "Symbolic Space and Mysticism in the Novels of Frank Waters," 13.
9. Broad, *Religion, Philosophy, and Psychical Research,* 242, italics in original.
10. See LeShan, "Physicists and Mystics."
11. See Larsen, *The Shaman's Doorway,* 28–29.
12. Waters, "Words," 234.
13. Knight, *The Wheel of Fire,* 11.
14. Campbell, *Creative Mythology,* 25.
15. Waters, "Mysticism and Witchcraft," 70.
16. Grigg, "Frank Waters and the Mountain Spirit," 45, italics in original.
17. Melville, *The Confidence-Man,* 271. In any edition, this quotation is in chapter 44.
18. Williams, *In the American Grain,* 120.

BIBLIOGRAPHY

PRIMARY SOURCES

Bibliography and Letters

Tanner, Terence A. *Frank Waters: A Bibliography, with Relevant Selections from His Correspondence.* Glenwood, Ill.: Meyerbooks, 1983.

Novels by Frank Waters

Below Grass Roots. New York: Liveright, 1937.
Diamond Head, by Frank Waters and Houston Branch. New York: Farrar, Straus, 1948.
The Dust within the Rock. New York: Liveright, 1940.
Flight from Fiesta. Athens: Swallow Press/Ohio University Press, 1987.
The Lizard Woman. Austin, Tex.: Thorpe Springs Press, 1984. Originally published as *Fever Pitch,* New York: Liveright, 1930.
The Man Who Killed the Deer. New York: Farrar & Rinehart, 1942; Denver: University of Denver Press, 1950; Denver: Sage Books, 1958; Chicago: Swallow Press, 1968; New York: Pocket Books, 1971; Athens: Swallow Press/Ohio University Press, 1989.
People of the Valley. New York: Farrar & Rinehart, 1941; Chicago: Swallow Press, 1969.

Pike's Peak. Chicago: Swallow Press, 1971; 1st paperback ed., Athens: Swallow Press/ Ohio University Press, 1987.

River Lady, by Frank Waters and Houston Branch. New York: Farrar & Rinehart, 1942.

The Wild Earth's Nobility. New York: Liveright, 1935.

The Woman at Otowi Crossing. Rev. ed., Athens: Swallow Press/Ohio University Press, 1987; originally published, Denver: Swallow Press, 1966.

The Yogi of Cockroach Court. New York: Rinehart, 1947; Chicago: Swallow Press, 1972.

Other Books by Frank Waters (selected)

Book of the Hopi. New York: Viking, 1963.

The Colorado. Rivers of America Series. New York: Rinehart, 1946; 1st paperback ed., with a new preface by the author, Athens: Swallow Press/Ohio University Press, 1984.

The Earp Brothers of Tombstone. New York: Clarkson N. Potter, 1960. Bison Book reprint, Lincoln: University of Nebraska Press, 1976.

Masked Gods: Navaho and Pueblo Ceremonialism. Albuquerque: University of New Mexico Press, 1950; reprint, Chicago: Swallow Press, 1969.

Mexico Mystique: The Coming Sixth World of Consciousness. Chicago: Swallow Press, 1975; 1st paperback ed., Athens: Swallow Press/Ohio University Press, 1989.

Midas of the Rockies: The Story of Stratton and Cripple Creek. New York: Covici-Friede, 1937.

Mountain Dialogues. Athens: Swallow Press/Ohio University Press, 1981.

Pumpkin Seed Point. Chicago: Swallow Press, 1969.

To Possess the Land: A Biography of Arthur Rochford Manby. Chicago: Swallow Press, 1974.

Other Works by Frank Waters (selected)

Conversations with Frank Waters. Edited by John R. Milton. Chicago: Swallow Press, 1972.

Cuchama and Sacred Mountains, by W. Y. Evans-Wentz. Edited by Frank Waters and Charles L. Adams. Athens: Swallow Press/Ohio University Press, 1982.

Eternal Desert. Photography by David Muench. Phoenix: Arizona Highways, 1990.

Frank Waters: A Retrospective Anthology. Edited by Charles L. Adams. Athens: Swallow Press/Ohio University Press, 1985.

"Frank Waters: Interview by Charles Adams." In *This Is About Vision: Interviews with Southwestern Writers,* edited by William Balassi, John F. Crawford, and Annie O. Eysturoy. Albuquerque: University of New Mexico Press, 1990: 15–25.

"The Regional Imperative." In *Sundays in Tutt Library with Frank Waters,* edited by Katherine Scott Sturdevant. Colorado Springs: Hulbert Center for Southwestern Studies, The Colorado College, 1988: 45–55.

"A Saturday with Frank Waters." *Writers' Forum* 11 (1985): 209–21.

"Visions of the Good: What Literature Affirms and How." Paper presented at Winona, Minn., 16 July 1986.

"The Writer's Sense of Place: A Symposium." *South Dakota Review* 13 (Autumn 1975): 6–9.

Periodical Publications by Frank Waters (selected)

"Man and Nature: An Indivisible Unity." *New Mexico Magazine* 52 (May 1974): 16–21.

"*The Man Who Killed the Deer:* 30 Years Later." *New Mexico Magazine* 50 (January 1972): 16–23, 49–50.

"Mysticism and Witchcraft." *South Dakota Review* 15 (Autumn 1977): 59–70.

"A New Look at an Old Worldview." *Studies in Frank Waters* 10 (1988): 117–28.

"Notes on Alan Swallow." *The Denver Quarterly* 2 (Spring 1967): 16–25.

"Notes on Los Angeles." *South Dakota Review* 19 (Spring-Summer 1981): 14–23.

"Prelude to Change." In "Frank Waters' 'Prelude to Change,' " edited by Charles L. Adams. *Nevada Historical Society Quarterly* 24 (1981): 250–54.

"Quetzalcoatl versus D. H. Lawrence's *Plumed Serpent.*" *Western American Literature* 3 (Summer 1968): 103–13.

"Relationships and the Novel." *The Writer* 56 (April 1943): 105–7.

"Words." *Western American Literature* 3 (Fall 1968): 227–34.

SECONDARY SOURCES

Adams, Charles L. "Frank Waters." In *A Literary History of the American West,* edited by Thomas J. Lyon, sponsored by the Western Literature Association. Fort Worth: Texas Christian University Press, 1987: 935–57.

———. "A Frank Waters Chronology." *Studies in Frank Waters* 9 (1987): 73–79.

———. "Frank Waters: Western Mystic." *Studies in Frank Waters* 5 (1982): 1–11.

———. "The Genesis of *Flight from Fiesta.*" *Western American Literature* 22 (November 1987): 195–200.

———. "Las Vegas as a Border Town: An Interpretive Essay." *Nevada Historical Society Quarterly* 21 (1978): 51–55.

———. "*Pike's Peak.*" *Writers' Forum* 11 (1985): 195–208.

———. "Tailings from the Pike's Peak Load." In *Sundays in Tutt Library with Frank Waters,* edited by Katherine Scott Sturdevant. Colorado Springs: Hulbert Center for Southwestern Studies, The Colorado College, 1988: 27–44.

———. "*The Woman at Otowi Crossing,* revised edition." *Western American Literature* 23 (1988): 45–50.

Adridge, Dorothy. "Little London: 1885 Census Shows Colorado Springs Was Hub of Activity." *Colorado Springs Gazette Telegraph,* 26 May 1985.

Arieti, Silvano. *Creativity: The Magic Synthesis.* New York: Basic Books, 1976.

Auerbach, Erich. *Mimesis: The Representation of Reality in Western Literature.* Translated by Willard Trask. Garden City, N.Y.: Doubleday Anchor Books, 1957.

Barnett, Lincoln Kinnear. *The Universe and Dr. Einstein.* 2d ed., rev. New York: William Sloane Associates, 1948.

Bennett, John Godolphin. *Gurdjieff: Making a New World.* London: Turnstone Books, 1973.

Bergson, Henri. *Creative Evolution.* Translated by Arthur Mitchell. New York: Random House, 1944.

Blackburn, Alexander. "Frank Waters." In *Dictionary of Literary Biography Yearbook: 1986,* edited by J. M. Brook. Detroit: Gale Research, 1986: 343–55.

———, ed. "Frank Waters: The Colorado College Symposium." *Writers' Forum* 11 (1985): 164–221.

————. *The Myth of the Picaro: Continuity and Transformation of the Picaresque Novel, 1554–1954*. Chapel Hill: University of North Carolina Press, 1979.

Bohm, David. *Wholeness and the Implicate Order*. London: Routledge & Kegan Paul, 1980.

Bolen, Jean Shinoda. *The Tao of Psychology: Synchronicity and the Self*. New York: Harper & Row, 1979.

Booth, Wayne C. *The Rhetoric of Fiction*. Chicago: University of Chicago Press, 1961.

Bradbury, Malcolm. "Style of Life, Style of Art and the American Novelist in the Nineteen Twenties." In *The American Novel and the Nineteen Twenties*, edited by Malcolm Bradbury. Stratford-upon-Avon Studies, vol. 13. London: Edward Arnold, 1971: 10–35.

Bredahl, A. Carl, Jr. *New Ground: Western American Narrative and the Literary Canon*. Chapel Hill: University of North Carolina Press, 1989.

Broad, C. D. *Religion, Philosophy, and Psychical Research*. London: Routledge & Kegan Paul, 1953.

Brooks, Cleanth. *The Hidden God: Studies in Hemingway, Faulkner, Yeats, Eliot, and Warren*. New Haven: Yale University Press, 1963.

————. *William Faulkner: The Yoknapatawpha Country*. New Haven: Yale University Press, 1963.

Brundage, Burr Cartwright. *The Fifth Sun: Aztec Gods, Aztec World*. Austin: University of Texas Press, 1979.

Bucco, Martin. *Frank Waters*. Austin, Tex.: Steck-Vaughn, 1969.

Campbell, Joseph. *Creative Mythology*. Vol. 4 of *The Masks of God*. London: Secker & Warburg, 1968.

————. *The Hero with a Thousand Faces*. 2d ed. Bollingen Paperback. Princeton: Princeton University Press, 1972.

————. *Myths to Live By*. New York: Viking Press, 1972.

————. *Occidental Mythology*. Vol. 3 of *The Masks of God*. New York: Penguin Books, 1976.

————. *Oriental Mythology*. Vol. 2 of *The Masks of God*. New York: Penguin Books, 1976.

————. *The Power of Myth*. With Bill Moyers. Edited by Betty Sue Flowers. New York: Doubleday, 1988.

————. *Primitive Mythology*. Vol. 1 of *The Masks of God*. New York: Penguin Books, 1976.

————. *The Way of the Animal Powers*. Vol. 1 of *Historical Atlas of World Mythology*. London: Summerfield Press, 1983.

Capps, Walter Holden, ed. *Seeing with a Native Eye: Essays on Native American Religion*. New York: Harper & Row, 1976.

Capra, Fritjof. *The Tao of Physics: An Exploration of the Parallels between Modern Physics and Eastern Mysticism*. 2d ed., rev. Boulder, Colo.: Shambhala, 1983.

Church, Peggy Pond. *The House at Otowi Bridge: The Story of Edith Warner and Los Alamos*. Albuquerque: University of New Mexico Press, 1959.

Cowley, Malcolm. "A Natural History of American Naturalism." In *Critiques and Essays on Modern Fiction, 1920–1951*, compiled by John W. Aldridge. New York: Ronald Press, 1952: 370–87.

Crook, John Hurrell. *The Evolution of Human Consciousness*. Oxford: Clarendon Press, 1980.

Cumming, Jill. "Joseph Dozier (1842–1925), 435 East Bijou Street" and "Frank J.

Waters (1902–   ), 435 East Bijou Street." In *The Shooks Run Inventory of Historic Sites,* published by the City of Colorado Springs, 1978.

D'Arcy, Martin Cyril. *The Sense of History: Secular and Sacred.* London: Faber & Faber, 1959.

Davis, Jack L. "The Whorf Hypothesis and Native American Literature." *South Dakota Review* 14 (1976): 59–72.

Dölz-Blackburn, Inés. "Imagery and Motifs in Frank Waters' *People of the Valley:* An Introduction." *Studies in Frank Waters* 7 (1985): 57–73.

Donne, John. *Songs and Sonets.* Edited by Theodore Redpath. London: Methuen, 1956.

Donoghue, Denis. *The Sovereign Ghost: Studies in Imagination.* Berkeley and Los Angeles: University of California Press, 1976.

———. *The Third Voice: Modern British and American Verse Drama.* Princeton: Princeton University Press, 1959.

Eliot, T. S. *The Complete Poems and Plays, 1909–1950.* New York: Harcourt, Brace, 1952.

———. *Selected Essays.* 3d ed. London: Faber & Faber, 1966.

Emerson, Ralph Waldo. *The Complete Essays and Other Writings of Ralph Waldo Emerson.* New York: Modern Library, 1950.

Empson, William. *Seven Types of Ambiguity.* 3d ed. London: Chatto & Windus, 1963.

———. *Some Versions of Pastoral.* New York: New Directions, 1950.

Engelberg, Edward. *Elegiac Fictions: The Motif of the Unlived Life.* University Park: Pennsylvania State University Press, 1989.

Ettin, Andrew V. *Literature and the Pastoral.* New Haven: Yale University Press, 1984.

Evans-Wentz, W. Y. Introduction to *The Tibetan Book of the Dead,* compiled and edited by W. Y. Evans-Wentz. 3d ed. London: Oxford University Press, 1960: 1–81.

———. *Tibetan Yoga and Secret Doctrines.* 2d ed. London: Oxford University Press, 1958.

Falck, Colin. *Myth, Truth and Literature: Towards a True Post-Modernism.* Cambridge: Cambridge University Press, 1989.

Faulkner, William. *The Hamlet.* New York: Vintage Books, 1964.

Ferguson, Marilyn. *The Aquarian Conspiracy: Personal and Social Transformation in Our Time.* Los Angeles: J. P. Tarcher, 1980.

Fiedler, Leslie A. *The Return of the Vanishing American.* New York: Stein & Day, 1968.

Fleck, Richard F. "Psychic Landscape." In *Dictionary of Literary Themes and Motifs: L-Z,* edited by Jean-Charles Seigneuret. Westport, Conn.: Greenwood Press, 1988: 1005–9.

Fletcher, Angus. *Allegory: The Theory of a Symbolic Mode.* Ithaca, N.Y.: Cornell University Press, 1964.

Franklin, H. Bruce. *The Wake of the Gods: Melville's Mythology.* Stanford, Calif.: Stanford University Press, 1963.

Friedman, Edward H. *The Antiheroine's Voice: Narrative Discourse and Transformations of the Picaresque.* Columbia: University of Missouri Press, 1987.

Gilinsky, Alberta Steinman. *Mind and Brain: Principles of Neuropsychology.* New York: Praeger, 1984.

Gladstein, Mimi Reisel. *The Indestructible Woman in Faulkner, Hemingway, and Steinbeck.* Ann Arbor, Mich.: University Microfilms, 1986.

Gleick, James. *Chaos: Making a New Science.* New York: Penguin Books, 1988.

Gonzales, James A. "Like Eyes of Gold: The Images that Define Maria del Valle." *Studies in Frank Waters* 7 (1985): 77–97.

Gordon, David J. *Literary Art and the Unconscious.* Baton Rouge: Louisiana State University Press, 1976.

Govinda, Lama Anagarika. *Foundations of Tibetan Mysticism.* New York: E. P. Dutton, 1960.

Greg, Walter W. *Pastoral Poetry & Pastoral Drama.* New York: Russell & Russell, 1959.

Grider, Daryl. "Rightness with the Land: Spirit of Place in the Novels of Frank Waters." Ph.D. dissertation, University of Tennessee, 1980.

Grigg, Quay. "Frank Waters and the Mountain Spirit." *South Dakota Review* 15 (Autumn 1977): 45–49.

———. "*Man, Woman, People:* An Arachnology." *Studies in Frank Waters* 10 (1988): 51–64.

Harding, M. Esther. *Psychic Energy: Its Source and Goal.* New York: Pantheon Books, 1947.

Heilbrun, Carolyn. *Toward a Recognition of Androgyny.* New York: Alfred A. Knopf, 1973.

Hick, John. *Faith and Knowledge.* 2d ed. Ithaca, N.Y.: Cornell University Press, 1966.

Highwater, Jamake. *The Primal Mind: Vision and Reality in Indian America.* New York: Meridian Books, 1981.

Hoffman, Frederick J. *Freudianism and the Literary Mind.* 2d ed. Baton Rouge: Louisiana State University Press, 1957.

Honig, Edwin. *Dark Conceit: The Making of Allegory.* New York: Oxford University Press, Galaxy Books, 1966.

Hornsby, Bill. "Frank Waters: 'Dean' of Western Writers," *Denver Post,* 9 September 1990.

Hoy, Christopher. "The Archetypal Transformation of Martiniano in *The Man Who Killed the Deer.*" *South Dakota Review* 13 (1975–76): 43–56.

———. "The Conflict in *The Man Who Killed the Deer.*" *South Dakota Review* 15 (1977): 51–57.

James, Henry. *The Art of the Novel: Critical Prefaces.* New York: Charles Scribner's Sons, 1934.

Jung, Carl G. "Answer to Job." In *The Portable Jung,* edited by Joseph Campbell, translated by R. F. C. Hull. New York: Penguin Books, 1976: 519–650.

———. "The Archetypes and the Collective Unconscious." In *Two Essays on Analytical Psychology,* by Carl G. Jung, translated by Cary F. Baynes. New York: Pantheon Books, 1953: 88–111.

———. "Commentary on 'The Secret of the Golden Flower.' " In *Alchemical Studies,* by Carl G. Jung, translated by R. F. C. Hull. Princeton: Princeton University Press, 1967: 1–56.

———. *Man and His Symbols.* Garden City, N.Y.: Doubleday, 1964.

———. *Memories, Dreams, and Reflections.* Edited by Aniela Jaffe, translated by Richard and Clara Winston. New York: Pantheon Books, 1963.

———. *Modern Man in Search of a Soul.* Translated by W. S. Dell and Cary F. Baynes. New York: Harcourt, Brace & World, 1933.

———. "Psychological Commentary on 'The Tibetan Book of the Dead.' " In *The Tibetan Book of the Dead,* translated by R. F. C. Hull. 3d ed. London: Oxford University Press, 1957: xxxv–lii.

————. *Psychology and Religion: West and East.* Translated by R. F. C. Hull. New York: Pantheon Books, 1958.

————. "The Psychology of the Child Archetype." In *Essays on a Science of Mythology: The Myths of the Divine Child and the Mysteries of Eleusis,* by C. G. Jung and C. Kerényi, translated by R. F. C. Hull. Bollingen Series 22. Princeton: Princeton University Press, 1969: 70–100.

Karl, Frederick R. *American Fictions 1940–1980: A Comprehensive History and Critical Evaluation.* New York: Harper & Row, 1983.

Kerényi, C. [or Karl]. "The Primordial Child in Primordial Times." In *Essays on a Science of Mythology: The Myths of the Divine Child and the Mysteries of Eleusis.* By C. G. Jung and C. Kerényi, translated by R. F. C. Hull. Bollingen Series 22. Princeton: Princeton University Press, 1969: 25–69.

Kermode, Frank. Introduction to *The Tempest,* Arden Shakespeare Paperbacks. London: Methuen, 1964: xi–xciii.

Klein, David Ballin. *The Concept of Consciousness: A Survey.* Lincoln: University of Nebraska Press, 1984.

Knight, G. Wilson. *The Wheel of Fire.* Rev. ed. London: Methuen, 1949.

Koestler, Arthur. *The Act of Creation.* New York: Macmillan, 1964.

Kostka, Robert. "Frank Waters and the Visual Sense." *South Dakota Review* 15 (Autumn 1977): 27–30.

La Barre, Weston. *The Peyote Cult.* 4th ed., enl. Hamden, Conn.: Archon Books, 1975.

Langer, Susanne K. *Philosophy in a New Key: A Study in the Symbolism of Reason, Rite, and Art.* 3d ed. Cambridge, Mass.: Harvard University Press, 1963.

Larsen, Stephen. *The Shaman's Doorway: Opening the Mythic Imagination to Contemporary Consciousness.* New York: Harper & Row, 1976.

Leavis, F. R. *The Great Tradition: George Eliot, Henry James, Joseph Conrad.* New York: New York University Press, 1973.

Lecomte du Noüy, Pierre. *Human Destiny.* New York: Longmans, Green, 1947.

Lee, Dorothy. *Freedom and Culture.* Englewood Cliffs, N.J.: Prentice-Hall, 1959.

Lefever, Ernest W. and E. Stephen Hunt, eds. *The Apocalyptic Premise.* Washington, D.C.: Ethics and Public Policy Center, 1982.

LeShan, Lawrence. "Physicists and Mystics: Similarities in World View." *Journal of Transpersonal Psychology* 1 (1969): 1–20.

Levin, Harry. *The Power of Blackness: Hawthorne, Poe, Melville.* New York: Alfred A. Knopf, 1970.

Lévy-Bruhl, Lucien. *The Notebooks on Primitive Mentality.* Translated by Peter Rivière, with a preface by Maurice Leenhardt. New York: Harper & Row, 1975.

Lorsch, Susan E. *Where Nature Ends: Literary Responses to the Designification of Landscape.* Rutherford, Madison, Teaneck, N.J.: Fairleigh Dickinson University Press, 1983.

Lynen, John F. *The Pastoral Art of Robert Frost.* New Haven: Yale University Press, 1960.

Lyon, Thomas J. "Does the Land Speak? Frank Waters and the Southwest." In *Sundays in Tutt Library with Frank Waters,* edited by Katherine Scott Sturdevant. Colorado Springs: Hulbert Center for Southwestern Studies, The Colorado College, 1988: 13–25.

————. *Frank Waters.* New York: Twayne Publishers, 1973.

————. "Frank Waters." In *Fifty Western Writers: A Bio-Bibliographical Sourcebook,* edited by Fred Erisman and Richard W. Etulain. Westport, Conn.: Greenwood Press, 1982: 509–18.

————. "Frank Waters and Small-'b' Buddhism." *Studies in Frank Waters* 5 (1982): 89–99.

————. "Frank Waters and the Concept of 'Nothing Special.' " *South Dakota Review* 15 (1977): 31–35.

Maling, Anne and Abiatha Willis. *The Dozier Family of Lower Norfolk County: A Reference.* Published in 1986 at 402 Harvard St., Norfolk, Va. 23505.

Malpezzi, Frances M. "The Emergence of Helen Chalmers." In *Women in Western American Literature,* edited by Helen Stauffer. Troy, N.Y.: Whitson Publishing, 1982: 100–113.

————. "Meru, the Voice of the Mountain." *South Dakota Review* 27 (1989): 27–34.

————. "A Study of the Female Protagonist in Frank Waters' *People of the Valley* and Rudolfo Anaya's *Bless Me, Ultima.*" *South Dakota Review* 14 (1976): 102–10.

Marinelli, Peter V. *Pastoral.* London: Methuen, 1971.

Marx, Leo. *The Machine in the Garden: Technology and the Pastoral Ideal in America.* New York: Oxford University Press, Galaxy Books, 1967.

Melville, Herman. *Collected Poems of Herman Melville.* Edited by Howard P. Vincent. Chicago: Hendricks House, 1947.

————. *The Confidence-Man: His Masquerade.* Edited by Elizabeth S. Foster. New York: Hendricks House, 1954.

————. *Moby-Dick, or, The Whale.* Edited by Luther S. Mansfield and Howard P. Vincent. New York: Hendricks House, 1952.

Mills, George. *The People of the Saints.* Colorado Springs: Taylor Museum of the Colorado Springs Fine Arts Center, n.d.

Milton, John R. "Intuition and the Dance of Life: Frank Waters." In *The Novel of the American West,* by John R. Milton. Lincoln: University of Nebraska Press, 1980: 264–97.

————. "The Sound of Space." *South Dakota Review* 15 (Autumn 1977): 11–15.

————. "Symbolic Space and Mysticism in the Novels of Frank Waters." *Studies in Frank Waters* 5 (1982): 12–27.

————. "Thoughts on Western Writers." *Writers' Forum* 15 (1989): 1–20.

Mobley, Ree. "Colorado Springs, 1905." *Colorado Springs Gazette Telegraph,* 11 January 1989.

Neumann, Erich. *Creative Man: Five Essays.* Translated by Eugene Rolfe. Princeton: Princeton University Press, 1979.

————. *Depth Psychology and a New Ethic.* Translated by Eugene Rolfe. New York: G. P. Putnam's Sons, 1969.

————. *The Great Mother: An Analysis of the Archetype.* Translated by Ralph Manheim. New York: Pantheon Books, 1955.

————. *The Psychological Stages in the Development of Personality.* Vol. 2 of *The Origins and History of Consciousness.* Translated by R. F. C. Hull. New York: Harper, Torchbooks, 1962.

Northrop, F. S. C. *The Meeting of East and West: An Inquiry Concerning World Understanding.* New York: Collier Books, 1966.

Ornstein, Robert E. *The Psychology of Consciousness.* San Francisco: W. H. Freeman, 1972.

Peat, F. David. *Synchronicity: The Bridge Between Matter and Mind.* Toronto: Bantam, New Age Books, 1987.

Potter, Charles Francis. "Coin of the Dead." Vol. 1 of *Dictionary of Folklore, Mythology, and Legend.* New York: Funk & Wagnalls, 1949, 1:241.

Powell, Lawrence Clark. "A Writer's Landscape." *Westways* 66 (January 1974): 24–27, 70–72.

Prigogine, Ilya and Isabelle Stengers. *Order out of Chaos: Man's New Dialogue with Nature.* New York: Bantam Books, 1984.

Rank, Otto. *The Myth of the Birth of the Hero.* New York: Journal of Nervous and Mental Disease Publishing, 1914.

Rascoe, Burton. "Two Worlds in Conflict." Review of *The Man Who Killed the Deer. Saturday Review of Literature* (13 June 1942): 71.

Rhine, Joseph Banks. *New World of the Mind.* New York: William Sloane, 1953.

Robinson, Cecil. *Mexico and the Hispanic Southwest in American Literature.* Tucson: University of Arizona Press, 1977.

Rudnick, Lois Palken. *Mabel Dodge Luhan: New Woman, New Worlds.* Albuquerque: University of New Mexico Press, 1984.

Sagan, Carl. *The Dragons of Eden: Speculations on the Evolution of Human Intelligence.* New York: Ballantine Books, 1977.

Schell, Jonathan. *The Fate of the Earth.* New York: Alfred A. Knopf, 1982.

Schneider, Daniel J. *D. H. Lawrence: The Artist as Psychologist.* Lawrence: University Press of Kansas, 1984.

Singer, June. *Boundaries of the Soul: The Practice of Jung's Psychology.* Garden City, N.Y.: Doubleday, Anchor Books, 1973.

Smith, Henry Nash. *Virgin Land: The American West as Symbol and Myth.* Cambridge, Mass.: Harvard University Press, 1950.

Smith, Robert W. "Frank Waters: An Appreciation." *Studies in Frank Waters* 7 (1985): 1–10.

Spencer, Elizabeth. "Emerging as a Writer in Faulkner's Mississippi." In *Faulkner and the Southern Renaissance,* edited by Doreen Fowler and Ann J. Abadie. Jackson: University Press of Mississippi, 1982: 120–37.

Spenser, Benjamin T. "Regionalism in American Literature." In *Regionalism in America,* edited by Merrill Jensen. Madison: University of Wisconsin Press, 1965: 219–60.

Sprague, Marshall. "Frank Waters: Narrator of the Region." *Colorado Springs Gazette Telegraph,* 2 February 1954.

Squires, Michael. *The Pastoral Novel: Studies in George Eliot, Thomas Hardy, and D. H. Lawrence.* Charlottesville: University Press of Virginia, 1974.

Stegner, Wallace. *One Way to Spell Man.* Garden City, N.Y.: Doubleday, 1982.

Steinbeck, John. *The Grapes of Wrath.* New York: Viking Press, Compass Edition, 1958.

Tanner, Jeri. "Time and Timelessness in *The Woman at Otowi Crossing.*" *Studies in Frank Waters* 11 (1989): 1–11.

Tanner, Tony. *The Reign of Wonder: Naivety and Reality in American Literature.* Cambridge: Cambridge University Press, 1965.

Tart, Charles T., ed. *Transpersonal Psychologies.* New York: Harper & Row, 1975.

Tedlock, Dennis and Barbara Tedlock, eds. *Teachings from the American Earth: Indian Religion and Philosophy.* New York: Liveright, 1975.

Teilhard de Chardin, Pierre. *The Phenomenon of Man.* Translated by Bernard Wall. New York: Harper, Torchbooks, 1961.

The Tibetan Book of the Dead. Translated by Lama Kazi Dawa-Samdup, ed. W. Y. Evans-Wentz. 3d ed. London: Oxford University Press, 1960.

Vickery, John and J. M. Sellery, eds. *The Scapegoat: Ritual and Literature.* Boston: Houghton Mifflin, 1972.

von Franz, Marie-Louise. *On Dreams and Death: A Jungian Interpretation.* Translated by Emmanuel Xipolitas Kennedy and Vernon Brooks. Boston: Shambhala, 1987.

————. "Science and the Unconscious." In *Man and His Symbols,* by Carl G. Jung. Garden City, N.Y.: Doubleday, 1964: 304–10.

Wain, John. *The Living World of Shakespeare.* Harmondsworth: Penguin Books, 1966.

Weber, Renée. *Dialogues with Scientists and Sages: The Search for Unity.* London: Routledge & Kegan Paul, 1986.

Wild, Peter. "Frank Waters: Rhythms of the Earth." *American West* 25 (June 1988): 12–13.

Wiley, Peter and Robert Gottlieb. *Empires in the Sun: The Rise of the New American West.* Tucson: University of Arizona Press, 1985.

Williams, William Carlos. *In the American Grain.* London: MacGibbon & Kee, 1966.

Woodroffe, (Sir) John. *The Serpent Power.* New York: Dover Publications, 1974.

Zukav, Gary. *The Dancing Wu Li Masters: An Overview of the New Physics.* New York: Bantam, New Age Books, 1980.

INDEX

Absalom, Absalom! *See* Faulkner, William

Absolute Consciousness (Atman, *Chit,* Dharma-Kāya, Self, Universal Mind, Universal Reality), xvii, 7, 11, 12, 14, 46, 54, 62, 63–64, 101, 130, 137, 138, 141, 149 n.3; in yogic doctrine, 43–45; approached by science, 67–68; as psychophysical energy, 113; in oriental mythology, 119–20; as idea of order, 137. *See also* Archetype; Buddhism; Conscience; Mysticism; Taoism

Adam Bede. See Eliot, George

Adams, Charles, 34

Allegory, 92, 99, 101, 104, 106–11, 137

American Fictions 1940–1980. See Karl, Frederick

Androgyny, 83, 85, 151 n.27. *See also* Archetype, of Divine Child

Angle of Repose. See Stegner, Wallace

Apperception, defined, 11

Archetype: as animated in myth, 9; of quincunx, 14, 17; of *axis mundi,* 14; of Mt. Meru, 14, 130; of *uroboros,* 22, 31–32, 48, 65; as problem in art, 22; of death and vision, 35, 44, 50–51, 154 n.25; of Buddhas, 36; of *picaro,* 38, 148 n.13; of golden sun, 64, 149 n.5; theory of, 67–68; of journey-return, 75–76, 82; of Divine Child, 83; of mandala, 115; of yin-yang, 119–20; of transfiguration, 130; of annunciation, 140. *See also* Cosmic Mother; Jung, C. G.

The Art of the Novel. See James, Henry

As I Lay Dying. See Faulkner, William Atman. *See* Absolute Consciousness

Atomic Age, 13, 14; as manifestation of materialism, 57; as release of physical energy, 63; history of, 114, 121, 122, 125

Austin, William: "Peter Rugg, the Missing Man," 19

Axis mundi (Immovable Spot, Tree of Life, World Navel): as apex of the cross, 4; as hub, 82; as "centering" of individual 83–84, 141–42. *See also* Archetype; Mythology

Bardo Thödol: as "Book of the Dead," 35; as "Bardo of Life," 51. *See* Evans-Wentz, W. Y.

Battle-Pieces. See Melville, Herman "The Bear." *See* Faulkner, William

"Being within." *See* Emergence

Benét, Stephen Vincent, 91

Bhagavad-Gita, 62

Bible, 16, 28, 59, 140; *Book of Job,* 54, 109, 111

The Big Rock Candy Mountain. See Stegner, Wallace

Billy Budd. See Melville, Herman

Blixen, Karen. *See* Dinesen, Isak

Bohm, David: *Wholeness and the Implicate Order,* xv, 12, 67, 68

Bolen, Jean: *The Tao of Psychology,* 119

Bradbury, Malcolm, 46

Bredahl, A. Carl, Jr.: *New Ground,* xviii

Broad, C. D., 139

Brooks, Cleanth, 8

Buddhism, 16, 49, 84, 104, 130, 131, 138; in Waters's outlook, xii; as Mahayana, 12, 35–37, 50–51; and yoga, 35, 36, 45. *See also* Mythology; Taoism

Campbell, Joseph, 83–84, 91, 95, 141; *The Power of Myth,* 117; *Creative Mythology,* 133–34

Capra, Fritjof: *The Tao of Physics,* 13, 113, 119

Cary, Joyce, 8

Cather, Willa: *My Ántonia,* 4; *Death Comes for the Archbishop,* 80

Chit (Sanskrit). *See* Absolute Consciousness

Church, Peggy Pond: *The House at Otowi Bridge,* 154 n.18

Clark, Walter Van Tilburg: *The Ox-Bow Incident,* 4; *The Track of the Cat,* 4

Clemens, Samuel Langhorne (pseud. Mark Twain): *Huckleberry Finn,* 30, 75, 101, 126–27, 143

Coleridge, Samuel Taylor: *Rime of the Ancient Mariner,* 20, 28

Comedy, aligned with pastoral, 74

The Confidence-Man. See Melville, Herman

Conrad, Joseph, 8, 21, 23, 99, 137; *Heart of Darkness,* 20, 23–24; *Victory,* 41–42

Conscience, 42–43, 80; as voice of Absolute Consciousness, 94, 101, 105, 106, 137. *See also* Gurdjieff, Georges

Consciousness, new world of. *See* Emergence

Cosmic Mother (Eternal Feminine, Great Mother): as *uroboros* in *Lizard Woman,* 24; and creative evolution, 28; as Good Mother and Terrible Mother, 31–32; as Dark Madonna in *Yogi,* 39, 40; as powers of the unconscious in *Pike's Peak,* 54; personified in *People,* 72, 82–83, 85; defined, 73; as archetype of creativity, 77; as feminine power of the unconscious in *Deer,* 100–101, 104–5, 106, 109–11; personified in *Otowi,* 128; as timeless power, 141

Creativity. *See* Mysticism. *See also* Vision, literary

Cultural primitivism, defined, 85

The Dancing Wu Li Masters. See Zukav, Gary

Dante Alighieri: *The Divine Comedy,* 53, 110

D'Arcy, Martin: *The Sense of History,* 103

Death Comes for the Archbishop. See Cather, Willa

Descartes, René, 113

Dharma Kāya. *See* Absolute Consciousness

Dickinson, Emily, 134

Dinesen, Isak (pseud. of Karen Blixen), 47

The Divine Comedy. See Dante Alighieri

Donne, John: "A Valediction: Forbidding Mourning," 131

Donoghue, Denis, 132

The Doors of Perception. See Huxley, Aldous

Dostoyevsky, Fyodor, 47

Duality: of mountains, xi, 3; of Waters's heritage, xii; of human existence, xiii; of nature, xiv; of Euro-Americans and Indians, xiv; of sexes, 5, 14, 15, 40–41, 109–11; of yin-yang, 12, 13, 14, 40; of pleasure-pain, 13; as polarities in oriental philosophy, 13–16; of good-evil, 13, 14; of consciousness-unconscious, 13–14, 15, 27–28, 54, 61–62; of positive-negative, 14; of earth-sky, 14; of light-dark, 14, 25; of reason-intuition, 14; of personal ego-impersonal Self, 14; of space-time, 14; of particle-wave, 14; of geological epochs, 14; of evolutionary stages, 14; of East-West races and cultures, 14; of people-place, 14; of ancient-modern America, 14; as inner conflict of characters, 14; as a philosophical stance, 15–16; of attraction-repulsion, 25, 40; of Terrible Mother-Good Mother, 32; as inherited codes of behavior, 51; as physiological basis, 66–67; of God in *Deer,* 109; displays crisis of identity, 135

Einstein, Albert: theory of relativity, 12, 65; mass-energy equation, 58; unity of worldview, 113; and Jung, 118. *See also* Time, nonlinear

Eliot, George: *Adam Bede,* 74

Eliot, T(homas) S(tearnes), 134; *The Waste Land,* xviii, 4; "Tradition and the Individual Talent," 5; *Four Quartets,* 16, 44, 127

Emergence ("Being within," evolution of consciousness, increased awareness, new world of consciousness, self-fulfillment, self-realization), xiv–xv, 3, 16–17, 18, 22–23, 27, 31–33, 35, 39–40, 47, 48, 64, 85–86, 109, 135; as redemptive vision, xvii, xviii, 114–15, 116–17, 123–24; as creative mythology, xvii, 3, 16–18, 65, 72, 100–1, 108, 110–11, 127–29,

151; evinced in contemporary history, 17–18; in Mesoamerican and Southwestern Indian cosmogeny, 17, 97, 98–99, 100–101, 120, 126, 138; and oriental philosophy, 17, 35, 138; as reconciliation of polarized powers, 17, 54, 71; unrealized in *Yogi,* 43, 45; as field of scientific discovery, 66–67; distinguished from cultural primitivism, 71; resembles Jung's individuation, 100; as allegory in *Deer,* 107; and synchronicity, 120. *See also* Absolute Consciousness; Mysticism

Emerson, Ralph Waldo, 5, 19, 29, 30, 59, 141; "The Over-Soul," 134

Epic, 52–53

Eternal Feminine. *See* Cosmic Mother

Evans-Wentz, W. Y.: *The Tibetan Book of the Dead,* 35, 37–38, 44, 45, 50, 51; *Tibetan Yoga and Secret Doctrine,* 35, 44, 45; as influence on Waters, 138

Everyman, 107

Evolution of consciousness. *See* Emergence

Faith, defined, 70

Falck, Colin: *Myth, Truth and Literature,* 1, 132–33

Faulkner, William, xvi, xviii, 4, 10, 47, 134, 137, 139; sexism in, 5, 7, 86, 87; limited worldview of, 5; nihilism of, 7–9; *Absalom, Absalom!,* 6; *As I Lay Dying,* 6; "The Bear," 6, 46; *Go Down, Moses,* 6, 7, 126–27; *Light in August,* 6, 74; *The Sound and the Fury,* 6, 143; *The Hamlet,* 86, 87

Fear of Flying. See Jong, Erica

Ferguson, Marilyn, xvii

Fitzgerald, F. Scott: *The Great Gatsby,* 46, 75, 143

Fletcher, Angus, 99

Forster, E. M., 8

Foundations of Tibetan Mysticism. See Govinda, Lama Anagarika

Four Quartets. See Eliot, T. S.

Frank Waters. See Lyon, Thomas J.

Freud, Sigmund: theory of personal unconscious, 12; theory of repression, 60, 77

Frost, Robert, 20, 75

Genre, literary. *See* Allegory; Comedy; Epic; Imaginary voyage; Pastoral; Tragedy

Gladstein, Mimi, 86, 87

Go Down, Moses. See Faulkner, William

Gorman, R. C., 92

Govinda, Lama Anagarika: *Foundations of Tibetan Mysticism,* 36–38

The Grapes of Wrath. See Steinbeck, John

Great Mother. *See* Cosmic Mother

Grider, Daryl, 35

Grigg, Quay, xi, 142

Gurdjieff, Georges, 153 n.15. *See also* Conscience

The Hamlet. See Faulkner, William
Harding, M. Esther: *Psychic Energy*, 115
Hardy, Thomas, 74
Hawking, Stephen, xv
Hawthorne, Nathaniel, 139; "Young Goodman Brown," 20; *The Scarlet Letter*, 86, 143
Heart of Darkness. See Conrad, Joseph
Heilbrun, Carolyn, 86
Hemingway, Ernest, xvi, 8, 30, 139; limited worldview of, 5; sexism in, 5, 86
Hick, John, 70
Highwater, Jamake: *The Primal Mind*, 98
Hoffman, Frederick J., 22
Honig, Edwin, 99, 110
Horgan, Paul, 4
The House at Otowi Bridge. See Church, Peggy Pond
Huckleberry Finn. See Clemens, Samuel Langhorne
Huxley, Aldous: *The Doors of Perception*, 97

I Ching. See Wilhelm, Richard
Idylls of the King. See Tennyson, Alfred
Imaginary voyage, 20–21
Immovable Spot. See *Axis mundi*
Increased awareness. *See* Emergence
Indian Tribes: Arapahoe, xi, 93; Cheyenne, xi; Navajo, xi, xii, 96, 100; Kiowa, xi; Ute, xi, 93; Hopi, 12; Cocopah, 25, 40; Yuma, 40; Mojave, 40; Pueblo, 78, 100, 123; Apache, 92
Indians, American: apperception of, xiv; myths and ceremonies of, xiv, 2, 10, 17, 84, 92–99, 103–4; cultural concepts of, 11, 54–55, 98, 104; Euro-American view of, 60; "Anasazi" social structure of, 96; nonverbal epistemology of, 102
Indians, Mesoamerican: myths of, 10, 12, 17, 24; time and space obsessions of, 14. *See also* Emergence
Irreducible Reality. *See* Absolute Consciousness
Irving, Washington: "Rip Van Winkle," 19

James, Henry, 139; *The Art of the Novel*, 107
Jeffers, Robinson, 134
Jong, Erica: *Fear of Flying*, 39
Joyce, James, 134
Jung, C(arl) G(ustav): aesthetics of, 9, 133–34; theory of archetypes of the collective unconscious, 12, 65, 67–68, 138; theory of synchronicity, 12, 68, 117–19, 138; on reconciliation of consciousness and unconscious, 13–14; on *uroboros*, 31; on Divine Child, 83; on individuation, 100; on reconciling symbol, 115; on *The Tibetan Book of the Dead*, 38, 51; *Modern Man in Search of a Soul*, 133. *See also* Archetype; Psychic energy; Synchronicity

Kafka, Franz, 99
Karl, Frederick: *American Fictions 1940–1980*, 4
Karma: as psychic residua, 38; as law of universal moral order, 45, 48–51, 137
Kerényi, Karl, 83
King Lear. See Shakespeare, William
Kluckholm, Clyde, 95
Knight, G. Wilson, 140
Koestler, Arthur, 113

La Barre, Weston, 97
La Farge, Oliver: *Laughing Boy*, 91
Langer, Susanne: *Philosophy in a New Key*
Lao Tzu, 13
Laughing Boy. See La Farge, Oliver
Lawrence, D. H., 8, 47, 74, 99; and Quetzalcoatl myth; *The Woman Who Rode Away*, 102; *The Plumed Serpent*, 154 n.19
"Leda and the Swan." *See* Yeats, William Butler
Levin, Harry, 19
Light in August. See Faulkner, William
Literature, American: regionalism in, xvii; shattered worldview in, xviii; relationship to the land in, xviii, stereotyping of western writers in, 5; confidence man in, 7; Puritanism in, 8–11; cosmic stance in, 16; dislocated characters in, 19–20; ambiguity in, 20; nightmare journey in, 20; naturalism in, 24, 146–47; motif of confinement in, 30; wondering vision in, 30; Transcendentalism in, 30; and ideal of forging new consciousness, 46; social protest in, 46; theme of virgin land in, 59; pastoralism in, 75; sexism in, 85–87; conscience as moral indoctrination in, 101; and Native American novels, 102; counterpointing in, 126–27
Long Day's Journey into Night. See O'Neill, Eugene
Look Homeward Angel. See Wolfe, Thomas
Luhan, Mabel Dodge, 102, 103, 105, 146 n.5
Lynen, John F., 75
Lyon, Thomas J.: *Frank Waters*, xii, xiv, xvi–xvii, 44

Macbeth. See Shakespeare, William
McNickle, D'Arcy: *The Surrounded*, 102
Maharshi, Bhagavan Sri, 14, 146 n.22
Malpezzi, Frances M., 130
Manfred, Frederick, 4

Mann, Thomas, 134
Marx, Karl, 108
Marx, Leo, 46, 74–75
Melville, Herman, xvii, 4, 5, 99, 134, 145 n.6;
    Moby-Dick, 8, 16, 20, 28, 47, 53, 59, 60, 92,
    107, 137, 143; *Battle-Pieces,* 16; *Billy Budd,*
    16, 106; *The Confidence-Man,* 143
The Merchant of Venice. See Shakespeare,
    William
Milton, John R., 136
Moby-Dick. See Melville, Herman
Modern Man in Search of a Soul. See Jung,
    C. G.
Momaday, N. Scott, 102
Moyers, Bill, 117
My Ántonia. See Cather, Willa
Mysticism: as experience of unity, 10; and
    parapsychology, 12; and science, 12, 67–68,
    112–14, 117, 139; oriental, 13; and Chris-
    tianity, 70; and creative function of mystics,
    116–17; concept of chakras in, 131; defined,
    139–40
Myth, Truth and Literature. See Falck, Colin
Mythology: and literary vision, 1; as basis of
    knowledge, 9; oriental, 10, 11–12, 31, 48,
    62; psychological interpretation of, 33; of
    Greek Fates, 47; occidental, 48, 59, 75;
    functions of, 59, 133–34, 142; mythogenetic
    zone of, 72, 114; and pastoral, 73–76; of
    death and resurrection, 79; of axial rock, 84;
    of covenant between men and animals, 91,
    95; of Fisher King, 122

Narrative of Arthur Gordon Pym. See Poe,
    Edgar Allan
Neumann, Erich, 22, 31–33, 119
New Ground. See Bredahl, A. Carl, Jr.

Oedipus Rex. See Sophocles
O'Neill, Eugene: *Long Day's Journey into
    Night,* 20
Order out of Chaos. See Prigogine, Ilya
Ornstein, Robert, 66
"The Over-Soul." *See* Emerson, Ralph Waldo
The Ox-Bow Incident. See Clark, Walter Van
    Tilburg

Pastoral: defined, 73–76; and *People,* 137; and
    regionalism, 151 n.6
Pauli, Wolfgang, 68
Peat, F. David: *Synchronicity,* 83, 113, 114,
    118–19
"Peter Rugg, the Missing Man." *See* Austin,
    William
Philosophy in a New Key. See Langer, Sus-
    anne
The Plumed Serpent. See Lawrence, D. H.

Poe, Edgar Allan: *Narrative of Arthur Gordon
    Pym,* 20, 28
Power to Become. *See* Absolute consciousness
Prigogine, Ilya: *Order out of Chaos,* xv, 67, 68
The Primal Mind. See Highwater, Jamake
Psychic Energy. See Harding, M. Esther
Psychic energy, 63, 113, 153 n.2
Psychic landscape. *See* Spirit of place

Quetzalcoatl: as God-Redeemer, 2, 12, 57, 124,
    154 n.19

Rascoe, Burton, 91
Relativity Theory. *See* Einstein, Albert; Time,
    nonlinear. *See also* Road of Life
Rime of the Ancient Mariner. See Coleridge,
    Samuel Taylor
"Rip Van Winkle." *See* Irving, Washington
Rivera, Diego, 46
Road of Life: as Mesoamerican myth, 2–3; as
    cosmic circle, 115. *See* Emergence. *See also*
    Taoism
Rock-Around-Which-Moving-Was-Done. See
    Axis mundi
Roethke, Theodore, 134
Romeo and Juliet. See Shakespeare, William

Sacred Mountains, xii, 3, 14, 63; as places of
    eucharistic ceremony, 64. *See also* Spirit of
    place
Sagan, Carl, 66
The Scarlet Letter. See Hawthorne, Nathaniel
Self. *See* Absolute Consciousness
Self-fulfillment. *See* Emergence
Self-realization. *See* Emergence
The Sense of History. See D'Arcy, Martin
Serpent power, 24, 109, 131
Sheldrake, Rupert, xv
Siddhartha Gautama, 36
Silko, Leslie Marmon, 102
Shakespeare, William: retributive justice in,
    45; as visionary, 47; vision of tragedy in, 53;
    The Merchant of Venice, 29; *The Tempest,*
    75, 81; *King Lear,* 107, 140; *Romeo and Ju-
    liet,* 125; *Macbeth,* 140
Sophocles: *Oedipus Rex,* 42, 107, 111
The Sound and the Fury. See Faulkner,
    William
Spencer, Elizabeth, 7, 8
Spirit of place, 4, 10, 14, 20, 23, 26, 32, 33,
    34–35, 41, 62, 63, 136; as psychophysical
    reciprocity, 30–31; and aesthetics of fiction,
    46–47; Indian atonement with, 55, 58–59;
    as point of entry into numinous world, 70;
    defined, 147 n.1. *See also* Mysticism; Unity
Stegner, Wallace: *Angle of Repose,* 4; *Big
    Rock Candy Mountain,* 4

Steinbeck, John, xvi, 139; sexism in, 5, 86–87; *The Grapes of Wrath,* 4, 80, 86–87
Stewart, George: *Storm,* 46–47
Storm. See Stewart, George
Stratton, Winfield Scott, xiii, 56, 149 n.4
The Surrounded. See McNickle, D'Arcy
Swallow, Alan, 91
Synchronicity, 12, 83, 124–25, 154 n.13; defined, 68, 118–20. *See also* Jung, C. G.; Peat, F. David; Taoism
Synchronicity. See Peat, F. David

Tanner, Tony, 30
Tantrism. *See* Govinda, Lama Anagarika
The Tao of Physics. See Capra, Fritjof
The Tao of Psychology. See Bolen, Jean
Taoism, 104, 138; and synchronicity, 119–20. *See also* Buddhism
Teilhard de Chardin, Pierre, xvii
The Tempest. See Shakespeare, William
Tennyson, Alfred: *Idylls of the King,* xviii
Thoreau, Henry David, 5, 30, 59
The Tibetan Book of the Dead. See Evans-Wentz, W. Y.
Tibetan Yoga and Secret Doctrine. See Evans-Wentz, W. Y.
Time, nonlinear: as timelessness, 9, 15, 17, 88, 124, 128; in relativity theory, 12, 118; as quality of character, 39; in spatial cosmology, 48; concept of, 62, 64–65; as available mind function, 66; as dynamically evolving reality, 72; as eternity, 117; as basis of emergence, 123; in creative mythology, 133; dramatized in characters who embody essence, 135–36; as geometry of spirit, 142; and "becoming," 143. *See also* Emergence; Mysticism
Tonantzin. *See* Cosmic Mother
The Track of the Cat. See Clark, Walter Van Tilburg
"Tradition and the Individual Talent." *See* Eliot, T. S.
Tragedy, 60–61, 62, 137, 142; causes of, 11, 59–60, 65; defined, 30, 45, 53–54, 57, 137; and the American West
Tree of Life. See *Axis mundi*
Turner, Frederick Jackson: frontier thesis, 53, 81
Twain, Mark. *See* Clemens, Samuel Langhorne

Unity: intuitive Amerindian concept of, xiv–xv; as interconnectedness of all living systems, 3, 11–13, 46–47, 57, 58, 70–71, 110; of microcosm-macrocosm, 11, 36, 47, 62, 69–70, 78, 83; symbols of, 12; as theme in *Lizard Woman,* 24; in brain's architecture, 66–67; as quest of science, 67–68; dramatized as completeness of identity, 135. *See also* Absolute Consciousness; Mysticism; Mythology
Universal Mind. *See* Absolute consciousness
Universal Reality. *See* Absolute consciousness
Upanishads, 62

"A Valediction: Forbidding Mourning." *See* Donne, John
Victory. See Conrad, Joseph
Virgin of Guadalupe. *See* Cosmic Mother
Vision, literary: nature of, 5, 8–10; as search for unity, 36–37; transcendental function of, 47; in composition of *Deer,* 90–91; and analogical thinking, 107–8; and mythic mode of consciousness, 128, 132–33; and mysticism, 139–40; as projecting central meaning, 141

The Waste Land. See Eliot, T. S.
Waters, Frank: dual nature of, ix; literary reputation of, x–xi, xvi, xviii, 4, 5; family background of, xi–xiii, 145 n.9, 150 n.14; vision of, xvii, 33, quest of, 1–3; compared with Faulkner, 4–9; mysticism of, 5; mystical experience of, 10, 35; acquainted with American West, 20, 34, 57–58, 76; not a Buddhist, 35; early search for literary stance, 49; philosophical maturity of, 57; composes *Deer* in Taos, 90–91; influenced by Jung after 1941, 100; composes *Otowi,* 114; honored by Colorado College, 134; not categorized by influences, 136–37
Waters, Frank, as author of Works: *Below Grass Roots,* xi, 52; *Book of the Hope,* 4, 6, 57; *The Colorado,* xiii–xiv, 6, 10, 20, 49, 71, 76; *Diamond Head,* 146 n.18; *The Dust within the Rock,* xi, 52, 57; *The Earp Brothers of Tombstone,* xiii; "Easy Meat," xii; *Flight from Fiesta,* 15, 146 n.18, 154 n.9; Letter to Mabel Dodge Luhan of 14 February 1941, 102–5; *The Lizard Woman [Fever Pitch],* xii, 12, 19–33, 48, 65, 72, 109, 135, 143, 146 n.4; *The Man Who Killed the Deer,* xiii, xvii, 4, 6, 7, 12, 14, 72, 90–111, 137, 138, 141–42, 143, 152 n.7; *Masked Gods,* xiii, xiv, 3, 6, 14, 50, 57, 65, 84, 95–99, 101, 114–15, 123; *Mexico Mystique,* xvii, 6, 10, 14, 98, 116, 124; *Midas of the Rockies,* xiii, 149 n.4; *Mountain Dialogues,* xvii, 3, 6, 12, 14, 17, 98, 100, 120, 138; "Mysticism and Witchcraft," 141; *People of the Valley,* xiii, xvii, 6, 7, 8, 12–13, 14, 15, 69–89, 135, 137, 139, 142, 143; *Pike's Peak,* xi, 6, 7, 8, 12, 15, 29, 52–68, 72, 134–35, 137, 138, 139, 142, 143; *Pumpkin Seed*

Point, 2, 6, 11, 17, 18, 57, 58–60, 65, 101; "Relationships and the Novel," 46–47; *River Lady,* 146 n.18; *To Possess the Land,* 15; "Visions of the Good: What Literature Affirms and How," 46–47; *The Wild Earth's Nobility,* xi, 6, 52, 60; *The Woman at Otowi Crossing,* xiii, xv, xvii, 6, 7, 13, 14, 15, 18, 72, 86, 112–31, 135, 138, 142, 143; *The Yogi of Cockroach Court,* xii, 6, 8, 12, 14, 15, 34–51, 72, 135, 137, 138, 142, 143

Waters, Frank, as artist: theme of search for unity, xvii, 35, 53, 135–36, of human solidarity, 43, 46, of racial harmony, 55, thematic use of parts of speech, 59, 61–62; omniscient point of view, 6, 49, implied author, 49, 69, 81–82, multiple restricted points of view, 7; counterpointing, 7, 39, 61, 66, 69–72, 114, 121; metaphorical orchestration, 7; interior monologues, 7, 56–57; uses of irony, 7, 24, 29–30, 44, 49–50, 54, 78, 121–22, 125–26, 129–30; nonsentimentalized tone, 54–55, 86–89, 137; nondoctrinaire language, 15; imagery and symbolism of light, 15, 37, 40–41, 44, 51, 72, 83, 127–28, 130; structure, 22, 35, 91, 121; characterization, 22, 24, 38, 39–40, 62, 73, 77–78, 81–89, 115, 117, 121, 130, 147 n.8; spatial metaphors, 2–3, 27, 28, 38, 40, 46, 77, 78, 109–10, 136–37, 141–42; comedy and humor, 25, 122; ambiguity, 27; symbolism of unconscious, 32, of modern waste land, 35, of fish in *Yogi,* 51, of granite-adobe, 54, of dam, 76–77, of archaic rituals, 82–83, of Maria's blanket, 84–85, of the Deer, 92, 94, 101, 105–6, 108–9, of fertility, 108, of kiva, 123, of numbers, 130–31; stance of compassion, 41, 46, 48, 49; morality, 35, 107; use of scapegoat psychology, 60–61; contrast of individual and society, 63; avoidance of pathetic fallacy, 71–72; nonimpersonation of Native American consciousness, 102, 106; "centering" of protagonists, 127; technique of witness-bearing, 128–30; technique of "flashforward," 129; rhetoric of negative universals, 137

Waters, Frank, as philosopher: 10–11; of literature, xvi–xvii, 7–8, 47; of universal moral order, 6, 47, 105, 107–8; of common humanity, 8, 15, 103–4; on death, 15, 50, 131; on cosmology, 28; on human sexuality, 39–40; on evolution, 47–49; on problem of alienation, 55, 105; on epistemology, 62; and prophet, 66–68; on faith, 69–71, 72; on violence, 80–81; rejects apocalyptic thinking, 114–15; of mystical experience, 123–25; on ontology, 134, 141–43

Weber, Renée, 68

Welch, James, 102

West (region of U.S.): as center of space experience, 136

Whitman, Walt, 5, 19, 30, 134

Wilhelm, Richard: *I Ching,* 119–20

Williams, William Carlos, 143

Wholeness and the Implicate Order. See Bohm, David

Wolfe, Thomas, 5; *Look Homeward, Angel,* 137

The Woman Who Rode Away. See Lawrence, D. H.

World Navel. See *Axis mundi*

Yeats, William Butler: "Leda and the Swan," 140

Yin-yang. *See* Duality

Yoga. *See* Buddhism; Taoism

"Young Goodman Brown." *See* Hawthorne, Nathaniel

Zukav, Gary: *The Dancing Wu Li Masters,* 113

A NOTE ABOUT THE AUTHOR

Alexander Blackburn was educated at Yale and Cambridge (Ph.D) and is Professor of English at the University of Colorado, Colorado Springs, where he edits *Writers' Forum.* He is author of two novels and of a critically acclaimed study of the origins of modern fiction, *The Myth of the Picaro,* and has edited an anthology, *The Interior Country: Stories of the Modern West.*